THE SMITHSONIAN BOOK OF
NORTH AMERICAN INDIANS

THE SMITHSONIAN BOOK OF NORTH AMERICAN INDIANS

Before the Coming of the Europeans

by Philip Kopper

and the Editors of
Smithsonian Books

Smithsonian Books
Washington, D.C.

Trade distribution by
Harry N. Abrams, Inc.
New York, New York

THE SMITHSONIAN INSTITUTION
Secretary Robert McC. Adams
Assistant Secretary for Public Service
 Ralph Rinzler
Director, Smithsonian Institution Press
 Felix C. Lowe

SMITHSONIAN BOOKS
Editor-in-Chief Patricia Gallagher
Administrative Asst. Anne P. Naruta
Senior Editor Alexis Doster III
Editors Joe Goodwin, Amy Donovan
Assistant Editor John F. Ross
Senior Picture Editor Nancy Strader
Picture Editor Frances C. Rowsell
Assistant Picture Editor R. Jenny Takacs
Picture Assistant Jan L. Bell
Production Consultant Irv Garfield
Production Editor Patricia Upchurch
Production Assistant June G. Armstrong
Business Manager Stephen J. Bergstrom
Marketing Consultant William H. Kelty
Marketing Manager Margaret Kei Mooney

Copy Editor Duke Johns
Research James A. Knight, Gail Prensky
Picture Consultant
 Barbara G. Stuckenrath
Design Watermark Design
Special Art Greg Harlin/Stansbury,
 Ronsaville, Wood Inc.
Separations The Lanman Companies
Typography Type Studio, Ltd.
Jacket Printing
 Lehigh Press Lithographers
Printing and Binding
 Arcata Graphics/Kingsport

The Editors of Smithsonian Books
gratefully acknowledge the assistance
of Don D. Fowler, *Mamie Kleberg Professor of Anthropology and Historic
Preservation, the University of Nevada
at Reno, and Research Associate in
Anthropology, Smithsonian Institution;*
Linda S. Cordell, *Chairman, Department
of Anthropology, University of New
Mexico;* Alice B. Kehoe, *Professor of
Anthropology, Marquette University;* and
Vincas P. Steponaitis, *Associate Professor, Department of Anthropology, State
University of New York at Binghamton.*

Manufactured in the United States of
America

First Edition

5   4   3   2

Pages 2–3: Great Plains buffalo descend to drink
in a painting from the 1830s by Karl Bodmer;
pages 4–5: "White House" walls at Arizona's
Canyon de Chelly; pages 6–7: Cuello, an early
Mayan archaeological site in Belize; page 10:
Aztec feather shield preserved at Stuttgart,
Germany; page 12: Copper repoussé profile of a
male from Oklahoma's rich Craig mound at the
Spiro site; pages 14–15: watchers at New Mexico's
Casa Rinconada, a stone structure with astronomically aligned ports, see dawn light at the summer
solstice; pages 92–93: Exquisitely flaked flint
"earth monster" carries Mayan nobles to the
underworld; pages 266–267: Arizona's Canyon
del Muerto bears images of Spanish conquistadors
by an unknown Indian artist.

**Library of Congress Cataloging-in-Publication
Data**

The Smithsonian book of North American
Indians.

  Includes index.
  1. Indians of North America—Antiquities.
2. Indians of North America—Social life and
customs. 3. North America—Antiquities.
I. Kopper, Philip. II. Smithsonian Books
(Publisher)
E77.9.S54 1986   970.01   86-20239
ISBN 0-89599-018-0
ISBN 0-8109-1510-3 (Abrams)

CONTENTS

FOREWORD

The Americas have long been regarded as lands of immigrants. For nearly 500 years, Europeans, Africans and Asians have come to the New World, variously as explorers, settlers, slaves, indentured servants, contract laborers and tourists. (A few Norse seafarers stayed briefly in eastern Canada around A.D. 1000.) As we now know, and as this book relates, the early Europeans encountered peoples they called Indians who were themselves the descendants of immigrants. Their ancestors had come into the New World at various times over many millennia. In time some became farmers, and on this indigenous agricultural base, great civilizations arose in Mesoamerica and highland South America. Elsewhere in the Americas, cultural development took several courses as people adapted to, or "lived into," the various ecological and topographical conditions found on the two continents.

When the later immigrants arrived in North America from across the Atlantic, they found peoples as culturally diverse as the Inuit of the Arctic, the Iroquois of the Northeast, the Pueblo farmers of the Southwest and the great Aztec civilization of Mesoamerica. These and other Indians were sources of great wonder and puzzlement to the new European immigrants. Scholars and other thoughtful and curious folk speculated on who these people were: where had they come from and what was their history before Columbus arrived in 1492 and misnamed them?

For nearly two centuries answers to these questions remained essentially speculation, much of it far-fetched. But, beginning with Thomas Jefferson, inquiry into questions of American Indian cultural history was put on a more systematic, and ultimately scientific, basis. The course of the inquiry has been long and complex, due to the immensity of the topic and the nature of the archaeological record. Many questions remain uncertain or unanswered. As in any scholarly discipline, new data generate new hypotheses; old ideas are constantly being reexamined. The quest for new and more accurate knowledge is arduous—and it is full of excitement, both for archaeologists and interested lay persons.

This book does two things: it tells us about the quest, over the past two centuries, to understand and explicate New World culture history; and it tells us, in outline, what we think we know, at present, about that culture history. Both stories are full of interest. One is the complex and fascinating history of human adaptation to, and cultural development in, the New World over ten to twelve, perhaps twenty or more millennia. The other is the systematic attempt to understand and tell that history. The reader is invited to turn the page and begin both stories.

by Don D. Fowler
Mamie Kleberg Professor of Anthropology and Historic Preservation, University of Nevada at Reno; and Research Associate in Anthropology, Smithsonian Institution

THE PEOPLE

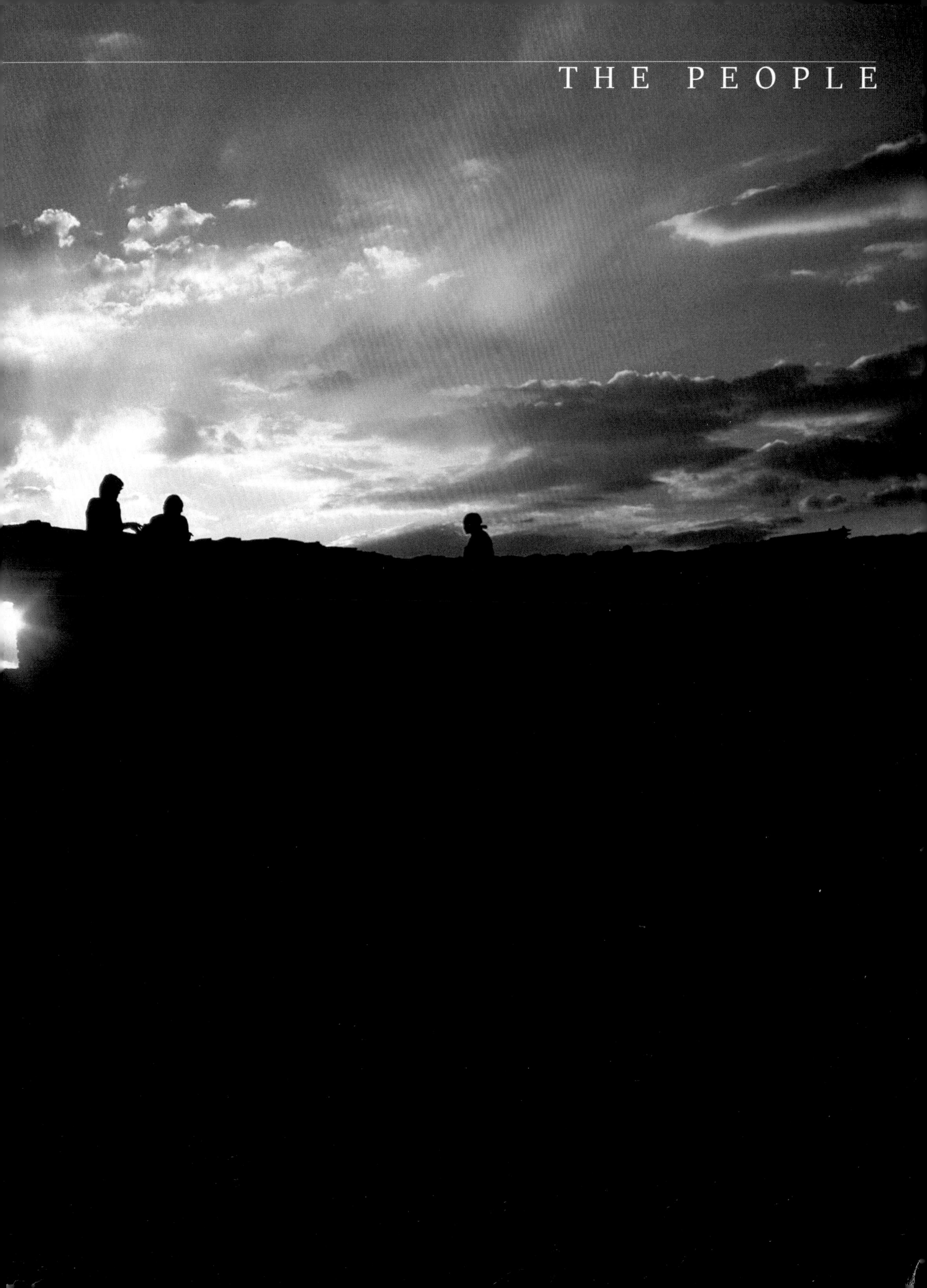

QUEST FOR THE PAST

We are real from the beginning of time.
—A Choctaw in 1985

 A century ago storytellers of the Pima tribe who lived around the Gila River Basin of southern Arizona related their people's beginning in this way: the Magician made the world, then realized it was not finished. "What he wanted on this earth was some beings like himself, not just animals." He shaped clay into figures of himself, built a *horno*, a clay oven, to bake them in and went off to gather firewood.

"Hanging around the way he usually does," Coyote, the Trickster, remolded the clay, which Man Maker the Magician placed in the oven without looking. When it was done he breathed life into an image, which then barked and wagged its tail. The Magician knew he had been fooled by Coyote, but did not undo his work when the Trickster asked "'What's wrong with it? Why can't I have a pretty animal that pleases me?'...That's why we have the dog; it was Coyote's doing."

When Man Maker made more images like himself and set them in the oven, Coyote pestered him to take them out too soon and the Magician said, "They're underdone. They're not brown enough. They don't belong here—they belong across the water someplace." And off he sent them. Then he tried again, but this time, after again taking Coyote's advice, he let them stay in too long. "Oh my. What's wrong? These are overdone. They're burned too dark....Maybe I can use them some other place across the water. They don't belong here."

Making two more figures, this time the Magician did not heed Coyote but took them out when he himself thought they were done. He breathed life into them. The two beings walked around, talked, laughed and behaved in a seemly fashion. They were neither underdone nor overdone. "These are exactly right," said Man Maker. "These really belong here; these I will use."

As Richard Erdoes and Alfonso Ortiz put it in *American Indian Myths and Legends*, many native Americans thought the White man was "one of the Creator's slight mistakes." Another mistake may have been that he only sent his underdone errors "across the water," where they did not stay put. Instead they returned to where they had been created, according to the lore of the Pima (who were neither more nor less ethnocentric than anybody else). There, by both intent and accident, they wreaked more havoc than even Coyote could cause.

Thereafter, much of the story belongs to history. Events occurring on this continent before Columbus—with the exception of those related in nearly forgotten Viking sagas—belong to prehistory, which by definition explores cultures whose stories were not recorded in writing.

The sciences, both social and biological, offer no support for the

A colorful selection of early North American artifacts from the Smithsonian suggests the richness of native American culture. Clockwise from the top: Acoma water jug (Southwest); Anasazi jar with handle (Southwest); Haida owl mask (Northwest); Columella beads (Southeast); Sikyatki polychrome bowl (Southwest); Mississippian monolithic stone ax (Southeast); Inuit water-bag handle (Arctic); Key Marco cat carving (Southeast); Mimbres bowl (Southwest); Iroquois wampum strings (Northeast). A pervasive symbol in the Southeast is the stylized hand, represented here in a silver disc, with a hand-and-eye motif, from the Fort Center site in Florida, top, and in what may have served as a paint palette from a Hopewell site in Ohio, above.

T his view of domestic life in a Nootka Sound house was illustrated by John Webber, who accompanied English Captain James Cook's survey of the Northwest Coast more than 200 years ago. Illustrations by Webber and other early eye-witness portraits, such as John White's rendition of an Inuit woman and child, above, still serve as an important source of information on pre-contact native life-styles.

notion that Europeans' arrival on this continent was a return. Furthermore, the event was much more significant than any mere "homecoming" could have been. The "discovery" of the New World has been called the most important event in the history of the Old. It opened two continents to avid colonization by expansionist Europeans and revealed a multitude of peoples whose existence shook the foundations of European thought.

Columbus encountered people "of very handsome bodies and fine faces" inhabiting what he presumed were the distant Indies, and so he dubbed them "los Indios." The misnomer stuck as Europeans tried to account for them even as the conquests began. In most of their languages the New World peoples called themselves the equivalent of "human beings," "humankind" or "people" and others something less. *Hopiti*, from which English derives Hopi, means "gentle people." Navajo call themselves *Dinneh*, meaning "people," in the sense of "the real people." According to one story, Indians of Canada's northern forests called their northern neighbors "eaters of raw meat," using a term that a Jesuit missionary transliterated as "Eskimos," which bore no relation to the name, *Inuit*, those northernmost people called themselves. Indians, like Europeans and others, all described their origins mythically: some said their ancestors came down to Earth on a rope. The Navajo appeared from the other direction: their ancestors were banished from a series of concentric worlds within this Earth because they misbehaved.

The savants of Europe overlooked an enormous truth while trying to

explain these peoples' origins within the context of the Bible, the basic document of European thought. The New World contained as varied a complex of human communities as the Old. Amerigo Vespucci described people with "no boundaries of kingdoms and princes, and no king." The Spanish conquistador Hernán Cortés encountered an empire that boasted astronomy, writing, monumental architecture and a vast and complex monarchy that ruled thousands of square miles and millions of people of a number of different tribes. Ancient mounds in the Ohio Valley were filled with stone and ceramic figures wrought by cultures long since gone into eclipse. In the Southwest stood abandoned towns that had been built by vanished people called Anasazi ("ancient enemies") and Hohokam ("all used up") in the tongues of their successors.

Insulated from the rest of the human race before the rise of complex civilizations, the Indians developed new strategies for hunting big game, such as mammoth and mastodon, and indeed new ways of living, both spiritual and physical, as they adapted to the continent they shared with the plants and animals upon which they depended for survival. While their contemporaries contrived metal tools and weapons halfway around the world, they raised stone technology to a matchless degree of artful utility and created metal ornaments of enduring beauty and artistic power. They successfully adapted to as many varied environments — arctic, desert, woodland, prairie, littoral, island and rain forest — as did the Old World's prehistoric or preindustrial ethnic groups. They developed pottery, basketry, irrigation, boats and more. At one time the societies of

"Ther was neur seen amonge vs soe cunninge a way to take fish," wrote artist John White during a late sixteenth-century visit to Virginia. Indians corralled fish in sophisticated weirs where they could spear them with long lances. The festooned North Carolinian hunter, above, painted by White, wore a complement of body paint, pearls and feathers to prepare for war or a solemn feast.

19

By the fifteenth century A.D., Tenochtitlán, shown in the model above, the imperial city of the Aztecs, was the center of a vast kingdom of tax-paying city-states stretching over most of central Mexico, the Mexican Gulf Coast and southern Mexico. As populous as any western European city at the time, metropolitan Tenochtitlán boasted a quarter of a million residents. A mural, right, from a temple wall in the Mayan city-state of Chichén Itzá depicts a waterside village scene.

the Western Hemisphere spoke nearly half the world's living languages. They peopled the lands and filled earth, sea and sky with pantheons of spirits. The triumphs and travails of the first Americans were as wondrous as those of any other peoples. The ancestral Indians, of course, had no known destination when they started out. Yet they populated one continent 6,000 miles long and 5,000 miles wide and ranged across another to the Strait of Magellan long before the Bronze Age dawned half the world away. If hunting alone could not sustain them (and it probably never did), some simply gathered wild plants, while others began nurturing them, perforce abandoning their nomadic freedom. In time many societies developed agriculture, domesticating wild plants, which made possible higher population densities and a degree of specialization of labor. This freed some to practice new crafts, others to contemplate (and placate) gods who ruled the uncertain forces of Earth, still more to engage in commerce, and a few to rule all the rest.

Into such realms came the White invaders, self-assured in the extreme, bringing with them a technology that aided them in their determination to conquer the peoples they confronted: large, seaworthy vessels; firearms and other iron and steel weapons and armor; and horses, animals unknown to the natives. The newcomers sought material wealth (Columbus had embarked to find a cheaper trade route to the Orient) and they set out to seize it any way they could.

Their inexorable drive to conquer, supported by guns, armor and mounts — and the unseen, unintended weapons of exotic diseases — made the newcomers irresistible, and the natives of the New World were vanquished and decimated. Many of those who survived had their bodies subjected to slavery and their souls to Christian conversion.

The remains of these peoples' past were often intentionally destroyed, overlooked as worthless or collected as curios. Monuments and temples of the great civilizations of Mesoamerica were often thrown down by the Spanish in their determination to bring Christianity to the Indians. The burial mounds of the East were most often leveled by the plow, for these "barrows" impeded the Europeans' agriculture.

In sum, as the colonists came in accelerating waves, many of the old peoples perished, while the remaining old cultures were altered almost beyond recognition. Yet tantalizing traces remained of what had been, clues to antiquity that posed innumerable questions for centuries.

Who built the ceremonial center of Copán in Yucatán with its ornately carved stelae? Who raised the fifteen-acre mound 100 feet high overlooking the Mississippi at Cahokia or the cliff palaces of Mesa Verde? What did the carved wooden cat represent before it became buried in

William Henry Holmes and his colleague, William Jackson, discovered this Anasazi house carved into a cliff face 700 feet above their campsite during a late-nineteenth-century geological survey expedition. Additional finds by the group among the hidden canyons of the Mancos River in southwestern Colorado revealed a remarkable complex of Anasazi cliff dwellings — today encompassed by Mesa Verde National Park. Holmes started out as expedition artist but later became chief of the Smithsonian's Bureau of American Ethnology.

A product of Caddoan artisans between A.D. 1200 to 1350, the ten-inch *Big Boy* effigy pipe, above right, was found in a burial mound at Oklahoma's Spiro site. A thousand-year-old Mayan grave ornament, below right, from Jaina Island off Mexico's Campeche coast portrays a woman weaving cloth on a backstrap loom stretched from her waist to a tree trunk. Indians of the region still employ the technique. From the same era, a Mayan cylindrical vase, above, depicts a scene from a ball game. Before two spectators, players in the foreground vie for the sport's large rubber ball, out of sight on the side of the vase.

When attached to a spear-thrower or atlatl, the banner stone, left, increased thrust and balance, enabling Indians of the Archaic period to throw their spears farther and more accurately. An important food source and burden carrier, the dog, represented on this late Mississippian drinking vessel, was the only domestic animal of the Southeast Indians.

the earth of Key Marco, Florida, where it would lie undisturbed for centuries? How did a piece of obsidian quarried in the Tetons find its way to the Ohio Valley when people traveled only on foot and by canoe? Why did fluted stone lanceheads—"Clovis points"—appear throughout the Americas some 10,000 to 12,000 years ago, then vanish from the stratigraphic record? What is the meaning of the Great Serpent Mound, a 1,300-foot-long earthen sculpture of a sinuous snake with something like an egg in its mouth? Whence came these people whose sacred tales told variously of descending from the sky, rising from earth and baking in Man Maker's kiln? After raising their mythic cities, where did the "old ones" go?

In part because of the cataclysms that followed "contact" and in part because few Indians had writing systems, these questions begged answers until the birth of archaeology. Not long after the thirteen colonies made good his Declaration of Independence, Thomas Jefferson would excavate an Indian "barrow" and conclude that it had been raised by a succession of people whose antiquity he could not guess at. The innumerable mounds of the Ohio Valley attracted others as the nineteenth century saw the rise of both serious investigation and self-serving speculation. Philosophical societies were organized in Boston and Philadel-

Figures on a bowl, above, from the Southwest's Hohokam culture may depict a dance similar to those still performed by peoples of the region. Right, such adornments as elaborate body painting, extensive tattooing and the facial banding and hair braiding seen on this copper-embossed Mississippian profile from the Southeast, probably indicated an individual's status.

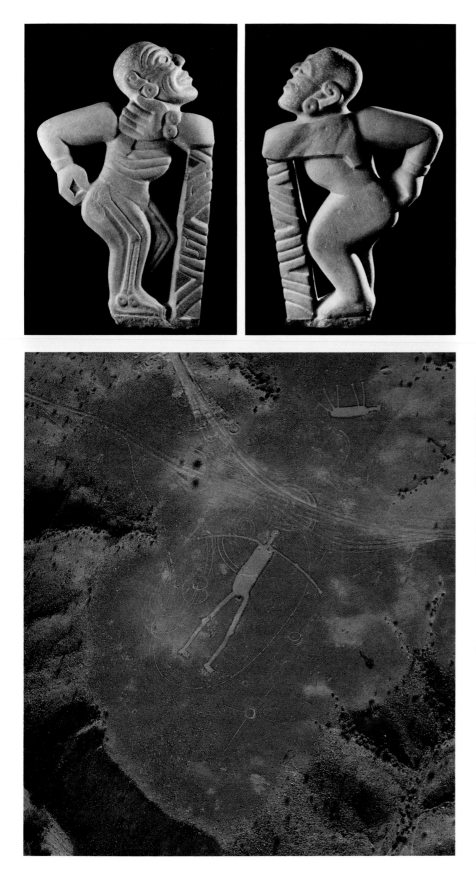

A diversity of human forms illustrates the variety of prehistoric North American Indian art: stone carvings of an old man and a young one leaning against a staff appear on opposite sides of the same Huastec sculpture from northeastern Mexico of the early eleventh century, left; the desert of southern California near Blythe bears an enigmatic gravel outline of a human figure 150 feet long, bottom left; the two-foot-tall effigy figures of a man and woman carved in marble were found with the remains of four individuals in the Etowah, Georgia site's mortuary temple mound.

Coyotes played a prominent role in the myths of many North American Indian cultures. A Hopewellian tobacco platform pipe from Ohio bears one, above, and a modern-day Navajo sand painting of a creation legend shows another, below. According to Navajo tradition, the Coyote stole a flame from the Fire God (lower left-hand corner) and brought it to the first man and woman (upper left-hand corner), leaving a zigzag trail of embers. Above right, a winsome Anasazi woman holding twigs dances for all eternity in a wall painting from northern Arizona.

phia. James Smithson, an English naturalist who never saw the United States, bequeathed a fortune to endow an American academy "for the increase and diffusion of knowledge among men." The Smithsonian Institution's first publication would be a study of these ancient mounds.

Interest in the native past of America grew hand in hand with the proliferation of universities and academies, with the development of the systematic sciences. While classical archaeology in the Old World has always been allied with the humanities and history of art, observers of natural phenomena in the New World—its exotic flora, fauna, geology and topography—launched the distinct traditions of American archaeology. Evolving out of natural history, American archaeology became part of the hybrid humanistic science, anthropology. Only a complex of disciplines could be used to piece together the aboriginal past, because America's ancient civilizations left such perplexing and diverse fragments: architectural ruins, folklore preserved by oral traditions, finely made stone weapons that survived tens of thousands of years, scattered shards of pottery, mortuaries rich in ritual goods and offerings, stores of grain, traces in the earth where posts once supported dwellings. From these clues the family of sciences and humanities called American archaeology has been painstakingly reconstructing the pasts of the original Americans for a hundred years or more. Now it is this book's goal to sketch the sometimes detailed and more often dim images of a puzzle that lacks more pieces than will ever be found.

All of us born on this continent descend from immigrants, no matter how recent or distant. It follows that a decent respect for the sensitivities of *all* ethnic groups prompts a word about nomenclature. When referring to specific living people, I shall endeavor to use the collective English noun that they use to name themselves. When speaking of a vanished native group or culture, I will use the name applied by archaeologists, usually one adapted from the place where the culture's artifacts were first unearthed. (Thus, following established practice: "Clovis" designates a material culture, consisting in this case of stone projectile points and scrapers, originally found in association with ancient bison bones at a "type site" near Clovis, New Mexico. "Clovis" does not refer to a people; Clovis-style stone tools were used by many Paleo-Indian peoples and have been found in nearly every part of North America.)

When referring to native North Americans in general, I will use the term that Columbus hopefully and mistakenly coined: Indian, the first single term that distinguished these various people from the rest of humankind. I hope no people of aboriginal descent will take offense, and let me state in advance that none is intended.

Skilled artisans at the site of eastern Spiro, Oklahoma, carved cedar to create this antlered mask, adorned with shells. Shamans may have danced wearing this mask, seeking good luck for hunters.

Bits of decayed flesh cling to the skull face of the Aztec god of the underworld, Mictlantecuhtli, who is squatting back to back with Quetzalcoatl, here portrayed as god of the wind in a portion of the fifteenth-century Aztec manuscript called the Codex Borgia. Death is symbolized by the position of the gods over the elongated, upside-down skull and Quetzalcoatl's jawlike knee decorations.

For light skinned (or "underdone") Americans of other ethnic origins, I will adapt Peter Farb's serviceable example from *Man's Rise to Civilization*, and use the term "White" with a capital W, except occasionally when referring specifically to Europeans who were the first to record their encounters with the Indians.

This book is both a work of prehistory that explores North America's preliterate cultures and one of history that involves the development of archaeology. The principals in this work, like Homer's heroes, are far removed. We may only know them through their scant remains and fascinating traces. They must be the stars of this narrative, while the archaeologists who have done the work of discovering them are featured players, messengers who bring the news. Without these men and women—both professional investigators and many amateurs—there would be no story to tell, because without archaeology the pre-Columbian past would remain largely unknown. As for the villain or antihero or trickster, we have one of those as well: time, which has caused such mischief in covering the tracks of all who came before us.

As my manuscript grows, the pile of its pages is weighted down by a worked, gray stone, an artifact found by a Washington boy near the Potomac River in the 1890s and generously given me by the boy who owned it next, the finder's now aging nephew, Henry W. Darmstead. A Smithsonian archaeologist confirmed my first suspicion: it is "a fully grooved ax" made from a cobble chosen for its roughly oval shape and slender proportion. Its business end, long since broken by use, was ground to a fairly keen cutting edge. The groove running completely around it was painstakingly "pecked" out chip by tiny chip with another stone until the indentation was deep enough to secure a wooden haft lashed with hide or sinew thongs. "It's not diagnostic to any age—except Archaic or later," Dennis Stanford told me, meaning that it's no more than about 10,000 years old. "Everybody except Paleo-Indians made them everywhere." Beyond that, little can be told from the artifact itself. Long since removed from where it lay, it cannot be "associated" with other telltale objects. It has no "context," no traces of organic material that the modern laboratory can date, no data-clad provenance, no scientific significance. The trickster Time has obscured its origins, its past. Yet I like its shape, its heft, and the fact that it is inscrutable. Let us find the people who made such a thing and wielded it to fell a sapling or fight a foe in the sunshine days of the prehistoric past. ✳

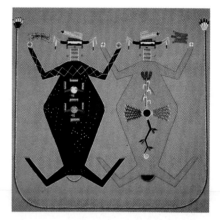

Lines of sacred pollen link the mouths and genitals of Father Sky and Mother Earth, creation's two halves, in this twentieth-century Navajo sand painting. Father Sky's night-black body also holds symbols of the sun, moon and stars of the Milky Way. Mother Earth appears with four sacred plants—corn, beans, squash and tobacco—growing out of an underworld wellspring.

THE IMMIGRANTS

 From time to time during the Pleistocene Epoch, which lasted between two and three million years, much of the world's water was locked in glacial ice while sea levels fell considerably. The Bering and Chukchi seas, shallow bodies of water today, were dry then, and in their place lay Beringia, a "lost continent" whose heartland would be submerged and reemerge several times during the relatively brief glacial periods.

The mechanics of glaciers are well understood, even if their causes remain unclear. Throughout the Pleistocene, Earth's climate underwent extreme fluctuations, especially of temperature and precipitation in the higher latitudes. During periods of severe cold, so much snow built up on the ground (and on the sea ice) that some survived the short summers; more fell each year than melted and ran off or evaporated, which produced an annual net gain in the buildup of snow. Canada's glaciers grew to perhaps nearly two miles thick near their centers—though this is not to say that ice-age people faced a mile-high "wall" of ice. At its margins the ice may not have been more than tens or hundreds of feet thick. But these were awesome barriers. Even if people had chosen to scale these heights, they could not have found food atop the ice—there no plants grew and thus no animals browsed.

In Africa, Europe and Asia, human beings became essentially "modern" during the ice ages. During the last ice age in Europe, Neandertal people, *Homo sapiens neanderthalensis,* began to bury their dead with ritual ceremony and grave goods. *Homo sapiens sapiens,* anatomically modern and culturally more sophisticated humans, succeeded the Neandertals. These people filled the Old World, leaving numerous examples of shelters, symbolic objects, carvings and paintings of animals, and weapons. They worked stone into knives, scrapers, spear points and a variety of other tools with extraordinary skill. Generation by generation they spread, until some occupied Siberia and eventually Beringia. There is no reason to believe that these people knew where they were going—or even that they knew they were going anywhere. Beringia should not be seen as just an avenue of transit, but as a place where people lived, some of whom moved on.

The term "migration" mistakenly implies intentional relocation, when actually the pace might have been so slow that each generation of immigrants thought they were simply moving to the next overlook or game-rich valley. When they moved deliberately, it may have been to follow a herd of caribou on its annual migration. When they explored, it may have been to discover where the flocks of waterfowl nested or wintered. As for the actual pace, it might have been determined by

Traveling into the New World across the Bering land bridge more than 12,000 years ago, humans and beasts alike faced scenes such as this one of Alaska's north slope—vast stretches of trackless tundra, broken only by long, winding rivers. Aside from people, the other migrants to North America included musk oxen, above; caribou; horses; a large, extinct form of buffalo; and woolly mammoths.

The First North American Immigrants

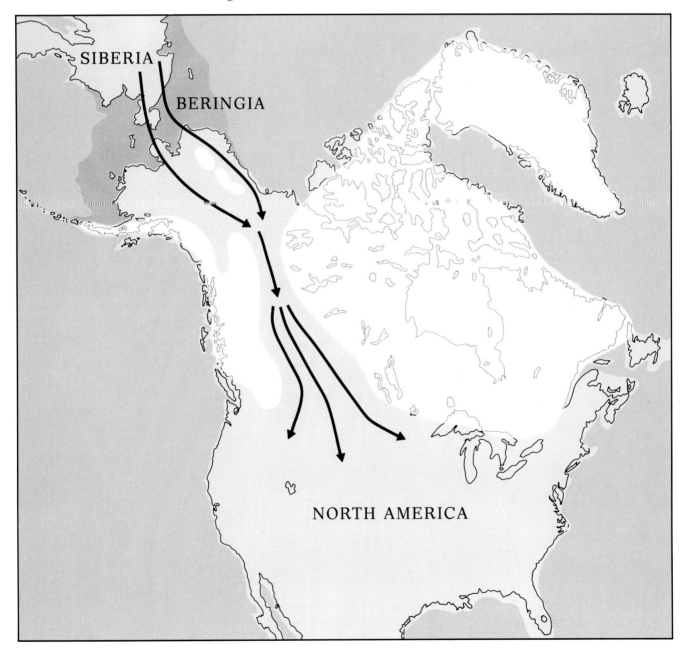

either one of two contradictory and equally human motives: the desire to stay put and the practical urge to move on. These first Americans may have lingered wherever they could make a living, which, before the rise of agriculture, meant where they found game. Even staying put, if the leader of a tribe moved his sleeping pallet only by the width of a bed each night, he would find himself ten miles away in a generation, or the distance from Canada to Nebraska in a millennium.

On the other hand, a school of anthropological thought holds that among hunting peoples the natural habit is to keep moving. This thesis maintains that when a hunting band finds a region particularly rich in game, it takes what it needs, notes the location for future reference and moves on, knowing it has found a living cache for the future. Those who preferred mammoths or mastodons as game might have borrowed from both life-styles. Ethnologists note that Africans who hunted elephants often followed a herd, waiting until they had learned the traits of its members before culling selected individuals—and leaving the most aggressive ones alone. Had the human invaders of the New World used this strategy, it could have meant a relatively fast transit down North America, across Mesoamerica and into South America, following one herd, then another. "Unmistakable signs" of ancient human occupation have been found near the tip of South America; people used Fell's Cave near the Strait of Magellan in Chile about 11,000 years ago. How much earlier must their first ancestors in the Americas have begun their unplanned trek down from Beringia? Although fierce controversies have raged for years over the date of the first human arrivals in the New World, archaeologists have reached no consensus. Their estimates range from 12,000 to 40,000 years ago, with most experts suggesting dates between 12,000 and 20,000 years ago. (In 1986, charcoal from a fire pit at a rock shelter site in Brazil was radiocarbon dated at 32,160 B.C. However, such early dates have proved to be in error before, and only further research will conclusively establish the age of this exciting find.)

What of their routes? While geologists can describe the glaciers' extent and duration with some certainty, many archaeologists contend that they have not defined the glaciology of Beringia with enough precision to serve prehistorical studies conclusively. At issue, for example, are the presumed locations of ice-free refuges in what is now Alaska, biotic oases similar to those in the ice-clad regions of northern Scandinavia today. The locations of the ancient Alaskan refuges play a critical role in estimating when migrations could have occurred, since people could not have crossed extensive inland glaciers. If and when they followed the Pacific coast remains a matter of conjecture because the ancient shores

During the Pleistocene Epoch, great global downturns in average temperature locked much of the earth's water into ice, reducing the level of the sea by as much as 300 feet. The shallow Bering Strait separating Siberia from Alaska became a natural land bridge that scientists call Beringia. Already well versed in the harsh realities of survival at northern latitudes, Asian Paleo-Indians moved into the New World, perhaps in pursuit of grazing animals. Mile-high glaciers prevented human passage beyond Beringia for most of the ice age. During certain periods, though, the Cordilleran and Laurentide ice sheets parted just enough to permit an ice-free passage into the heart of the continent. The view of northern Alaska near the Brooks Range, above, may resemble some of the landscape that the early immigrants to the New World encountered.

they followed have long since been inundated by the rising ocean and lie beyond the reach of archaeological excavators. In fact, most experts feel the shore from lower Alaska southward was not a likely route, for the steep coast lacked accessible beaches and was broken by rugged fjords. Still, a consensus holds that even during the height of the Wisconsin glaciation (the most extensive), the Laurentide ice sheet covering much of the northern continent never completely fused with the Cordilleran ice sheet of far western Canada. Between them lay a narrow ice-free corridor from Beringia to the southern interior. Presumably the human immigrants, living in small hunting bands, followed this corridor as they moved slowly south.

The territory that these bands entered presented a unique combination of circumstances. Such New World animals as the camel and horse had extended their ranges to the north and then west into the Old World; ancestral bison, moose, elephant and caribou had come the other way to browse or graze the colder regions of North America. Yet away from the glaciers this continent nurtured an array of mammals that the Old World had never known.

Whether from Old World or New, many Pleistocene mammals grew to extravagant size. Ground sloths reached twenty feet in length, mammoths stood fourteen feet at the shoulder and a beaver, with teeth the size of a woodsman's ax, grew as large as a black bear. There were horses and camels still about in North America and a bison with a six-foot span of horns, though the largest moose had antlers measuring eight feet across. Sustained by a flora adapted to the cool, wet conditions of the time, these browsers and grazers themselves supported a similarly impressive menagerie of predators.

The giant short-faced bear, *Arctodus simus,* was a long-limbed predator bigger than a grizzly, but much more highly adapted for running; it must have been the continent's most formidable carnivore. Some saber-toothed cats had eight-inch canines. An American lion, *Panthera leo atrox,* was larger than any of today's lions and rivaled in size any cat that ever lived. The dire wolf, *Canis dirus,* probably one of the mammals that evolved in South America, was the largest of the canine family. Giant teratorns, vulture-like birds with wingspans of fifteen feet or more, attended the predators' kills. It was into this realm that the first human immigrants walked, with a well-developed arsenal of weapons and hunting skills honed by thousands of years of Old World hunting experience.

Some experts have suggested that the late arrival of human hunters in North America was a critical factor in the extinction of many species of

Asian migrants discovered an astonishing variety of mammals in North America. In the upper left-hand corner of this Smithsonian mural a small group of hunters battles a twenty-foot-long ground sloth. Other animals, some now extinct, include: woolly mammoths (right and center background), moose (left background), short-faced bear (center), grizzly bear (right center, on snow), Dall sheep (center foreground), saiga antelope (right fore-gound), woodland musk ox (left center), horse (far left foreground), lionlike cats (right center), long-horned bison (left background), wolf (center), arctic fox (left foreground), wolverine (right background) and badger (right foreground).

For a time, Paleo-Indian hunters shared the North American continent with saber-toothed cats whose enlarged canines often grew eight inches long. These were specially adapted for slashing through the long hair and thick skin of large, slow-moving herbivores. Clear evidence that the stone-tipped spears of early Indian hunters could penetrate the skins of elephant-like mammals is found in this broken spear point, lodged in a mastodon bone.

large animals. In Africa, these prehistorians argue, the fauna, both large and small, had evolved shoulder to shoulder with the primates that included ancestral humans. As the genus *Homo* had arisen and eventually emerged as a predator in the Old World, the rest of the biological community had evolved, too. Predators—humans among them—threatened any edible animal's survival in the Old World, and the variety of African wildlife that survived into the Pleistocene presumably evolved traits that enabled them to adapt to the hunters. But in North America the animals evolved without humans in their midst. Suddenly, these animals found themselves confronting a species against whom they had no defenses. Their evolved behaviors only sufficed to protect them from other quadrupeds. One species that barely managed to survive demonstrates the significance of encountering a new predator. The musk ox, a gregarious ungulate, developed an effective defense against pack hunters like wolves. When threatened, these grazers do not panic and stampede—their slow, clumsy flight would provide little protection against fleet and tireless wolves. Instead they stand their ground bunched tightly, with the adults surrounding their young, ready to fight off attackers approaching from any direction. Such a static defense would be little more than an invitation to human hunters in open country, which may be why the once wide-ranging musk ox nearly vanished.

Eventually, a warming climate and perhaps other factors placed serious stress on the big herbivores as the Pleistocene's last glacial period waned; new flora replaced favored grasses and other plants; new temperature ranges and changed rainfall patterns added to the havoc. But the human hunter added a new factor in the survival stakes and may have helped push a number of large vegetarians over the brink of extinction, among them the mastodon, the mammoth and the long-horned bison, together with many of the carnivores that preyed upon them.

By archaeological definition, Paleo-Indians are those whose artifacts have been found with the remains of extinct megafauna—the huge vanished mammals of the Pleistocene. Notably this group includes those people who made the style of projectile points called Clovis points after the New Mexico site at which they were first found in 1932. Clovis projectile points have since been discovered all over North America, from Nova Scotia to Mexico, from the tundra to the mangroves. Similar stone points have also appeared in the Andes and Tierra del Fuego in South America. Many of the datable Clovis points appear to have been used from around 9500 B.C. to 8500 B.C., though older and younger sites also exist. One of the abiding mysteries of North American archaeology involves a complex of related questions. Where did the Clovis stone

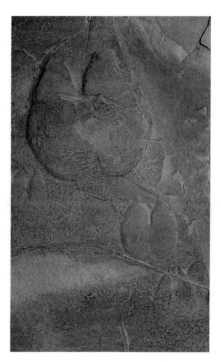

Fossilized footprints of a juvenile and adult camel were found in California's Death Valley National Monument. Camels were among the many large mammals roaming the North American continent before their extinction at the end of the Pleistocene. Changing climate may have placed them in jeopardy, a circumstance perhaps augmented by human predation.

In confrontation since Pleistocene times, a modern grizzly and moose face off in Alaska's Denali National Park, just as their ancestors may have 15,000 years ago. This time the mother was able to defend her calf.

points come from originally? How did they become ubiquitous so fast? Why did they disappear so suddenly?

Clovis stone point styles seemed to appear in full flower, yet they obviously derived from older traditions dating far into the Eurasian past. But archaeologists have not reached a consensus on the prior evolution, except to agree that Clovis points marked a transition from Old World stone toolmaking traditions.

Made of almost any variety of fine-grained or glass-like stone such as chert, chalcedony or obsidian, Clovis points are not only beautifully crafted, they are formidable weapons, three to four inches long and extremely sharp. It is possible that the points were designed to be hafted with sinew to a short wooden or bone handle, which in turn was fitted into a socket on a longer shaft to make a sharp-tipped lance. Thus the hunter need carry only one heavy shaft and several replaceable heads to be well armed. On the other hand, the points may have been fitted to light shafts to be hurled with an *atlatl,* a term archaeologists borrowed from the Aztec word for a spear-thrower. The atlatl was a simple and ingenious device, a sort of launch-pad handle that provided extra mechanical advantage by adding length to the hunter's arm.

Along with projectile points, and the spears they tipped, Clovis people made a variety of other tools, including scrapers, hammers, bone awls and needles. Nonetheless, their possessions seem to have been scant; evidently these people lived in traveling bands. Clovis campsites typically contain the remains of prey that became extinct at the end of the Pleistocene: mammoths, mastodons, sometimes long-horned bison or horses, as well as animals still living today, such as caribou. Their travels carried them afar; before their toolmaking tradition disappeared, Clovis point makers had reached Nova Scotia, the Yukon and the Andes.

Other archaeologists suspect that Clovis people were not quite so nomadic but returned regularly to semipermanent campsites. Further, they may have had a "technology" far more advanced than previously assumed. Witness the 11,000-year-old Thunderbird site in Virginia's Shenandoah Valley. Among middens and toolmaking debris, excavations revealed a perplexing pattern of nearly invisible "postmolds." These stains appear in the ground after wooden posts decay and, over time, turn into new earth. The new earth retains its distinctive color for a long time and can be detected by a careful archaeologist. The pattern at Thunderbird was very faint, the molds barely inches deep in farmland that had been plowed for nearly 300 years, but chemical tests ascertained that the earth of the molds was younger than the surrounding ground. Errett Callahan, an expert in paleolithic technol-

At Folsom, New Mexico, bones of an extinct bison were uncovered beside the flint spear point that killed the creature, providing irrefutable archaeological proof of humans' early arrival in the New World. The hunter of this animal must have lived at least 10,000 years ago, the time when *Bison antiquus* became extinct.

ogy (including the many arts of toolmaking), was commissioned to raise a structure based on the postmold pattern, using only tools and techniques available to Paleo-Indians. His building is an eye-opener, because accounting for all the postmolds produced a surprisingly sophisticated shelter. University of Delaware professor Jay F. Custer, another specialist in the region's archaeology, put it this way when he first saw it: "Paleo-Indians weren't *supposed* to put that much effort into a house."

An experimental archaeologist by trade, Callahan used fire-hardened hickory sticks to punch post holes in the earth. He cut saplings with stone axes hafted in fire-bored wooden or deer antler handles. Setting green saplings in the post holes and bending them into a shelter frame tied with bark or rawhide thongs, he raised a convincing oval framework more than thirty-six feet long. He found some anomalous postmolds along the north side of the primary ring and, determined to account for every stain in the original pattern, he decided they could have held uprights for a wattle windbreak. Another row of seemingly out-of-place molds ran through the stone-age house. Callahan postulated that these became uprights for a baffle to reduce interior drafts and conserve the heat from two hearths serving the thirty-odd people in the house. There were no signs of the hearths themselves within the discovered postmold pattern. That there should have been hearths is clear. This region, which experiences temperatures as low as zero in modern winters, was somewhat colder 11,000 years ago, when snowfall might have measured forty inches a year. But no hearths were found. Possibly they were destroyed by plowing during the historic period. And, of course, there are other possible interpretations for the entire scenario. What appear to be post-hole patterns for one long house may be post holes for two houses built on almost the same site at different times. No one can be sure from existing evidence.

The task of piecing together the Paleo-Indian past is an undeniably difficult one for the archaeologist. Callahan adopted a novel approach. By personally living off the land using only stone-age tools for a period of months, he hoped to discover that technology's capabilities. He follows a basic tenet: "absence of proof is not proof of absence." There remain many fascinating truths to discover, or hypotheses whose validity may be demonstrated by a long stint in the wilderness or by building a house with archaic tools. Witness the revealing efforts to discover how Paleo-Indians lived on the western plains.

A classic example of such archaeological sleuthing is found in Joe Ben Wheat's analysis of the Olsen-Chubbuck bison kill site near Big Sandy Creek in southeastern Colorado. About 8,500 years ago, hunters ambushed a bison herd on the plain, then stampeded nearly 200 of them into the natural trap of a narrow arroyo—a dry gulley. In blind panic the animals ran to escape, only to stumble and meet their deaths in the little ravine.

The ancient shambles was exposed by wind erosion in 1957 after several years of drought had wasted an already semiarid region. Gerald Chubbuck, an amateur archaeologist who had visited the area for many years, came upon it in December and collected several projectile points of a post-Clovis style termed Scottsbluff. Notifying Wheat, a curator at the University of Colorado Museum, he returned with another skilled amateur, Sigurd Olsen, and dug about a third of the site until the professionals embarked on a major excavation the following summer.

Here is what Wheat and his party found when they uncovered the ancient arroyo. From a shallow start, the little gulch ran eastward and in the course of 200 feet broadened from eighteen inches to a width of twelve feet while cutting its way to a depth of seven feet. Within a stretch of 170 feet lay about fifty skeletons that Chubbuck and Olsen excavated and 143 more that Wheat's team unearthed: forty-six mature bulls and twenty-seven young ones; sixty-three adult cows and thirty-eight immature ones; sixteen calves, some only a few days old. Wheat reported his findings nearly twenty years ago in *American Antiquity*, the journal of the Society for American Archaeology, and in *Scientific American:* "The bones were found in three distinct layers. The bottom layer contained some thirteen complete skeletons; the hunters had not touched these animals," presumably because they lay beneath others

A team of scientists led by the Smithsonian's Dennis Stanford used flaked stone tools to cut up a dead elephant in an attempt to learn more about how hunting peoples may have butchered fallen mammoths 12,000 years ago. Hacking, sawing and chopping with tools of obsidian—natural glass—replicas hafted onto wooden handles, Stanford found the labor involved in this task "tremendous" but certainly possible. One surprising observation made by the team was that the degree of wear on the tools, calculated by equipment seen in the center photo, was substantially less than originally expected—raising new questions about standard explanations for the heavily abraded cutting edges found on many prehistoric tools.

that were wedged in too tightly to be removed. Of the complete and nearly complete skeletons at the bottom of the gulch, twenty-one faced from southeast to southwest, a few faced east or west, while none faced toward the northern half of the compass.

Reconstructing the event that brought these animals to such a pass, Wheat analyzed the lay of the southward-sloping land as it must have been. Since the arroyo ran across the drainage, it could not owe its origin to the mechanics of normal runoff. He surmised that it began instead as a bison trail worn in the dry ground by animals making their habitual way to the nearby river. Frontiersmen in the nineteenth century noted that bison trails typically approached rivers at right angles, a bit of information that had interesting implications when integrated with other details gleaned from the site.

However opportunistic Paleo-Indians might have been on occasion, this kill was no accident but a carefully planned event. In order to bring it off, the ancient hunters apparently learned where and when a bison herd made its way to water. Only then could they have deployed themselves in advance and driven the animals into the natural trap. This took planning, organization and a sound knowledge of the herd's habits. All this was suggested by the topography, the site and by lance points found in the skeletons of the intact bison at the bottom of the heap—animals that the Indians had not been able to retrieve and butcher. The positions

Skilled flint worker and experimental archaeologist, Errett Callahan knaps a Clovis point, a style of spear point favored by Paleo-Indians as long ago as 10,500 B.C. in many parts of North America. It takes Callahan two hours to reduce a grapefruit-sized piece of Texas chert to a point ready for hafting to a wooden shaft. He uses a variety of tools made of stone and moose antler to create the points. The last step is the creation of a flute or depression in the side of the point to facilitate its attachment to a shaft. An example of a possible prehistoric vise, fashioned out of a forked stick wrapped with sinew, holds the point and prevents its fracturing while the Clovis flute is flaked off by a single blow from an antler tool.

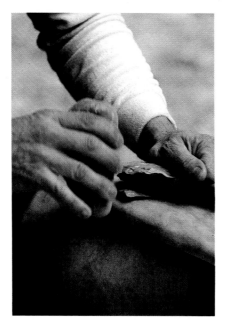

of the lance points showed Wheat that some of the hunters rose from ambush along the herd's eastern flank when the frightened animals approached, thus forcing them toward the draw. Few animals were trapped in the shallower western end of the arroyo, but it is fair to assume that another group of hunters was posted on the western flank to keep the whole herd from making an end run around the trap.

These animals were *Bison occidentalis,* a species of bison extinct today. Assuming that they shared the weak eyes and sharp nose of *Bison bison* (the surviving historical species), they could be approached warily so long as the hunters' scent did not reach the herd. This, of course, required the hunters to approach a grazing or water-bound herd from downwind. Most of the doomed leaders—the undisturbed carcasses—were headed south and none north. It follows that they were running south when they came to the arroyo and stumbled down its steep side to be maimed, smothered or trapped by animals that followed the leaders over the edge. The wind must have been blowing from the south, Wheat reasoned, and the hunters launched their attack from the north. The presence of calves indicated to Wheat that the kill occurred in late May or early June. (Recently, scholars have revised the seasonal date of the bison jump to late summer or early fall. During the last five years, George Frison, at the University of Wyoming, developed and used new dating techniques and information unavailable to Wheat when he

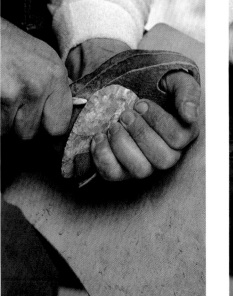  

Smithsonian archaeologist Dennis Stanford, second from left, and colleagues, above, test a prehistoric spear-thrower, the atlatl, an implement that enhances the thrusting power of a stone-tipped spear. Stanford demonstrates proper throwing form, right, in a series of strobe-lighted photographs. He pierced a 4-inch-square target at forty yards, a testimony not only to skill but also to the special handling characteristics of a well-made atlatl.

excavated the site. Frison found that the calves were several months older than originally thought, pushing the date from spring to summer.)

When bison panic, "the herd has a tendency to close ranks and stampede in a single mass," Wheat wrote. (Unlike musk ox, they could not be counted on to huddle together and stay put when attacked.) "If the herd encounters an abrupt declivity such as the Olsen-Chubbuck arroyo, the animals in front cannot stop because they are pushed by those behind. They can only plunge into the arroyo, where they are immobilized, disabled or killed by the animals that fall on top of them." Some that survived the fall no doubt struggled and escaped; others were dispatched by the hunters. Then the carcasses were hauled up onto the plain and butchered, a process that could be explained in part with the help of practical ethnology.

"The way in which the butchering units were grouped suggests that several bison were moved into position and cut up simultaneously," Wheat wrote. "Since foreleg units, sometimes in pairs, were found at the bottom of each pile of bones it seems reasonable to assume that the Paleo-Indians followed the same initial steps in butchering that the Plains Indians did in recent times. The first step was to arrange the legs of the animal so that it could be rolled onto its belly. The skin was then

cut down the back and pulled down on both sides of the carcass to form a kind of mat on which the meat could be placed. Directly under the skin of the back was a layer of tender meat, 'the blanket of flesh'; when this was stripped away, the bison's forelegs and shoulder blades could be cut free, exposing the highly prized 'hump' meat, the rib cage and the body cavity and its prized organs.

"Having stripped the front legs of meat, the hunters threw the still-articulated bones into the arroyo. If they followed the practice of later Indians, they would next have indulged themselves by cutting into the body cavity, removing some of the internal organs and eating them raw. This, of course, would have left no evidence among the bones. What is certain is that the hunters did remove and eat the tongues of a few bison at this stage of the butchering, presumably in the same way the Plains Indians did: by slitting the throat, pulling the tongue out through the slit and cutting it off. Our evidence for their having eaten the tongues as they went along is that the tongue bones [hyoids] are found throughout the deposit instead of in one layer or another." Then the exposed rib cages were addressed and ribs broken off—perhaps by using a leg bone with the hoof attached for a hammer, as Plains Indians did.

And so it went, as the butchers cut the spine away from the pelvic

A rain shower fifty years ago eroded a gully near Dent, Colorado, exposing the 11,000-year-old remains of a successful Paleo-Indian mammoth hunt. Denver Museum of Natural History investigators, above, found evidence that Paleo-Indian hunters stampeded a group of mammoths into the gully, dispatching twelve by boulders and Clovis-pointed spears. With other sites such as Clovis, Dent provides reliable dates for early human presence in the New World.

girdle, then dealt with the hind legs, removing meat as they went. Wheat found special significance in the way that the neck vertebrae were "draped over the front" of the skulls, indicating that the neck meat had been cut off. For Plains Indians, neck meat was too tough to eat "in its original state." They dried it for later use as pemmican. "The fact that the Paleo-Indians cut off the neck meat strongly suggests that they too preserved some of their kill."

Wheat found no indication that these ancient hunters removed bison brains, as their successors did. On the other hand, "historical accounts of butchering by Plains Indians indicate no such efficient system" as "the high degree of organization displayed by the Paleo-Indians."

Finally, Wheat estimated the hunters' numbers. On the basis of modern butchering data he projected the amount of food that this kill yielded—56,640 pounds of meat plus five tons of organs and fat. On the basis of historical records, he reported that a feasting Indian adult "could consume from ten to twenty pounds of fresh meat a day." Further, a newly killed animal was deemed palatable for as long as a month. Then juggling all these data with notions of how heavy a load nomads could carry, Wheat suggested that the kill provided a band of 150 Paleo-Indians with food for about a month. The dry pemmican could have lasted much longer, indefinitely for all practical purposes, while the fresh meat would have gotten quite "high" in the heat of summer. But for a people living before the amenities of modern food processing and storage, this lode undoubtedly represented a dietary treasure.

Now viewing retirement through the haze from his constant pipe, Joe Ben Wheat urges us to stay alert to the plain fact that "ancient people faced the same problems that we do": to provide themselves with clothing, utensils, shelter and the comforts of life—as they lived it. Paleo-Indians got all this and more from the bison, whose hide provided material for shelters and clothing, whose bones provided ornaments and tools like needles, whose sinews provided cord and lashings. A bison herd on the hoof was their supermarket, and offered innumerable goods, including meat in giant packages.

Wheat's advice points out another lesson that we ought not to forget. Whoever would call the earliest Americans "primitive" ought to consider bagging a bison herd on foot. Better that we consider their capabilities, their skills, their foresight and strategies. Paleo-Indians colonized the continent! ✳

Brilliant deductions by archaeologist Joe Ben Wheat revealed remarkable detail — from time of year to prevailing wind direction — of a large Paleo-Indian bison kill that occurred in southeastern Colorado some 8,500 years ago. Nearly 200 bison were funneled into an arroyo and killed at the Olsen-Chubbuck site.

THE INHABITANTS

In the fullness of time the ancient immigrants to the Americas became inhabitants of a new land offering environments as varied as its eventual human societies. The result was the emergence of cultures of spectacular diversity. Discovering how these cultures developed remains one of the Herculean challenges facing archaeology. Today most evidence of ancient life must be gleaned painstakingly from the soil.

First, civilization—a relatively high level of cultural and technological development—did not come full-blown into the New World; instead, civilization evolved from simpler beginnings here, and did so several times over. The variety of prehistoric American cultures is too divergent for all to have sprung from a single root stock at a single time. Rather, a host of independent cultures arose. Some peoples developed considerable sophistication and seemed bent on continuing to flower; others peaked, then went into decline; others seem to have settled into a stable relationship with each other, their neighbors and their land.

The first Americans were isolated from what Europeans long believed to be the only seats of civilization in the Middle and Far East. Yet they developed complex systems of agriculture, pottery, weaving and monumental architecture. There also arose such amenities as artistry in sculpture, ceramics and fabrics; oral literature of epic depth and complexity; and a practical tradition of astronomical observation that enabled development of a more accurate calendar than contemporary Europe could boast in 1492.

Many of these elements will be discussed in the regional chapters that constitute *Land and Culture*. For now, let us consider two fundamental processes that led to diverse civilization in America: the growth of agriculture and linguistic development.

The rise of agriculture must be counted among prehistory's seminal happenings. It occurred more than once, in the Old World, of course, and—independently—in the New. Although the reasons for the early domestication of plants are not known, it seems likely that people began the process by managing the environment and growth of wild plants that produced some desirable food or fiber. Evidence from central Mexico indicates that, perhaps as long ago as 9,000 years, people began to manipulate the ancestral stocks of today's corn (maize) to produce a larger "ear." By 5,000 years ago, domesticated plants in Mexico included corn, beans and squash, and many others. Once agriculture arrived in what is now the southwestern United States, it was adopted in several forms by several peoples who—it deserves emphasis—must have been predisposed to it for reasons of their own. Despite obsolete theories

A mural, opposite, painted on the wall of the balcony of the National Palace in Mexico City by Diego Rivera, Mexico's famed artist, portrays the Totonac people of eastern Mexico tending the maize fields and preparing tortillas. In a series of such murals, Rivera evokes the history of his country from ancient times. Above, a hunter flexes a bow in this petroglyph from Michigan.

49

to the contrary, it did not just happen inevitably through some "natural" course of events or some innate bent for "progress."

As University of New Mexico archaeologist Linda S. Cordell has aptly summarized, many scholars just a generation ago assumed that humans invented agriculture "as an almost natural outgrowth of an 'evolutionary trend' toward more complete control over the environment." Consequently the development of agrarian ways did not need to be explained but could be taken for granted. Recently, however, a number of "very important studies of modern hunters and gatherers dispelled a number of ethnocentric myths about the hunting and gathering way of life." For example, numerous observers have noted that hunter-gatherers invest less labor in obtaining food than do farmers. Typically they work two days a week rather than the four to six days that preindustrial farmers must toil in fields. Further, while farmers' children in preindustrial societies are routinely put to work, foragers often do not depend on the help of their young. Few humans seem to want to work harder than necessary (witness our modern love of "laborsaving" devices). It follows that people who turned to more laborious lifeways were either compelled to do so or found some special advantage in it. For these reasons and others, Cordell concludes that the adoption (or development) of agriculture should not be seen as an essentially "natural" tendency. Rather, the causes are complex and usually dependent on local conditions which are extremely difficult to reconstruct today.

C lay animal figurines from ancient Snake-town in south central Arizona may represent female deer and were perhaps part of a Hohokam fertility rite. Similarities among the figurines suggest the craftsmanship of a single artisan.

However, archaeologists did not need to look far to discover a likely motive for prehistoric Indians to become farmers in the Southwest. One of the simplest reasons is the nutritional imperative. People must eat. The rule applies even in a region where the abundance of wild food sources varies substantially, sometimes from year to year and often from century to century, in climatic cycles. Given a relatively fertile period when ample rain falls each year to sustain wild plants (which in turn support animals), human populations might easily increase. On the other hand, when droughts reduce available wild foods, even a stable human population, to say nothing of a growing one, must augment normal forage sources. In both cases—in times of wild plenty or natural want—prehistoric people would be compelled to find ways to feed themselves that were not purely dependent on the whims of nature. They might turn to the most elementary forms of horticulture not because of any inherent evolutionary bent, but simply because their appetites exceeded what nature's larder supplied.

This is not to say that agriculture developed overnight, but rather over a span of millennia. The traditional beginning of agriculture is usually placed sometime in the Archaic period, after the Paleo-Indians had been forced to forsake their dependence on declining herds of the biggest game. Indians did not suddenly become innovators; more likely they were quite conservative, following their ancient living habits as long as possible. The Southwesterners who first practiced rudimentary

Karl Bodmer, a Swiss artist on an expedition up the Missouri River during the 1830s, painted a buffalo skull perched atop a cairn and suggested that it was an Assiniboin medicine sign, a magical device used as a buffalo lure by hunters of the Great Plains. Bodmer's watercolors, along with the written accounts of German naturalist Prince Maximilian of Wied, provided a vivid picture of the vanishing lifeways of the Plains Indians.

51

Evolved from ancient Mexican strains, modern corn or maize grows in a field at Navajo National Monument in northern Arizona, opposite. Inhabitants of Wupatki pueblos near today's Flagstaff, Arizona, ground dried maize kernels with grindstones called a metate and mano, above. Ripe ears of corn adorn the headdress of the Mixtec god of maize, right, from Oxaca, Mexico.

agriculture remained mobile much of the year. The people of the Southwest's Cochise culture, for example, planted seeds in the course of springtime wanderings. Then they returned to the planting site when the plants were ripening—just as they knew to arrive at places where known wild foods grew in time to harvest them.

The first maize in America north of Mexico, found in New Mexico's Bat Cave, has been dated by the University of Michigan's Richard Ford at about 1000 B.C. Its promise of a more certain food supply had consequences that can only be described as revolutionary. These ramifications included a multitude of changes both in technology and living habits. Further, many of these changes were interdependent.

Using wild cereals requires some sort of milling tools to remove husks and grind grains into flour. The simplest innovations were grinding stones. A milling stone itself, however, is heavy, clumsy to move and difficult to make—something not to be discarded out of hand. A seasonally nomadic tribe, which understandably preferred to travel light, would be

Virginia Indians grill shadlike fish in Theodore de Bry's engraving, right, adapted from a late sixteenth-century drawing by John White. Carved with a bird symbol, the jasper plummet from Louisiana's Poverty Point, above, may have served as a weight for fishing nets or lines.

inclined to leave it near the area of cultivation, then return to use it when the crop matured.

By simply planting seeds and letting them grow without care or even taking advantage of "volunteer" seeds left after wild plants were consumed the year before, the most casual sort of agriculture can be practiced while a nomadic lifeway continues. But maximizing a crop's yield requires nurturing the plants and that in turn means settling down at least for the length of a growing season. When a people settled down—even for a season—they encountered new sets of constraints. For instance, nomadic foraging involves finding limited supplies of fresh food frequently, while staying put requires a self-sustaining source of fresh food (that is, reliable animal herds) or long-term storage. The advantages of containers more waterproof, insect-proof and rodent-proof than baskets must have become obvious. However it happened that pottery was invented (or adopted), there were practical needs for it, incentives for its development. As agriculture moved north, pottery followed.

Most dramatically, perhaps, it behooved farmers in the dry Southwest to assure the availability of water lest the crop perish in a midsummer drought. It was imperative that they develop ways of marshaling a scant water supply and manipulating it—an irrigation system. In turn, building such a system may have implied a major construction project, which depended on long-term communal cooperation and efficient organization of a work force.

Taken separately, all these factors involved the evolution of new activities, which in turn depended on the discovery and use of dramatically different skills and tools than those that served hunter-gatherers. Taken together, these changes called for new allocations of energy and new kinds of social organization. The rise of agriculture opened dramatic new opportunities for people who changed their way of living, but also required major changes in living habits. It is hardly stretching the point to suggest that a commitment to agriculture is tantamount to revolution.

Although anthropologists have traditionally held that in many, if not all, environments, the rise of agriculture and the adoption of sedentary living patterns were linked, it appears that peoples in many regions adopted sedentary or semi-sedentary ways without also adopting intensive agriculture. In the Northeast, Northwest and Southeast lived peoples who combined sedentary habits with hunting-gathering, and practiced limited agriculture, if any at all.

At Poverty Point, a 3,500-year-old site in northern Louisiana, several thousand people may have lived a sedentary existence, apparently almost entirely without agriculture (see Chapter 8). Some archaeologists have suggested that this remarkable center supported itself by hunting, fishing and foraging for wild plants. While Poverty Point's reason for existence remains something of a mystery, evidence indicates that it may have been a major trading hub as well as a ceremonial center.

From the evolution of sedentary cultures grew civilizations bewilder-

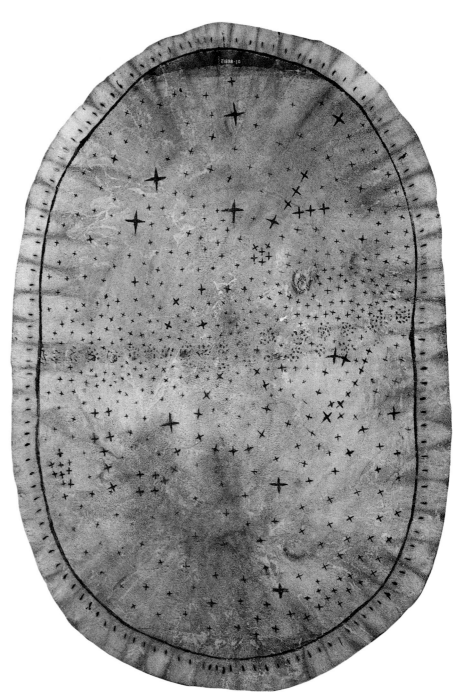

S tar groupings and patterns important to Skidi Pawnee cosmology are represented on a leather sky, right, from the historical Plains period. Pawnee priests probably employed it for ceremonial rather than astronomical purposes. A detail of a Navajo petroglyph in sandstone, above, appears to depict a humpbacked god next to a circular symbol of the cosmos. Fringed with eagle feathers, the hump contains water and seeds.

ing in their complexity. In fact, the signal trait of native America is its spectacular cultural heterogeneity. No better example exists of this than language—"American Babel" in University of Minnesota ethnologist and linguist Robert F. Spencer's terms. As many as 200 languages, some as different as Chinese is from German, existed in North America. More languages were spoken in California alone than are native to Western Europe. The extreme diversity of native American tongues suggests that they were not imported; rather they developed here from several primitive ancestral stocks.

Would knowledge of those origins provide a key to some of the puzzles of the native American past? It would appear that relationships among the languages should reveal past movements of peoples, their connections and separations. But that cannot yet be done.

Two linguistic techniques, glottochronology and lexicostatistics, illustrate some of the basic problems. Glottochronology traces closely related languages back to a common root by analyzing changes in sound that occur at a fairly regular rate. However, in a millennium a language changes more than 20 percent of the elementary words and structures it shares with related languages. Simple arithmetic then leads to the conclusion that if two languages split off from a common stock by 3000 B.C., almost all their shared words would have vanished by the time serious linguistic study began a century ago—even if the offspring languages avoided other influences, which is rarely the case. Lexicostatistics analyzes words held in common by distantly related languages, but this, too, is a chancy business among long-lived tongues, especially ones that have borrowed back and forth and influenced each other after descending from unrelated stocks.

While tentative groupings of languages do help scholars interested in linguistic relationships, Smithsonian linguist Ives Goddard dispels the notion that living languages can be traced back to explain the mysteries of migration and prehistoric origins. The way languages work and changes occur in people's manners of speaking are far too complex for that, as are the tangled connections between language, culture and environment. A useful example lies in the more familiar realm of Europe's Romance languages. People inhabited the Italian peninsula, Iberia and Gaul long before the rise of Rome or even the appearance of Latin. Iberia in particular had strong native linguistic traditions, yet languages closely related to Latin came to the fore. The reason is simple enough: a governing class came to speak the language of imperial Rome, and in time that language, Latin, filtered down through the societies of Portugal, Spain, France and Italy. It even made significant contributions to a Germanic

A rock wall painting found in New Mexico's Chaco Canyon may tell the story of a supernova that appeared near the crescent moon on July 4, 1054. The hand mark may have denoted the spot's sacred status among the Anasazi of the area.

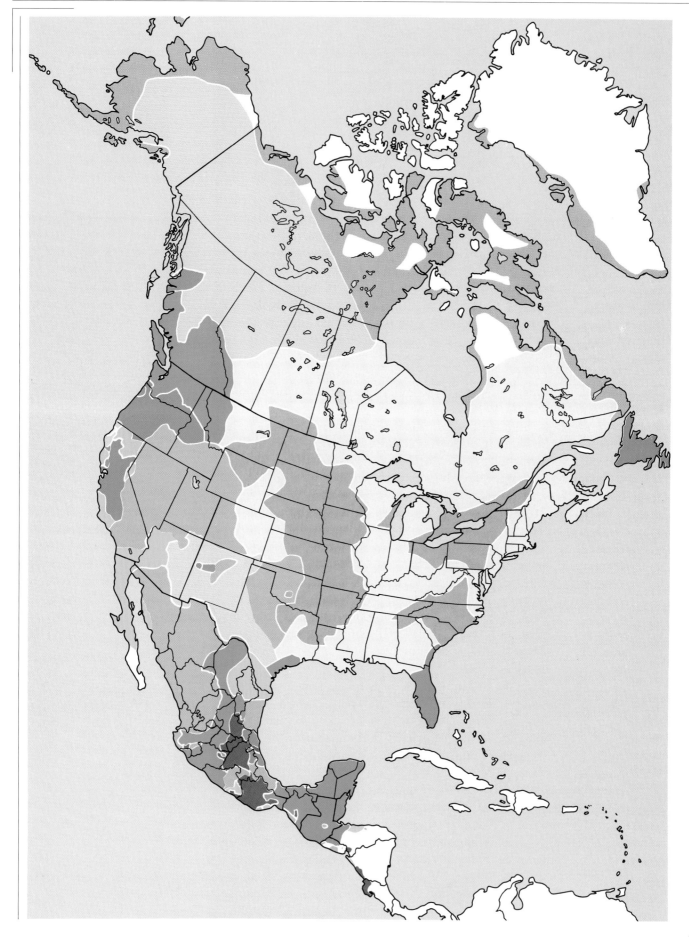

North American Indian Language Groups

Eskimo-Aleut

Na-Dene

Macro-Algonquian

Macro-Siouan

Hokan

Penutian

Aztec-Tanoan

Oto-Manguean

Undetermined

Linguists believe that at least 200 languages and perhaps many more were spoken in North America at the time of European contact. These languages were mutually unintelligible: an Owascan from New York State would have had as much difficulty communicating with a Pima from the Southwest as with a Mandarin from China.

The map at left divides these languages into large groups called phylums. The languages within one group are related to each other but have no apparent relation to those of another group.

Each group consists of a number of families composed of distinct but related languages. The Seneca, Mohawk and Cherokee languages fall into one family, the Iroquoian, in the same way that French, Spanish and Italian are part of the Romance family. Linguists believe that at the time of contact about seventy-three language families existed in North America. In fact, more families existed in California alone than in all of Europe. Within each family may be many languages; within each language are dialects.

Linguists face many difficulties in studying prehistoric North American languages, since all except Mayan were unwritten. (However, because a language is not written does not mean that it is in any way "primitive" or unsophisticated.)

Information for the language map was compiled by University of Indiana scholars C. F. and F. M. Voegelin in 1966 after the classificatory consensus reached by the First Conference on American Indian Languages.

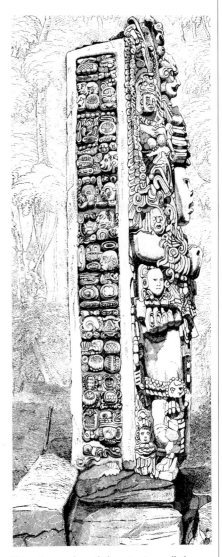

Using pictographs and phonetic signs called glyphs — the only writing system ever developed in prehistoric North America — Mayan scribes immortalized the exploits of a prince on this twelve-foot-tall stela from Copán in Honduras. The illustration was drawn by Frederick Catherwood, who with John L. Stevens traveled in Central America during the years 1839 and 1840.

The wooden box, above, held eagle feathers worn by the Ojibwa of Wisconsin on religious occasions. Pictographic inscriptions on the outside of the lid helped ritualists remember the words of songs sung at annual ceremonial gatherings. A historic era Tlingit shaman's charm, right, took the form of a five-inch-long spirit canoe carved in the shape of a sea lion and an octopus, carrying seven spirits.

language, English, after Roman influence was felt in the empire's northern realms. Thus the spread of Latin reflects political events but could hardly be used to uncover settlement patterns or population movement.

The example demonstrates that clear relationships between languages do not prove much more than the likelihood that ancestors of the people who speak them were somehow connected in the past. But connected when and how? By blood, trade, accidental proximity or conquest? Those who study linguistics can only answer that historical Indians who speak Algonquian tongues must share linguistic roots. This observation means that the ancestors of latter-day speakers shared some experience or ancient connection, but just what sort of connection,

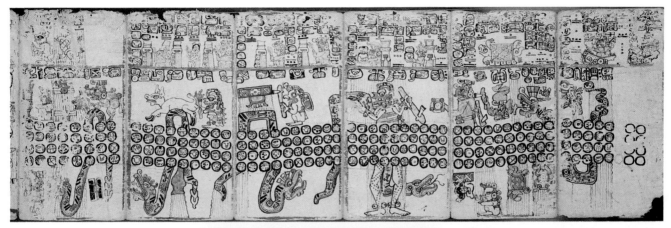

P rogression of a serpent image through pages of the Madrid Codex, above, one of a very few surviving Mayan manuscripts, may chronicle the movement of a constellation through the sky in A.D. 1400. The Maya accurately recorded the dates of historical happenings through a calendrical system based on sophisticated mathematics and astronomical events. Left, ivory "story knives" were used by Inuit girls of the Yukon to illustrate stories, tales and legends in wet mud or sand.

The Aztec solar deity stares fiercely from the Stone of the Sun, an intricately carved basalt disk more than ten feet in diameter that contains a wealth of information about the complexities of the Aztec cosmos, ritual and calendar. Surrounding the god, four rectangular symbols represent earth, wind, fire and water. Two circular images of claws clenching human hearts may signify the Aztec practice of human sacrifice; hieroglyphs note important dates in the past.

when it was forged and when broken remain mysteries. The small family bands of the Great Basin spoke Shoshonean languages that are related to Aztec, the tongue of one of America's mightiest prehistoric kingdoms. In California, the Yurok, Karok and Hupa had such similar cultures that even specialists cannot tell their artifacts apart, yet their languages are mutually unintelligible. Since the end of prehistoric times in the Southwest, the several pueblo-dwelling peoples have displayed nearly identical cultural traits, yet they speak languages of four separate families, tongues whose semantics and syntax indicate the fact of distinct origins but not how or when they occurred.

Some Indian languages are guttural, others melodic, others marked by "cracked consonants." Athapaskan languages, apparently the next-to-last family to reach the New World, are tonal, as are many oriental tongues — which might suggest an as-yet unproven connection to Mandarin or Thai. However, thus far only the Eskimo-Aleut family, the very last to arrive, has revealed a possible if still undefined kinship with a Eurasian language family. The languages of America have no demonstrated roots in the Old World; they all arose here, evolving from unknown, ancient stocks.

This, of course, does not make them inferior to European tongues in any way — only different. As Robert Spencer suggests, "suffice it to note that the American Indian languages, as finished systems, can express fully as wide a range of thought as can the languages of Europe.... What is clear, when American Indian linguistic structures are considered, is that the rules of Latin grammar have no [universal] application." Indo-European languages typically share an organizing principle in the importance placed on time (through verb tenses) and on distinctions between nouns (things, which are inherently stable) and verbs (actions, which are perforce transitory). Many Indian languages were built on other linguistic principles.

Differences among Indian languages offer intriguingly distinct ways of talking. Unlike many European languages, some are not preoccupied with the placement of events in past, present or future time, but rather with an action's duration or repetitious nature. In Kwakiutl a speaker must say whether an object is seen — both by the speaker and whomever he is speaking about. In Navajo a subject must be revealed as definite or vague; a verb stem cannot avoid indicating that the object is round, long, animate or whatever; or that an act is in progress, habitual or brief. The Indian person, beast or thing can only be described in a much more rigorous range of contexts than English requires. This suggests to some scholars that Navajo speech reflects a perceived world in which

Twenty-year-old David Stuart, left, has already made significant contributions to the study of Mayan hieroglyphics, an interest he has nurtured since age nine. The enigmatic glyphs that decorate a stela, above, at the Mayan site of Tikal in Guatemala may have recorded a great leader's accomplishments.

people are subordinate and must order themselves in relation to their surroundings.

Perhaps more telling than the structure of Indian languages is their surviving body of lore or oral literature. This information—the realm of ethnology, not archaeology—can sometimes be helpful in fleshing out pictures of prehistoric life, belief and wisdom in a manner that potsherds, ossuaries and artifacts can only suggest. Still, it is a world often neglected. As pioneer ethnologist Henry Rowe Schoolcraft exclaimed upon discovering the wealth of Indian narrative, "Who would have imagined that these wandering foresters would have possessed such a resource? What have all the voyagers and remarkers from the days of Cabot and Raleigh been about, not to have discovered this curious trait, which lifts up indeed a curtain, as it were, upon the Indian mind, and exhibits it in an entirely new character?"

Indian myth is as rich as any literature, and it bears mention that some Western epics—for instance, the *Iliad* and the *Odyssey*—derived directly from oral traditions that may have recorded information as accurately as writing. The advantage of written records, of course, is that the audience need not be within earshot of the narrator nor even live in his or her time. Other than that, some studies have documented that literate people often have far less ability to remember accurately what they hear than do the nonliterate. In any event, Indian lore relates events that seem historical and highly symbolic myths as well.

According to the Ojibwa, there came a time when snow covered the world higher than the tops of spruce trees and Squirrel led the freezing people into the sky in search of warmth. There they found leather bags containing rain, snow, storms, cold and sunshine, which they stole from the bear guarding them. On the long way home, Squirrel cut up one bag to patch his moccasins. That bag held warmth, which escaped and melted the snow, flooding all earth. Then an Old Man on a raft saved animals in pairs, which took turns diving deep into the water until Duck brought up a bit of mud from which dry land took shape.

Historical Inuits spoke of old and young stories, while the Winnebagos knew sacred or simply human-told tales and the Pawnees true or false ones. The Navajo have special regard for stories passed down from the beginning of time—"when the world was soft." These are accepted as pure truth and distinguished from later stories that have been contrived by storytellers, however wise they may be. Similarly, as we shall see in the next chapter, archaeology and its kindred disciplines seek to discover what truths they can about prehistoric Indians, the first immigrants who became cultured inhabitants of the Americas. ✳

A painted, ceramic elder recounts tribal myths and legends to children in this twentieth-century sculpture, *Storyteller,* crafted by Cochiti Pueblo artist Helen Cordero, above. Opposite, ancient Mesoamericans prepare a temple frieze in one of Diego Rivera's modern epic murals that adorn the National Palace in Mexico City.

THE INVESTIGATORS

Consider the difficult task of the archaeologist. Precious few direct links connect the present and the pre-Columbian past, forcing scientists to base most of their theories on archaeological evidence, the mute testimony of objects in the earth. The historic period following the European invasions saw more evidence of the past destroyed than can ever be regained. The reasons involved European intent, Indian acquiescence, greed, biological accident and a host of other factors belonging properly to social or political history but not to the history of archaeology.

Contact introduced a series of cataclysms that shattered the continuity of every Indian society. The demographic map of the Americas was virtually remade even before European colonists arrived in any numbers. A "minor" encroachment such as de Soto's expedition from Florida to the Mississippi in the 1540s left whole villages decimated, immediately by the sword, weeks later by disease. Elsewhere, ecosystems were quickly upset, as when followers of Hernán Cortés drained the Valley of Mexico's irrigated farmlands or *milpas*. From the Atlantic to the Pacific, contact created wholesale change.

In short, then, what sound knowledge we have of pre-Columbian America has been uncovered through archaeology which attempts to separate confirmed fact from fable and supposition. As a hybrid science, even as a complex of sciences and humanities studies, archaeology has had mixed success in the course of almost two centuries. Called a single discipline for the sake of convenience, it has a history that sometimes seems as complex and ramified as the bygone civilizations it explores.

Each stage of archaeological thinking has arisen not in a vacuum but within the context of its time. It may seem quaint or unspeakably wrongheaded today—just as today's hottest fashion may appear hopelessly naive tomorrow. Like any other intellectual pursuit, it must be the product of its time and may thus reflect the best—or sometimes the worst—that a period had to offer.

Seeds of interest in antiquity were sown in fourteenth-century Italy by humanists seeking aesthetic and philosophical ideals in the classical civilizations of Greece and Rome. The Renaissance was still alive in Europe when the New World was "discovered" and explored. Consequently the priests who followed Cortés to Mexico made some serious inquiries into the native past even as they set out to destroy the living cultures. Missionaries such as Diego de Landa, who was sent to convert some 300,000 inhabitants of the Yucatán Peninsula in Mexico, alternately used the pen and the sword. Inspired by Renaissance traditions, de Landa interviewed Mayan elders about their languages, religions and

Evidence from a temple mound at San Lorenzo, left, and other southern Mexican sites convinced archaeologist Matthew Stirling of the existence of an elaborate Mesoamerican culture predating the Mayans. Strongly opposed for twenty years, his theories were upheld by other finds and radiocarbon analysis. At least three centuries older than that of the Mayans, the sophisticated Olmec culture thrived more than 3,000 years ago in Mexico. Above, an archaeologist with the Texas Highway Department analyzes a grid map of a Paleo-Indian site uncovered by publicly funded construction work in central Texas.

In this volume published in 1801, Thomas Jefferson described his investigations of mounds near his Virginia home at Monticello. He concluded that the mounds were the work of ancestors of the Indians of his time, a view not generally accepted until 100 years later.

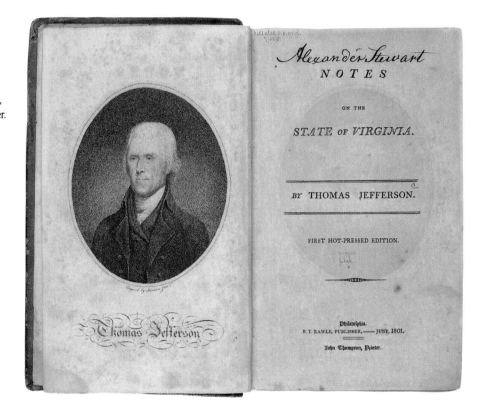

cultures even as he followed his own militant creed by destroying temples, burning books and slaying thousands. Gold and jeweled artifacts found in native shrines vanished into the treasuries of Spain, while a few precious fruits of scholarship were sequestered in monastic archives where they remained buried—lost, in effect—for centuries. By modern definition, most of these investigations were de facto ethnology: the study of living cultures. By the time they were uncovered, they could best be used by archaeology, the study of vanished peoples through their artifacts and other physical remains.

The first North American excavator seems to have been ahead of his time—in archaeology as in so many other realms. Thomas Jefferson, a father of the Republic, is also somewhat sentimentally called the father of American archaeology. He was a child of the Enlightenment, that eighteenth century epoch that encouraged the exploration of diverse realms, including both political and natural "philosophy." In *Notes on the State of Virginia,* a miscellany written in 1781 and 1782 for the secretary of the French legation in Philadelphia, Jefferson described his careful excavation of prehistoric remains, the continent's first archaeological "dig" worthy of the name.

Fur trading and other elements of White contact had greatly altered the lives of Virginia Indians by the time Captain John Smith established the first English colony at Jamestown. Smith's map of 1607 acknowledges the powerful Algonquian chief Powhatan and the Powhatan confederacy, thirty tribes allied against the spread of White influence. The marriage of Powhatan's daughter, Pocahontas, to John Rolfe brought a short period of peace, which was broken when White settlers pushed inland in search of land to plant tobacco.

The thousands of Indian mounds, scattered throughout eastern America between the Appalachians and the Mississippi, were the subject of popular curiosity and unsubstantiated myth. "That they were repositories of the dead, has been obvious to all," Jefferson wrote. "But on what particular occasion [they were] constructed, was a matter of doubt." Some stories held that Indians collected all their dead at certain times and interred them together. Others held that these "barrows" were mass graves of battle casualties. "There being one of these [mounds] in my neighborhood," wrote Jefferson, "I wished to satisfy myself whether any, and which of these opinions were just. For this purpose I determined to open and examine it thoroughly."

Jefferson noted the location, its proximity to what had been an Indian town, and its "spheroidical form" and dimensions: forty feet around at the base and seven-and-a-half feet high. He also noted it had been nearly twice as tall, and boasted trees a foot in diameter, before coming under the plow a dozen years earlier. "I first dug superficially in several parts of it, and came to collections of human bones, at different depths, from six inches to three feet below the surface. These were lying in the utmost confusion, some vertical, some oblique, some horizontal, and directed to

This mid-nineteenth-century cross section of a burial mound in Louisiana, with other romanticized portrayals of Indian sites, fed a yearning on the part of White Americans for a past as grand as that of the Old World.

every point of the compass, entangled, and held together in clusters by the earth."

Ruling out its use as a warriors' graveyard on account of a child's jaw found within, Jefferson then made some adroit conclusions: "Appearances certainly indicate that it has derived both origin and growth from the accustomary collection of bones [not of fresh corpses], and deposition of them together; that the first collection had been deposited on the common surface of the earth, a few stones put over it, and then a covering of earth, that the second had been laid on this, had covered more or less of it in proportion to the number of bones, and was then also covered with earth; and so on."

Jefferson remarked on other mounds in the vicinity and on the theories about who had made them. While "those aboriginals of America" might have come from Europe by boat via Iceland and Greenland, a more logical explanation was an Asian origin, since Captain James Cook recently had reported that only a narrow strait (the Bering Strait) separated the two continents. "The resemblance between the Indians of America and the eastern inhabitants of Asia, would induce us to conjecture, that the former are the descendants of the latter, or the latter of the former."

Jefferson's report was a model in several respects. First of all, he had not set out to prove a favored bit of hearsay (or disprove a heresy) but to discover "whether any, and which of these opinions were just." Second, he drew conclusions from what he observed. Third, his objective investigation revealed the presence of strata in the mound, and he understood their meaning. Distinguishable layers of earth separated layers containing human relics, indicating a series of depositions and thus distinct periods in time (though he did not belabor that point). Finally, in putting his findings in larger perspective, he supported a tentative conclusion about the Indians' origin.

This report made a telling contribution to archaeological science, although Jefferson's work and lesson in procedure were ignored for decades. The chief reason may be that his sober example was pushed into the background by a succession of fictions that their promoters termed theories. Though they were closer to fantasies, these speculations excited enormous interest. Convinced of their glorious destiny, the people of the young American nation hungered for an appropriately heroic past to rival the splendors of the Old World. Further, they sought swift rationales for nascent political and social policies and comprehensible explanations of some present-day facts that they found uncomfortable. As Robert Silverberg put it so succinctly in his definitive study, *The Mound Builders,* "Men in search of a myth will usually find one, if they work at it." And work they did.

As adventurers and settlers explored the western territories more carefully, the extent and variety of the mounds became awesomely apparent. There were some 10,000 in the Ohio Valley alone. Cahokia, a pre-Columbian settlement overlooking the Mississippi across from the trading post that became St. Louis, contained some 120 mounds. The largest, Monks Mound, was enormous: 100 feet high and covering nearly fifteen acres. In the northern regions they tended to be smaller (though one contained an estimated 311,353 cubic feet of earth), while perhaps more perplexing. Here were monuments in the shapes of birds, reptiles and fabulous beasts. Many of the mounds contained intriguing artifacts: pottery, weapons, ceremonial tools, exquisitely worked stones, artful symbols and exotic carvings. Inevitably people asked the obvious

E phraim Squier's and Edwin H. Davis's
excavations of mounds in southern Ohio
uncovered an unprecedented number of
artifacts and led to the Smithsonian's
first publication, *Ancient Monuments of the
Mississippi Valley,* brought forth in 1848.
Selected objects from their excavations of 200
mounds appear in a section from Davis's unpub-
lished portfolio, a curious vision of the development of art forms in ancient America.

question: who built the mounds? Surviving Indians, whose achievements and capabilities seemed drab by comparison, could not readily explain these antiquities, so the Whites conveniently provided explanations, each one more compelling than the last.

An early student of Indian origins was James Adair, who traded with the Cherokee and Chickasaw from South Carolina to northern Mississippi for thirty years. His *The History of the American Indians,* published in 1775, offered twenty-three arguments "in proof of the American Indians being descended from the Jews."

This notion that the Indians must descend from the Lost Tribes of Israel (mentioned in the Book of Kings) had a long life. First aired in the papal courts of the sixteenth century, it would be championed by such savants as William Penn and a president of Yale College. Pennsylvania's founder said Indians reminded him of Jews he had seen in London, while Ezra Stiles sought Benjamin Franklin's opinion to support his own that they were heirs of the Canaanites driven from Palestine by Joshua's Israelites. (Franklin thought perhaps the mounds were built by the Spanish explorer Hernando de Soto.)

Not surprisingly, the myths fed on each other, and their proponents borrowed bits of fact from random sources to reach new heights of fancy well into the nineteenth century. Herodotus had written that a Scythian king was buried with great treasure under "a vast mound," and Macedonian accounts revealed that Alexander the Great had buried a friend with due ceremony under "huge tumuli" during a Persian campaign. The Canaanites worshipped "in high places." Thus it must be obvious that people of similar greatness had built America's mounds, which could not have been raised by a native people now regarded as treacherous, ignorant and indolent savages standing in the way of the White man's progress. One nineteenth-century savant argued that Indians had sprung from Atlantis. Caleb Atwater, postmaster of Circleville, Ohio, in the 1820s, wrote that the ancient features in his neighborhood had been built by Hindu migrants from India, who abandoned them eventually and settled in Mexico. Governor DeWitt Clinton maintained that New York's mounds had been raised by Vikings.

After hypothesizing that the mounds were built by some noble race of other than North American origin, the theorizers would conclude that those people must have vanished under ignoble circumstances. Hence the moundbuilders had been overcome by some treacherous barbarians, who then spawned the Indians whom the mythmakers detested so hotly. In one of its uglier aspects, this argument (in its many forms) presupposed the legitimate right of another race (i.e., White Americans) to oust

Nineteenth-century scientists and luminaries attributed artifacts from the Southeast, such as this replica of a sandstone face from Ohio, to a variety of Old World cultures, certain that the ancestors of the Indians were incapable of fine craftsmanship. Such cultural chauvinism dies hard; it was not until the 1894 publication of an exhaustive Smithsonian report that proper credit was given to the forebears of America's own native peoples.

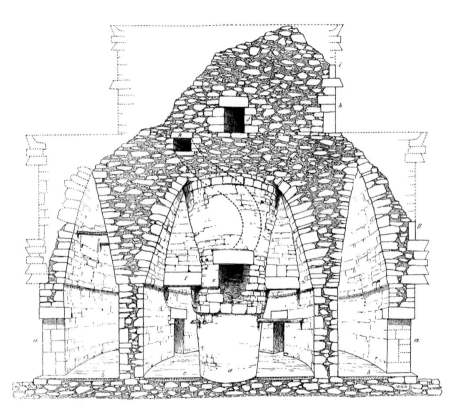

William Henry Holmes, shown above at the Smithsonian's Castle building with a friend, enjoyed a distinguished career as artist, archaeologist and museum director. The undated archival photograph of a National Museum of Natural History hall of Mexican archaeology, opposite, was probably taken just after Holmes's tenure as chief of the Bureau of American Ethnology from 1902 to 1909. Mayan glyphs adorn the wall, and Aztec pots rest in the cases. A model of the temple at the great Mayan city of Chichén Itzá appears behind the large Aztec calendar stone. At this site on the Yucatán Peninsula, Holmes's careful work during the mid-1890s led to a masterful collection of archaeological drawings, including one of the tower called the Caracol, left.

the ousters' heirs. Bruce G. Trigger, one of Canada's leading ethno-historians of the colonial era, concludes that Whites of the time deemed the Indians so biologically and culturally inferior that they saw them as "doomed to extinction."

Nonetheless, there were those who looked at the evidence with clear eyes. In 1829, James H. McCulloh, Jr., sifted through the available anatomical evidence to compare a small number of ancient skeletons with those of living Indians. In his view, which was poorly received, the moundbuilders and modern natives were of one race. Ten years later a Philadelphia doctor, Samuel G. Morton, published his study of ancient and contemporary Indian skulls, which found no important differences between them. Amid all the sound and fury of the moundbuilder mythology, some solid work was being done to illuminate America's antiquity.

As far back as 1790, Thomas Jefferson had appealed to "our philosophical societies" to collect "exact descriptions" of the mounds. The institutions Jefferson referred to served as the kind of civic initiator, intellectual moderator and brain trust that the university and (much later) the government commission would become. One was the American Antiquarian Society, founded in Boston in 1812 by Thomas Hart

North American Cultural Areas

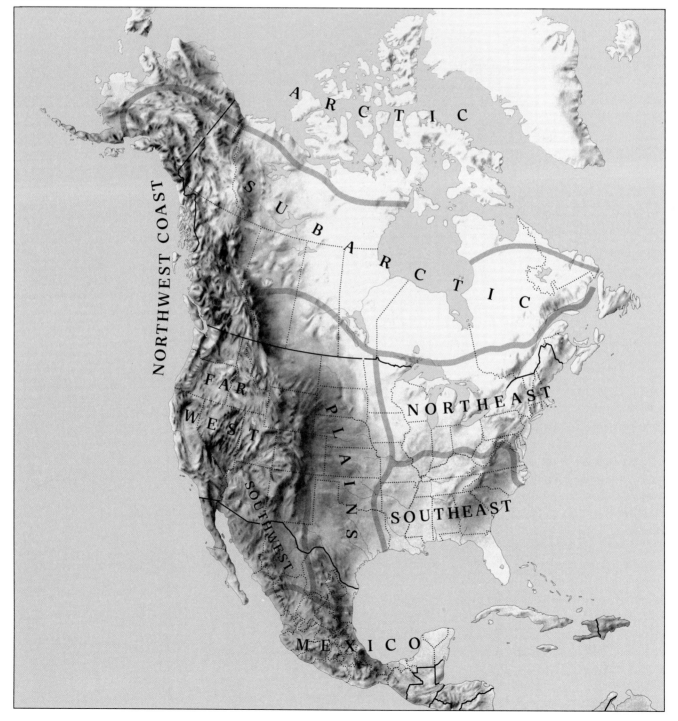

Benton, Henry Clay and others. Another was the American Philosophical Society, which Jefferson would serve as president. A third was the American Ethnological Society, founded in 1842 by his former Treasury Secretary, Albert Gallatin. Finally there was the Smithsonian Institution, whose contributions to the growth of American archaeology would be greater than that of all the others combined.

James Smithson was a wealthy English amateur scientist and member of the Royal Society who died in 1829. His will bequeathed a fortune "to found at Washington, under the name of the Smithsonian Institution, an establishment for the increase & diffusion of knowledge among men." After a chest of gold sovereigns was consigned to the Philadelphia mint and punched into United States specie worth $508,318, Congress haggled for eight years about accepting the money. John C. Calhoun, for one, said the Constitution did not permit the government to accept such a gift. But former President John Quincy Adams, then a leader in the House of Representatives, prevailed and the "establishment" was chartered in 1846. Its first Secretary, physicist Joseph Henry, intended the Institution to serve art, the physical sciences and natural science and to provide a clearinghouse for scientific literature through a major library system. As it happened, the first volume of its publications program dealt with Indian mounds.

In 1846, newspaper editor and mound explorer Ephraim George Squier and his backer, Edwin Hamilton Davis, both of Ohio, presented a paper on Indian mounds of the Ohio Valley to the American Ethnological Society, which was eager for more. A more ambitious work proved too large and expensive to be published by a private organization, so Albert Gallatin pressed it upon Joseph Henry. After Henry's stringent editing, it appeared as the first volume of the Institution's *Contributions to Knowledge,* an occasional series that Henry saw as the keystone of the Smithsonian's program.

Ancient Monuments of the Mississippi Valley was a landmark work, a systematic and intentionally objective description of the major mounds. Written largely by Squier, who ascribed the southern mounds to an unknown race, the volume nonetheless had lasting importance, especially since many of the mounds described were to be destroyed before they could be assayed by modern science.

Once involved in de facto archaeology, despite Henry's initial disinterest in the subject, the Smithsonian pursued it; four of the first eight *Contributions* dealt with American prehistory. Henry established a network of volunteers around the continent to report back on natural history and phenomena — including discovered Indian ephemera, relics and

T o delineate broad regions of prehistoric human habitation in North America, archaeologists often divide the continent into cultural areas roughly corresponding to its geographical and environmental zones. These cultural areas often overlap and their boundaries are broad and flexible rather than hard and fast.

G reat sandstone ruins mark an Anasazi village in Arizona's Canyon de Chelly, opposite, photographed by Timothy O'Sullivan in 1873. Two members of the survey team are dwarfed by the cliff ruins called the "White House." The trip that O'Sullivan accompanied as official photographer was one of many post-Civil War geographical expeditions. Above, explorer, geologist and anthropologist John Wesley Powell brought a diversity of talents to the Smithsonian's Bureau of American Ethnology. Among his many contributions as its first director, Powell, with the help of BAE linguists, determined by 1891 the first and still authoritative division of North American Indian tribes into linguistic stocks.

monuments. This curriculum grew under his direction for thirty years. Then in 1879, the year after his death, it took a new course, thanks to the unintentionally combined efforts of the next Smithsonian Secretary and a one-armed Civil War veteran named John Wesley Powell.

Resigning his commission after the war, Powell resumed his prewar position as a schoolmaster, but soon moved to a college, then undertook a geological expedition to the Rockies. Thereafter he became increasingly involved in surveys of the West, at first as a leader, later as an administrator. In Washington, he persuaded friends on Capitol Hill to establish the Bureau of Ethnology as an adjunct of the Smithsonian. His interests were primarily ethnological; he meant to study the living Indians including those he had met during his wide-ranging survey trips, but his research would prove critical in helping archaeologists relate the present to the past. Among many other accomplishments, Powell and the Bureau staff catalogued and classified the surviving North American native languages in a work that remains authoritative. The Smithsonian's new Secretary, Spencer F. Baird, no mean hand around the halls of Congress himself, convinced legislators to dedicate part of the new Bureau's budget — and thus its energy — to archaeological research.

This development in turn led to the final discrediting of the old mound-builders theories by Cyrus Thomas, head of the Division of Mound Exploration in what was by then the Bureau of American Ethnology. Thomas dispatched survey teams to conduct a broad sample of the most significant eastern mounds. Armed with the results of the teams' test excavations, he devised a new classification of monuments based on region and culture as indicated by artifacts. In the Bureau's *Annual Report* of 1894, he compiled a monumental array of data and argument to demonstrate that the mounds had been built in different periods by many cultures. None of them, he concluded, was exotic or "lost," except in the sense that, as Greece had lost her glory and Rome her grandeur, they had been eclipsed. This compendium settled the issue so far as science was concerned.

Toward the end of the century, one of John Wesley Powell's Smithsonian colleagues, Otis T. Mason, proposed one of the great practical concepts for comparative studies in anthropology, the notion of the "culture area." He divided the continent into eighteen geographic regions, each of them a distinct realm in terms of gross geology, climate and biota — in a word, an environment. In these defined areas each different society faced similar conditions, restraints and opportunities, and thus the ways they adapted — and their relative successes — could be compared and contrasted. Mason's useful scheme has also been refined, revised and

Frank H. Cushing, an anthropologist and archaeologist at the Smithsonian's Bureau of American Ethnology in the late nineteenth century, was a pioneer of ethnology, the study of traditional native lifeways. He spent years among the Zuni of the Southwest, learning their language and ceremony. Much later, he unearthed the Key Marco site in Florida, assembling a valuable collection of rare, remarkably well-preserved wooden artifacts, including this cat mask drawn by expedition artist Wells Sawyer.

simply changed over the years (as, for instance, when others divided the continent differently) because it works. A region's environment proves to be an influencing factor that limits or channels the practical strategies available to every culture that evolves within it. For example, inhabitants of an arctic coast cannot live by foraging for acorns any more than a woodland people can base their economy on hunting sea mammals. (The culture-area idea has also been abused. Occasionally environment has been erroneously interpreted as a determining factor that predestines the ultimate development of local cultures. In fact, the extent to which any culture becomes complex, warlike, artistic or sedentary, or achieves any other qualitative character has little to do with the environment. People can develop variously "creative" or predatory or any other kind of societies anywhere.)

The last decades of the nineteenth century witnessed marvelous discoveries and raw adventure. In the Southwest, Swiss-born Adolph Bandelier rode a mule thousands of miles in search of prehistoric sites. Traveling as lightly as possible, sometimes without even a blanket, he lived with descendants of prehistoric Americans and followed leads his Indian hosts provided. Thus he found a number of ancient settlements, among them, the ruins of Frijoles Canyon in what is now called Bandelier National Monument. In 1888, cattle rancher Richard Wetherill and his brother-in-law, Charles Mason discovered the spectacular ruins of Mesa Verde in southwestern Colorado while looking for strays in a snowstorm. Wetherill and his brother, John, spent years investigating Mesa Verde and other sites.

One of the most colorful ethnological and archaeological pioneers was the Smithsonian's Frank Hamilton Cushing, a prodigy and *enfant terrible* of sorts who made a lasting contribution to anthropology. Intrigued by Indian lore during his solitary boyhood, he published papers in the Smithsonian Annual Report before hiring on at twenty-two to join an expedition to the pueblos of the Southwest. There he stayed, with the permission of Powell and Secretary Baird, while the expedition went on.

The self-styled "doomed exile" was taken in by the Zuni governor, who told him, "If you do as we tell you, you shall be rich, for you shall have fathers and mothers, brothers and sisters and the best food in the world." In fact, he found the cuisine repulsive at first; indeed, life in the pueblo seemed intolerable for some time. But Cushing soon adopted Indian dress and diet (perforce) and learned to live like his hosts and to speak their language. He remained there for five years and virtually became Zuni himself, in due time obtaining membership in the secret and sacred Priesthood of the Bow.

80

In effect, Cushing invented at Zuni the total immersion approach to fieldwork and blazed an ethnographic trail for future investigators. He was perhaps the first ethnoarchaeologist to attempt to connect the pots and stones he saw in use with those he excavated. In the 1890s, Cushing discovered and partially excavated the Key Marco, Florida, site where he found many beautifully carved wooden artifacts and works of art more than 1,000 years old.

The Smithsonian's Bureau of American Ethnology remained in the vanguard of prehistoric studies at least until Powell's death in 1902. It continued to spearhead archaeological investigations even as universities began to establish the anthropology departments that collectively would take the lead in years to come.

Already a noted artist and illustrator, as well as a veteran of geological survey expeditions to the Southwest, William Henry Holmes established himself as one of America's leading archaeologists during this time. During his early career, Holmes worked for the Smithsonian, the United States Geological Survey and Chicago's Field Museum of Natural History. Later, back at the Smithsonian as a curator and as director of the Bureau of American Ethnology, he conducted archaeological expeditions to many parts of North America, and his classifications of pottery and stone tools earned him a secure niche in the annals of American archaeological history. (Returning to his first love, he ended his long and eventful career as the director of the National Gallery of Art.)

As discovery followed discovery, archaeologists developed a complex and still evolving array of procedures with one goal in mind: to preserve as much information as possible so that a site could be reconstructed in the laboratory at some future time and yield yet new insights into prehistory. Whether the data have been recorded on file cards or computer tape, one of the systematic archaeologist's prime purposes has remained the same from the late nineteenth century onwards: to record what an excavation uncovered, both in terms of specific objects and the layers of earth in which they were found. Knowing the precise location or "context" of artifacts remains crucial, because even today many layers of a clearly stratified site may conceal information that as-yet-undeveloped techniques may eventually provide ways to discover.

In archaeology, context is everything. Find a lance point embedded in a vertebra of *Bison antiquus* buried deep beneath layers of undisturbed soil, in context, and the excavator knows it must be at least 10,000 years old because that bison species became extinct then. Find the lance point in the bottom of a stream bed, where erosion has carried it, and it has lost all context. It cannot be traced to the ancient culture that created it.

The preeminent Smithsonian anthropologist of the early twentieth century, Czech immigrant Aleš Hrdlička almost single-handedly established the discipline of physical anthropology — the science dealing with the study of skeletal characteristics. An indefatigable traveler, Hrdlička collected human bones from all over the world, providing the Institution with a remarkable collection.

Archaeological fieldwork entails not only the recovery of artifacts but painstaking efforts to map their placement in three dimensions as well. Above, archaeologists at the Thunderbird Archaeological Park in Virginia hang plumb lines from a grid system to plot the precise position of Paleo-Indian stone tools. Archaeologists in New York reconstructed the dimensions of a long-vanished fourteenth-century Iroquoian longhouse at the Furnace Brook site near Syracuse, right, by carefully noting the "postmold patterns" — discolorations in the ground caused by the rotting of wooden posts that once supported the building. It measured 210 feet long by 22 feet wide. Different mapping techniques come into play when excavations probe the stacked layers of debris often found in caves. University of Texas archaeologists, oppo-site, establish a vertical profile of the Bonfire Shelter Cave in southern Texas where bone frag-ments from Paleo-Indian kills of big game have been found.

Find the lance point on the sidewalk in front of a museum, and it is again out of context. It cannot be presumed to be any older than the sidewalk on which it lies.

Although the importance of stratigraphic sequences had been under-stood in a general way even in Jefferson's time, stratigraphic excavating techniques were not appreciated or applied until the early 1900s, when American Museum of Natural History archaeologist N. C. Nelson used them during his excavation of a refuse dump at Pueblo San Cristobal, near Santa Fe, New Mexico. Meticulously recording the level of pottery fragments in the old dump, Nelson was able to establish a chronological sequence of pottery styles for the site.

The American Museum of Natural History had emerged as a leading institution in the field of anthropology in the latter part of the nineteenth century, as had the Field Museum of Natural History in Chicago and the University of California at Berkeley. Another was the Peabody Museum at Harvard, whose longtime curator, Frederic W. Putnam, has been called the "professionalizer" of American archaeology. Putnam helped found departments of anthropology at many institutions, bringing the field academic respectability and hastening the development of systematic techniques and more rigorous testing of theories of cultural evolution.

Archaeologists in the Laboratory

Archaeologists must start with artifacts and use these as building blocks toward an understanding of the larger context of prehistoric Indian behavior patterns. While artifacts have always come from the field, most of the synthesis takes place in the laboratory. There excavated materials—stone chips, broken bones, potsherds, pollen grains, snail shells, charcoal from fires and baked clay from fire pits—must be processed, analyzed and stored. Only then can archaeologists begin to ask—and answer—questions about the manner in which prehistoric Indians lived.

Of course, much of the fundamental lab work has changed little since the early days of American archaeology. Potsherds and stone points must be sorted and marked according to location, and potsherds are still laboriously pieced together to reconstruct a pot.

Traditionally, potsherds of different types were used to develop local and regional chronologies. When a shard was found above another, the one below was assumed to be older. Today, the soil around the shards is carefully analyzed for signs of disturbance, such as animal burrows, to make certain that the stratigraphy of the site is intact.

Researchers increasingly draw on the resources of unrelated sciences. Botanists offer important clues about ancient environments with studies of fossilized pollen. Chemists, geologists, wildlife ecologists, physicists and paleontologists bring their specialized training and knowledge to bear on archaeological questions. Coordinating interdisciplinary research programs enables archaeologists to gain better understanding of the behavior patterns of past peo-

Archaeologists paint tiny grid coordinates onto potsherds, top, to indicate their relationship to each other when they were found. Above, a University of Texas technician performs the painstaking task of pot reconstruction.

Director of the University of Texas Archaeological Research Laboratory, Dee Ann Story examines specimens at the university's collection of late prehistoric pottery, left. Top, Texas State Archaeologist Robert J. Mallouf analyzes stone projectile points for variations in manufacturing techniques. Above, Texas Historical Commission draftsman Ed Aiken prepares a site plan of a late prehistoric house from the Great Plains.

Director of the Smithsonian's Radiocarbon Dating Laboratory, Robert Stuckenrath, below, prepares a sample for radiocarbon dating, a process that measures the decay of carbon 14, an element present in all living organisms. Below left, Donald Lewis of the Center for Archaeological Research at the University of Texas examines a barium chloride solution mixed with crushed pottery to determine a mineral "fingerprint" of the clay. In some cases archaeologists can match the clay used to fashion a pot with its exact geographic origin.

ples. For example, the science of archeometry uses chemistry and other physical sciences to identify mineral elements in ancient pottery. Geologic variations in clay types imbue pottery with geographic source "signatures," and may help archaeologists trace ancient trade patterns. In the study of fracture dynamics, archaeologists work with physicists, anatomists and others to identify break patterns in animal bone and stone and to reveal ancient toolmaking and butchering techniques.

Thus, as the tools of other sciences are brought to bear on archaeological problems, archaeologists can expand the scope of their research, asking new questions and testing new hypotheses.

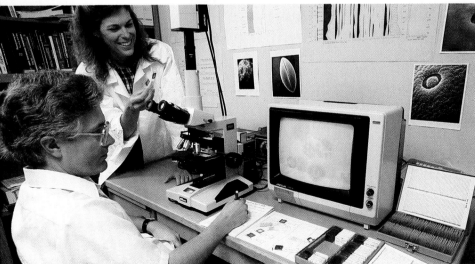

University of Texas geographer Stephen Hall and Assistant State Archaeologist and paleobotanist Glenna Dean-Seaman, left, study microscopic fossil pollen on a video screen for clues to climatic and environmental conditions present at an ancient Great Plains village. Above, Director of the Texas Archaeological Survey Solveig Turpin and her assistant examine an X-ray of a Pleistocene horse's leg bone for signs of butchering by Paleo-Indians. They believe that a blow from a hand-held hammer stone caused a fracture, after Paleo-Indians killed the horse by stampeding it over a limestone bluff at Bonfire Shelter in southern Texas more than 12,000 years ago.

As these institutions and many others established academic departments of anthropology and archaeology, the disciplines matured and diversified. Coming from Germany to the American Museum of Natural History and then to Columbia University, Franz Boas revolutionized anthropological thought. While spending a rugged year with Inuit on Baffin Island, Boas realized that their love of art and poetry was in no way inferior to their remarkable hunting skills. In essence, this influential scholar taught that all ethnic groups had virtually the same capacity for cultural achievement, and further that none was inherently superior or inferior. Rather, their developments reflected different strategies, choices and opportunities. This idea gave new energy to the study of all cultures and illuminated new areas of inquiry even in the study of extinct societies.

The first third of the twentieth century was an era of intellectual giants. Aleš Hrdlička, a strong-willed Czech who founded the Smithsonian's physical anthropology department in 1903, brought a worldwide perspective to the study of human diversity. But he also set back studies of early human presence in the New World by decades after he decided that Asians could not have come to this continent until after the end of the last ice age. Through his writings, he launched scathing attacks on any upstart scholar who suggested otherwise. Thus the issue was virtually closed until spear points found with extinct bison bones at the 10,000-year-old Folsom, New Mexico, site presented undeniable evidence of earlier human presence in the Southwest.

As the corps of archaeologists grew, the body of archaeological data multiplied exponentially and investigators found themselves working at cross purposes. For instance, each archaeologist typically named newly uncovered cultures and periods as he or she saw fit—though another excavator in the next county, state or river basin might be using entirely different nomenclature for the same culture phases. In 1927, Harvard-trained Alfred V. Kidder invited leading southwestern archaeologists to convene at his Pecos Pueblo camp for the first "Pecos Conference," which would become an almost annual meeting. Here the group drafted the "Pecos Classification," which defined eight cultural periods, Basketmaker I through III and Pueblo I through V. This classification marked the first substantial cooperative effort to establish an agreed-upon chronology and nomenclature for a region. Similar efforts would be repeated many times over in virtually every other area in later years.

The growing need for a common forum led to the founding of the Society for American Archaeology (SAA) in 1935. By that year in the midst of the depression, two things had become abundantly clear. For one, archaeology then lacked a voice loud enough to make itself heard.

(The Tennessee Valley Authority, soon to embark on a massive dam-building program, had just been created with little thought for the countless archaeological sites that would be flooded by dozens of man-made lakes.) Two, there was a vast amount of archaeological work waiting to be done, work of great potential significance for a nation that would soon become interested in its prehistory.

These two facts were reflected in both the subsequent institutionalization of archaeology through the SAA and the acceleration of what was then called "salvage archaeology." This kind of work has grown substantially ever since, largely through national legislation that requires archaeological surveys to precede the construction of highways, reservoirs and the like. Today, far more trained archaeologists perform survey and salvage work than so-called pure research; the discipline has become a presence in the mundane world of roads, dams and other public works.

After World War II, archaeology experienced a period of internecine upheavals so extreme that outsiders are hard-pressed to understand it. The arguments involved what came to be called the "new archaeology." In part the movement aimed at making prehistoric studies more "scientific" and less concerned with classification and typology of artifacts. Its champions were no longer satisfied with examining the past but, in the words of Yale anthropologist Frank Hole, now "sought to generate and test general laws that would explain all human behavior." More interested in explanation than description, the new archaeologists sought to explain past human behavior through the study of sites and the patterns (or lack

Above, professional looters bulldoze a site in the Southwest, obliterating the village ruins and the archaeological record in their search for valuable Mimbres pottery. Commercial exploitation of Indian sites, opposite, can be equally destructive.

More than 1,000 years ago, Anasazi masons constructed this wall, opposite, at New Mexico's Pueblo del Arroyo. Weathered wooden beams supported a floor within. Archaeologists use these beams to pinpoint construction dates through dendrochronology — the highly accurate science of tree-ring dating. A carved snake, left, guards the base of "Serpent Hill," the Great Temple at the Aztec capital of Tenochtitlán — today's Mexico City. Myth has it that the Aztec mother of gods and humans, Coatlicue or "she of the serpent skirt," gave birth here to Quetzalcoatl, the plumed serpent god and creator of humankind.

of them) of the artifacts scattered through them. Applying statistical techniques, experimentation, and an array of interdisciplinary scientific tools, they were able to extract a great deal more information — and new kinds of information — from archaeological sites about the behavior of the peoples who had inhabited them.

When the smoke finally cleared, it appeared that American archaeology had become — inevitably if not gracefully — a multitude of perspectives. When more than 2,000 interested people attended the fiftieth annual meeting of the SAA in 1985, the few charter members fondly recalled that in 1935 a standard hotel room had been large enough to accommodate the entire membership. By now archaeology had grown to embrace a variety of branches and specialties. To the despair of some old-guard members, modern archaeology had come to involve academics, contractors, federal and state bureaucrats, statisticians, cyberneticists and a host of others. Today it affects the routes of interstate highways and makes its mark on elementary school curricula. Some complained that careers could now be built on such specialties as the study of fossil feces or wear patterns in Paleolithic tools. Others expressed concern that North American prehistory had now grown too vast for a single mind to command. So be it. Teams of specialists could use their powerful new tools to help crack the secrets of North American prehistory. And if they argued with each other a great deal, so be it again. Spirited discussion of hypotheses is at the heart of the scientific method and therefore of good science. And science, the dispelling of old myths, attitudes and unsupported beliefs, is what archaeology is all about. ✷

THE ARCTIC

 The prehistoric settlement and permanent habitation of Arctic North America is a human miracle of the first magnitude. The continent's northern rim features a desolation of shingle beaches, sheer ice faces, stately beautiful mountain ranges, trackless tundra and snow fields without horizon. It is uniform only in its cold, its winter dark and its merciless disregard for the careless or the poorly equipped—a vehemently inhospitable place, not even quite a land so much as a frigid hydrosphere dominated by sea and ice.

The secret of the Arctic peoples' success lay in their deft adaptation to the circumstances they found. However grim their realm appears to us, it is one of the world's richest in accessible natural bounty. Of primary importance, sea and shore support an extravagant variety of sea mammals —whales, seals, walrus, sea lions. In addition, there were shellfish in the shallows; deep-water fish like cod and flounder; freshwater species in inland rivers; and anadromous salmon returning to upriver spawning grounds. Then there were the enormous flights of seabirds, shorebirds and migratory fowl that came each spring to breed, then brood and molt in coastal marshes and tundra ponds that never drained because of the underlying permafrost. Finally, on the mainland were caribou and musk oxen for the taking by those who learned to hunt the migrating herds. Even the arctic voles and lemmings, rodents no bigger than mice, provided food for those who sought their burrows for tiny caches of seeds. To exploit the resources of this frigidly bountiful land and sea required suitable technologies, skills and sheer bravery. In other words, the prehistory of the Arctic largely involved the acquisition and perfection of new technologies to exploit the resources found in the cornucopia of animal plenty—especially the varied fauna of the bordering seas.

While human presence in the far north can be inferred at very early times, the first substantiated occupation of the Arctic dates from no earlier than 9000 B.C.—or only half as long ago as some scholars believe North America first received human immigrants from Asia. (Then there are signs that people drifted north from elsewhere on the continent, descendants of groups that had crossed Beringia long before.) One of the earliest people to successfully settle in modern Alaska reached the tiny, southern Aleutian island of Anangula by 6750 B.C. and remained at least until 6250 B.C.—a span longer than White settlement in North America thus far. The place was virtually barren of vegetation—no trees and only a few berries and greens in summer, together with indigestible grasses. The long-lived settlement stood by the generous shore. Here were fish, shellfish and birds, and the sea mammals that sustained the village for 500 years: hair seals and sea lions in year-round residence,

Symbol of life in the barren reaches of the far north, the polar bear, opposite, has been the most feared and prized prey of many Arctic peoples since human occupation of this vast region began thousands of years ago. A carved wooden mask of the ancient Dorset culture of the Canadian high Arctic, above, represents a work of magic as well as art and was probably used in special ceremonies by shamans.

Arctic

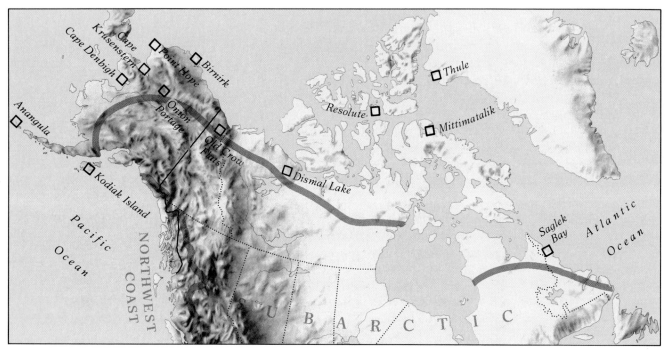

migratory fur seals and whales. Whether the Anangulans could chase the latter offshore is unknown, for no signs of boats have been recovered. Further, it's unclear whether this was an island in 6000 B.C. Sea level may have still been so low that it was part of an Aleutian peninsula.

In Anangula the houses were small, oval, semisubterranean structures with frames of driftwood covered with matting and live sod rooted in an insulating layer of earth. The distribution of excavated artifacts suggests to archaeologist Jean S. Aigner of the University of Alaska that this society apportioned its tasks much like historical Aleuts, its apparent descendants. "Women and girls worked inside the house, making clothing, grinding pigments and tending the stone lamp in which they burned sea mammal fat to provide heat and light." The men and boys spent their days atop the sod house, making tools and implements of stone, bone and driftwood and keeping a lookout for marine game. Each family made whatever it needed; there was neither specialization among families nor an apparent hierarchy. But there was vital cooperation, especially when it came to hunting.

"Considering how such prey (sea mammals) were probably hunted, the size and permanence of Anangula take on particular significance," Aigner wrote recently in a *Scientific American* essay. The village was

Habitans du Golfe de Kotzebue.

inhabited for twenty generations, longer than the existence of imperial Rome. "The number of houses and the distribution of other artifacts at Anangula suggest that roughly seventy-five people lived there at a time, or twice the minimum number called for by the style of hunting....A core group needed at least from six to eight families to ensure consistent success." (Behaviorists deduce the smallest size of a viable social group by assessing the risks of a people's lifeway. Were only two nuclear families to unite in a maritime society, for example, they would be vulnerable to inevitable disaster, because loss of a single boat at sea would wipe out all the hunters. Too many people living together, on the other hand, could strain the carrying capacity of an island in times of want.)

"If a community of that size is to survive through recurrent periods of scarcity, it must have highly developed hunting techniques. Not only were the (Anangulan) islanders' hunting techniques sound enough to support a large community but also they were reliable enough to support a permanent one." They maintained the village generation after generation, probably only going to seasonal camps from time to time. "When game is scarce, one obvious strategy is to pick up the village and move. The people of Anangula, however, were such skilled hunters, and locally available resources were so abundant, that the villagers did not have to

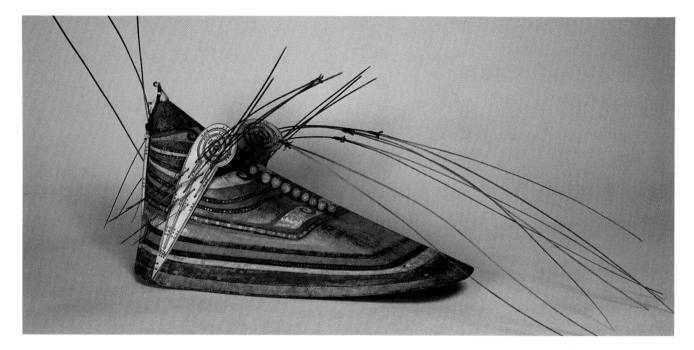

A painted wood Aleut hat, above, is distinctively adorned with carved ivory sidepieces, blue beads and sea lion whiskers. Worn only by hunters at sea, such as those depicted in this early nineteenth-century lithograph, opposite, the long-visored, pyramidal hats shielded the eyes from glare.

resort to such measures." When they finally abandoned Anangula it was because volcanic ash blanketed the place.

Inuit (or Eskimo) prehistory begins in earnest around 4000 B.C. with a distinct Northern Archaic tradition, then makes substantial innovative leaps with what archaeologists call the Arctic Small Tool tradition—a technology characterized by hafted one-half- to three-quarter-inch chisel-like blades used for working wood, bone and ivory. "By 2500 B.C. in the Kodiak region, people of the Takli culture had taken up the polishing of implements of slate," writes University of Oregon authority Don E. Dumond. This trait set Kodiak apart from the nearby Aleutians, where stone tools continued to be chipped rather than ground. Meanwhile, from the Alaska Peninsula north through Alaska and western Canada began to appear "peoples with a distinctive, miniaturized tool kit of delicately chipped" tools. Dumond suggests that the technology inherent in the microblades, burins and adz blades of the Small Tool tradition may have originated in Siberia. The Small Tool tradition is one of the first major indications that the Eskimo had the interest and ability to colonize the Arctic; it marks the beginnings of prehistory in the North American Arctic.

These people had bows and arrows but not stone lamps that burned oil fuel. Their harpoons, crude affairs compared with what came later, had "end blades" like chisels and were simply designed to stab quarry

like walrus. Nonetheless, new technology enabled groups of early Inuit to scatter widely — and no doubt often to perish when overwhelmed by local conditions. The Small Tool tradition gave way to a variety of local, short-lived cultures.

Soon two new cultures dominated the Arctic: the Norton culture around the Bering Sea and then all Alaska; and the Dorset culture that expanded east of the Mackenzie River, opening up virgin territory all the way to Greenland. These cultures produced important innovations. Among Norton peoples in particular, stone lamps appeared along with the first toggle-headed harpoons. Pottery in the Arctic was not to become highly refined or important, but techniques of making crude earthenware apparently came from Siberia, demonstrating continued links with Asia. Kayaks became common and evidently enabled Norton people to hunt small seals, sea otters and the like. The *ulu*, a crescent-shaped knife useful for cutting blubber, made its appearance.

About the same time, the Dorset culture appeared and spread throughout the eastern Arctic in a series of fits and starts whose causes have not yet been explained. These people had stone lamps but no pottery, perhaps because they may have been untouched by direct Asian influence. An expansive group, the Dorset people settled along coasts newly uncovered by retreating glaciers as the climate improved. They built several sorts

An Aleutian grass bag, above, exhibits the two-strand twining technique used almost exclusively by Aleut women to weave all manner of fine baskets. The Punuk culture of six or seven centuries ago produced the exquisitely carved ivory magic charms, top, which represent an Eskimo shaman propitiating a walrus to honor the animal's spirit.

99

Arctic, A.D. 350

Imaginative stories and songs help proto-Inuit peoples, the Ipiutak, to while away a long spring night at the ancient settlement of Point Hope in northwestern Alaska in this artist's depiction. Drawn to the coast in the spring and summer to harvest the rich resources of the Arctic Ocean, extended families crowded into semisubterranean sod houses reinforced with driftwood. Artifacts from nearby burial mounds suggest that the Ipiutak were perhaps the most accomplished artisans of all Arctic peoples. Archaeologists unearthed a wealth of carved ivory pieces including decorated harpoon heads, snow goggles, animal carvings and the elaborate ornamental band a man carves in the foreground. Artistry also took the form of facial tattoos and labrets — decorative pieces of ivory worn in holes in the cheeks.

Discovered in an ancient grave near Point Hope, Alaska, the masklike ivory image with decorative patterns at right was carved by Inuits of the Ipiutak culture, which began about A.D. 300 and lasted until about 1100. Ipiutak sites at Point Hope are known for their elaborate burial goods, as well as for the earliest use of iron in arctic Alaska. Below, a carved figure of a young walrus etched with a skeleton design may have been sewn to a shaman's garment to serve as a guardian spirit.

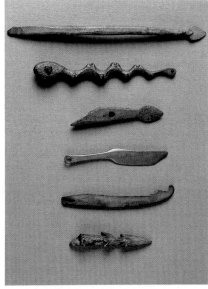

of dwellings depending on what material was handy: shallow pit houses, skin tents supported by ribs of beached whales and sod block houses. They used meteoric iron when they found it, and native copper for knives and projectile points. And they seemed to have adorned their implements for the sake of adornment. Like Norton people to the west, they hunted both caribou and small seals, but they concentrated on these alone and did not seem to seek different quarry. In this respect, they appear to have been essentially conservative, and that trait may have contributed to their demise.

Thule culture arose on Siberian and Bering Strait islands where whales, walrus and bearded seals were favored prey. It then leaped to the Alaskan mainland and in short order raced across the Arctic. Environmental factors, Robert McGhee of the National Museum of Man in Ottawa suggests, were a primary cause of the long Thule migration to the East. A continental warming trend broke up the summer pack ice, encouraging bowhead whales to seek the rich feeding grounds east of Alaska in the Beaufort Sea. Seaworthy boats and effective whale-hunting techniques enabled Thule hunters to pursue these bowheads ever eastward.

Thule communities were dominated by whaling captains, men who had the wherewithal to build, equip and maintain a boat. Historical analogy suggests that each captain also had the duty to support his

The upper half of a female figure rests within the shallow basin of a large oval stone blubber lamp, above left, from Alaska's Kenai Peninsula. Such lamps were used to burn animal fat, marrow or fish oil for illumination and heat. Above, small ivory objects from Point Hope, Alaska, include toy harpoon heads and a toy snow knife.

103

crew of a half-dozen men or so and their families, all of whom shared in the bounty of the chase. Each such leader was associated with a men's house in which boat and gear were maintained. This house was also the ceremonial center for both men's activities and the entire community's.

Sophisticated whaling technology grew hand in hand with the development of the whalers' social hierarchy. The seaworthiness of kayaks and larger umiaks enabled the Thules to chase whales, walruses and seals in the open water; throwing boards or atlatls and drag floats enabled them to kill and retrieve their quarry efficiently.

Within a century they were settling distant territories in the eastern Arctic and eclipsing Dorset communities. Thule expansion was aided by the fact that these versatile people had developed methods of hunting seals in winter ice and used dogsleds to improve transportation. "Perhaps the greatest advantage conferred by Thule culture...was not a specific technique but an overall adaptive flexibility," Jean Aigner writes. "Drawing on a wide range of techniques and a world view that supported settlement moves and changing hunting strategies, Thule groups routinely took a wider range of animals than...[previous people]...and used more locations. Such economic and social flexibility made it possible to maintain the equilibrium of the community under changing environmental conditions."

On Baffin Island in eastern Canada, Thule culture supported a long-lived population of perhaps 250 where previous cultures had been hard-pressed to sustain more than 150. Here they hunted bowheads, seals, walrus, caribou, polar bear and beluga whale. When the warming trend ended and both whale and caribou populations waned, these people simply changed their staples, adapted their hunting to other prey and took more small seals. They also split up into smaller groups and abandoned their shore-bound sod houses for snow houses built at the edge of the ice pack, where hunting could continue through the winter. Aigner concludes, "Under conditions of stress brought on by climatic change, people of the Thule culture responded with modifications of their way of life—in the locations and organization of settlements, in the tools and methods for subsistence and in the range and mixture of animals taken."

Not only did the Arctic peoples learn to cope with the extremes of their environment, they traveled vast distances, assuming in the words of the Smithsonian's Henry Collins "the greatest linear distribution of any people in the world." From the northeast coast of Siberia their territory spread an astonishing 6,000 miles to the shores of eastern Greenland. They may have traded directly or indirectly with peoples as

Caribou Eskimos, a group of independent bands that live in the central Arctic to the west of Hudson Bay, once carried out elaborate ambushes of caribou with the use of long, converging lines of cairns, or *inukshuks,* such as the one opposite, to drive the animals toward hunters concealed in shooting pits. Ivory carvings from the Dorset culture of arctic Canada, about 800 B.C. to A.D. 1000, include this piece of caribou antler, above, on which approximately sixty human and humanlike faces are carved.

E vidence of Norse presence in North America, iron boat rivets from a Viking ship overlie a map of the Ellesmere Island region, where excavations of the floor of a fourteenth-century Inuit sod house turned up not only these pieces but links of medieval chain mail and other Norse artifacts. The remains of the prehistoric dwelling were found on tiny Skraeling Island, several miles south of Ellesmere's Bache Peninsula, an area rich in archaeological deposits.

far-flung as those of Siberia, the Northwest Coast of North America, the Athapaskan of Canada, the Norse in Greenland and the Indians of the northeastern Maritime Provinces.

The Arctic has witnessed a variety of peoples moving across its beautiful, desolate reaches during the last 9,000 years or so. In late prehistoric times, descendants of the last wave of immigrants—calling themselves Inuit, and eventually being called Eskimo by the Whites— claimed the sinuous coastal regions and islands from Asia across the Bering Sea to Alaska and along the Arctic Ocean archipelago to the Atlantic and Greenland. Along the Aleutian Islands chain and nearby Alaskan mainland were their closest cultural and linguistic relatives, the Aleuts. Both Inuit and Aleut became essentially maritime people. The Arctic interior—and the adjacent Subarctic—became inhabited by another family of Indian cultures, people who spoke Athapaskan languages in the western part of this forested realm and, like the Algonquians to the east, wrested their living from game, notably caribou, and freshwater fish.

If it seems predictable that the continent's northernmost regions would be settled last, the reasons and results are surprising. Most waves of America's immigrants crossed Beringia and kept going slowly on, fanning southward and of necessity adapting to new environments once they had passed the great glaciers that covered most of Alaska and

Canada. As one archaeologist has written, "The journey ... undoubtedly took millenniums, but it was by no means time wasted. Indeed, the journey may have served as a laboratory" for testing and perfecting new hunting methods, social strategies and adaptations to specific parts of the high latitudes. By 7000 B.C., when the last waves of immigrants appeared, they may have found their way south blocked—or occupied by earlier arrivals, which would have amounted to the same thing. Yet the ancestors of the Aleuts and Inuits may also have remained in the far north because they liked this realm of sea-freezing cold—they were already adapted to cold-climate living. Having arrived when the glaciers were retreating, they found new territory as soon as it opened.

Far more threatening to these peoples—and there were several groups —would have been a temperate or tropical place teeming with plants and small animals. Like the Paiute foragers in historical Utah whose idea of paradise was a place with many rabbits, the original northerners found plenty in a place that offered conditions resembling those they had known before. What are more remarkable—or perhaps instructive— are the ways in which they embellished life in the frigid north. Then as now, the climate was generally one of the most rigorous on Earth and the environment the most demanding, yet the Arctic peoples developed often highly stylized, bold, yet graceful styles of art. Furthermore, their

Excavating prehistoric living sites in the Ellesmere Island region, archaeologist Peter Schlederman, at left in the photograph above, discovered Inuit remains dating back 4,300 years and, in 1978, surprising clues of contact with the Norse. Here he and a student examine artifacts from a site on Skraeling Island. Schlederman's excavation of a late Dorset culture longhouse on Knud Peninsula just south of Bache Peninsula produced countless miniature blades of chert and a wealth of carved animal figurines, including this polar bear head, above left.

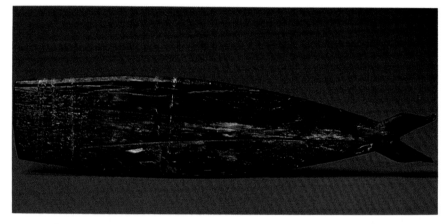

Rising at roughly the same time as the Dorset culture began its sudden decline — about A.D. 1000 — the Thule culture spread eastward across the Canadian Arctic to Greenland. A maritime people, the Thule were superb hunters and preyed upon many species, including seals, walrus, caribou, polar bears and the giant baleen whales of the Arctic seas. The winged design of the ivory needle case, above, is characteristic of the late Thule period. Such needle cases were carved to hold bodkins, with which women sewed sealskin. A cutout of baleen, or whalebone, above right, may have celebrated the rare killing of a sperm whale.

sense of artistry was applied not only to palpable objects — tools, utensils and weapons — but in the realms of song, instruments and oral literature.

"Only in the Southwest did music play so great a role" as among the northern people, according to John Bierhorst, a translator and writer on native American lore. "Only among the Pueblos and perhaps the Iroquois was the art of fiction so highly developed." On the basis of recent observations he offers a common-sensical explanation that seems to apply to the prehistoric Arctic as well: "Stories were needed, if for no other reason than to help fill the endless winter night. At its best, this eminently practical approach to storytelling gave rise to a secular entertainment industry unexcelled by any other native American culture." In Greenland, storytelling became a profession as good narrators came to live by their art, spinning out yarns and introducing a masterpiece with the challenge, "No one has ever heard this story to the end," then stretching it until the audience fell asleep. Another historical viewpoint suggests that "a new song or joke introduced into Alaska makes its way from one scattered camp to another and may turn up in Greenland a year or so later."

This points out another intriguing aspect of the Inuit in particular: for the most part, their dialects remain mutually understandable from Siberia to Greenland. Thus their narratives could spread equally far so long as groups or travelers encountered each other from time to time, probably a frequent occurrence among these far-ranging peoples. Appreciated more widely than their folklore, the Inuits' useful goods have always seemed to involve far more complexity, energy and skill than practical utility required. It seems never to have been enough just to make a useful tool; the tool was made to be beautiful. "That fact has interesting implications for theories about the beginnings of art," as Peter Farb wrote. "In the far north, where humans must face the constant threat of

starvation, where life is reduced to the bare essentials—it turns out that one of these essentials is art. Art seems to belong in the basic pattern of life of the Eskimo, and of the neighboring Athapaskan and Algonquian Indian bands as well."

Consider an eighteenth-century trader's experience in northern Canada. In the middle of winter, Samuel Hearne followed a single set of strange snowshoe tracks to a hut where he found a stranded woman who had been eking out an existence alone for seven months. Hearne wrote, "It is scarcely possible to conceive that a person in her forlorn situation could be so composed as to contrive or execute anything not absolutely essential to her existence. Nevertheless, all her clothing, besides being calculated for real service, showed great taste, and no little variety of ornament. The materials, though rude, were very curiously wrought, and so judiciously placed as to make the whole of her garb have a very pleasing, though rather romantic appearance."

Making beautiful tools, one line of reasoning suggests, might have arisen from practical concerns, given the slender margin for error in the Arctic. Supposing that Inuits pleased the spirits of their pantheon by adorning harpoons with animal effigies, in practical terms the extra care involved in decoration may have contributed to a finer weapon, one less likely to fail when used. Though all subsistence economies by definition lack frequent surpluses of food, life in the plant-scarce north can be sustained only by hunting; in some respects survival here was more perilous than in the southerly hardwood forests, where a variety of plant and animal food sources was available during much of the year. At least, if one silent arrow missed its mark, a deer left tracks that could be followed; it did not swim away into the trackless sea as would an Arctic seal or whale.

Characteristic artifacts of the Thule culture, which lasted from about A.D. 1000 to 1700, include this ivory fish lure with incised skeleton design, above left, and wooden snow goggles, above, which were worn to prevent snow blindness while hunting.

During the course of a culture's evolution, this devotion to crafted perfection would have become part and parcel of de facto religious tradition—a reflection of the hunter's cosmology—and thus also served the spiritual life. We say that beauty lies in the eye of the beholder, yet in the dangerous north, beauty may have been a form of insurance against weapons that might fail; thus the higher the degree of aesthetics, the more food at hand.

Other anthropologists have rejected the art-as-utility concept. Ethnologist Franz Boas, associated with Columbia University for most of his career, and a student of the Inuit, argued in *Primitive Art*, published in 1927, that "aesthetic pleasure is felt by all members of mankind.... The very existence of song, dance, painting and sculpture...is proof of the craving to produce things that are felt as satisfying through their form, and of the capability of man to enjoy them." Thus, while a set of aesthetic canons may have served to enhance community cohesiveness, the Inuit valued art for its own sake, and appreciated artistic talent whether in poetry, song or carving.

Adding another wrinkle, traditions of decorative carving themselves evolved in a curious manner that Smithsonian investigator Henry Collins outlined nearly fifty years ago in his chronology of Bering Sea Eskimos on St. Lawrence Island. Over the course of more than 2,000 years the carving did not become more elaborate per se; rather it became more economical, even minimalist, to borrow a term from modern art. Design elements were simplified as if the Eskimo artist/toolmaker had abandoned extravagant decoration in order to depict more purely the essence of a bird, beast or fish.

Typically, every adornment depicted a real or fabulous animal so as to please its spirit, its *inua*—through bestial flattery. The inuas were known to dislike ugliness, and the spirit of a bird or seal that was slain by a rude weapon would carry that message to its kind in the spirit world. On the other hand, the spirit of an animal that was well slain and handled with honor would return in the body of a similar animal and repopulate the Earth. Like virtually every other aboriginal group, the Inuit believed that all animals and even inanimate things had vital spirits that people must properly respect or suffer the consequences.

The keys to ultimate adaptation and habitation of the Arctic were flexibility and versatility, aided by a most inventive and ingenious technology. Also, it seems possible that each successive culture, ending with the Thule, came to more intimately understand a broader range of animals through their more varied hunting. In this development might they have better served inua? ✻

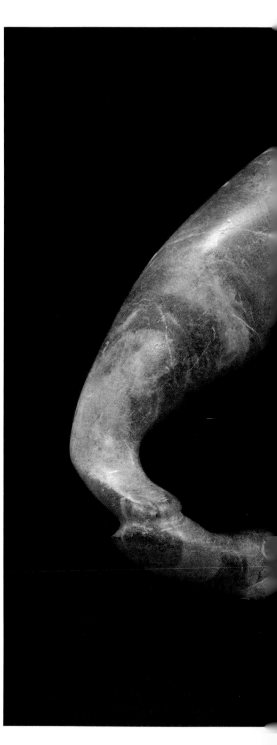

The polar bear, an ancient Eskimo — or Inuit — motif, receives contemporary treatment in this modern soapstone sculpture, *Bear on Ice,* by Manno, from Cape Dorset on southeast Baffin Island. The bear seems to stare at his reflection in mirrorlike ice.

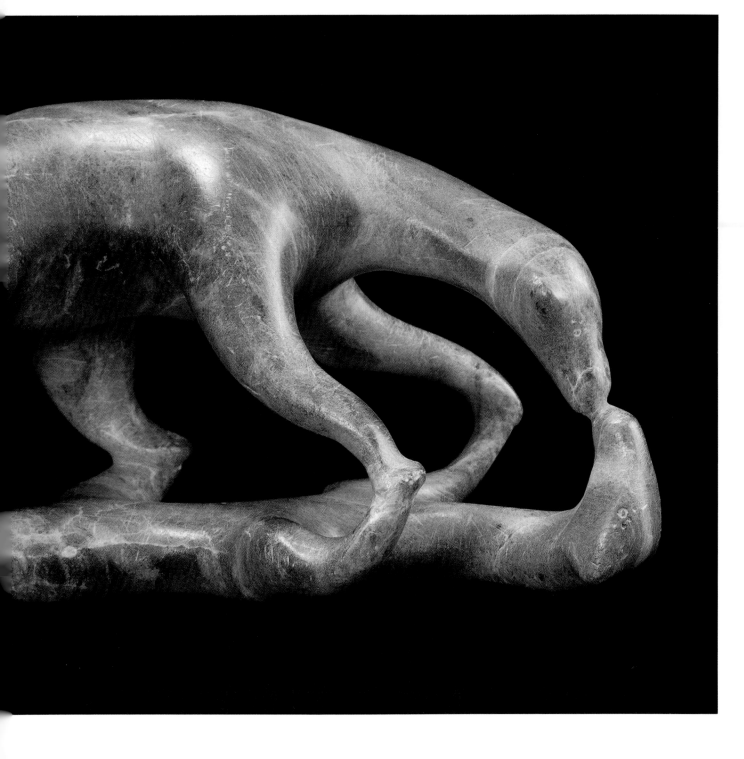

THE SUBARCTIC

With the coming of spring ten millennia ago, caribou migrated northward along habitual routes through Alaska's heartland toward their summer grazing grounds. They crossed the Kobuk River at a ford now called Onion Portage where Paleo-Indians lay in ambush—as would uncounted later generations of hunters—waiting for their quarry to enter the ford, where they could be easily killed. Though weapons and cultural traditions have changed, inhabitants of the Subarctic return to this spot even to this day.

This prime example illustrates how geography, seasons and types of animal life have enforced a remarkable continuity among the Subarctic peoples. Referring to northeastern Canada, Canadian archaeologist James V. Wright believes that these peoples maintained "a degree of cultural uniformity perhaps unequalled in the rest of North America.... In addition to cultural continuity through space, the prehistory of the Shield is characterized by cultural continuity through time. [The Shield Archaic period of Canadian prehistory takes its name from the Precambrian Shield, a great geological formation that underlies most of eastern Canada.] The northern Algonquians at the time of initial contact with Europeans followed a way of life that had not changed significantly for more than 7,000 years."

No other North American region compares with the Subarctic in size—two million square miles—and consistent habitat. This land of forests, bogs, mountains and bleak tundra stretches between the coasts of Labrador and Alaska. Within it are four sub-regions: the Precambrian Shield arcing from Labrador through Ontario to northeastern Alberta, northern Saskatchewan and the Northwest Territories; beyond, the mountainous Cordillera lying west of the Mackenzie River basin; the Alaskan Plateau and southern Alaska comprise the rest of the region. At these latitudes the winters are cold, long and dark. The summers of forty to sixty frost-free days are too short to sustain most cultivated crops. "Ethnologists generally recognize that the existence—physical, societal, and cultural—of the hunting peoples of the subarctic expanse has been sharply and immediately keyed to the terrain and its subsistence resources," writes the University of Iowa's June Helm in the Smithsonian's multivolume *Handbook of North American Indians*. A sharp language boundary west of Hudson Bay bisects the region into two linguistic realms, Algonquian to the east and Athapaskan to the west, but that boundary matters little in terms of lifeways. It may reflect ancient relationships, yet "linguistic heritage has but secondary implications for the comprehension of cultural adaptations, lifeways and influences for change among the native peoples of the subarctic," Helm continues.

Crowning the barren tundra with stands of spruce, a glacial gravel deposit called an esker winds its way past the myriad lakes of the Thelon River valley region of Canada's Northwest Territories, opposite. Oases of green amidst a vast northern desert of bedrock, muskeg and water, eskers often shelter foxes and wolves and provide travel routes for caribou, whose trails can be seen here. The rectangular covered container with etched decoration of lines and chevrons, above, was fashioned from birchbark by Cree-speaking Indians near Obedjiwan in Canada's Quebec Province. Birchbark was a vital resource for peoples of the forested areas of the southern Subarctic, especially the Algonquians of the east.

Subarctic

Wright attributes the region's cultural uniformity to a unique constellation of cultural and geographic factors. Travel was possible via lakes and rivers: in summer, people used canoes; in winter, snowshoes and sleds. Second, forest fires devastated areas as large as 10,000 square miles, driving out or consuming all denizens—including humans. Also, given the low carrying capacity of the enormous region and the need to relocate often, people lived in small hunting bands, maintaining loose social ties. They traced kinship through both male and female to maximize every person's connections. Polygamy occurred in both its forms: polygynous men often married their wives' sisters while polyandry enhanced women's economic security. Finally, the difficulties of surviving in the boreal forests discouraged outsiders.

Both the Algonquian and Athapaskan peoples sustained themselves largely on the two subspecies of New World reindeer: the woodland and barren-ground caribou (respectively, *Rangifer tarandus groenlandicus* and *Rangifer tarandus caribou*). These animals were the staple, though human hunters took moose, snowshoe hare and other game as they found it. They hunted by stalking, driving and ambush, as well as by snare and deadfall. They attacked both bear and beaver in their winter dens. Where caribou were not plentiful, they hunted moose, a difficult

Migrating seasonally in great herds such as that shown above, caribou provided many of the peoples of the Subarctic with food and the basic material for tools, weapons, clothing and shelter. The fluted spear point of obsidian, right, discovered near the Koyukuk River in Alaska, dates from between 11,000 and 9000 B.C. Such points were among the most characteristic tools of Paleo-Indian hunters.

An unknown artist of the Naskapi of northern Quebec painted a complex design — possibly a sun symbol — on this section of caribou skin, above right. Above, the finely tanned caribou-skin outfit, a man's summer costume, was made by the Kutchins of western Alaska. The shirt is decorated with red, black and white beads, highly prized dentalium shells and red ochre, as are the trousers and attached moccasins and mittens.

task since these animals rarely congregate in any numbers. They also took deer, elk, Dall sheep, musk ox, mountain goat and whatever else their range provided: beaver, woodchuck, marmot, muskrat, porcupine, arctic ground squirrel and various smaller rodents. But Subarctic fauna are notably cyclical in their abundance. The snowshoe hare peaks in ten-year cycles, rodent species in three- or four-year cycles. When each wanes, its predators decline and turn to other quarry such as ptarmigan, whose numbers then also fall steeply. These cycles discouraged consistently large populations of most animals, thereby also inhibiting human growth.

Salmon, whitefish and pike were important wherever they occurred, and waterfowl contributed to the larder, especially during molting season when they could be caught by hand. Throughout the Subarctic, black bear was prized because of its abundant fat, which added calories to the diet of these cold-climate dwellers. Since ice-age mammals such as mammoths and mastodons were almost certainly extinct when people arrived, the Subarctic Paleo-Indians probably always depended on the caribou. From the caribou, the people obtained food, hides and material for many implements from bones for netting needles to rawhide for fishlines and thongs. They ate the meat fresh or they preserved it by sun-drying or smoking, then pounding it into powder and mixing it with fat to make pemmican. They made containers from mammals' and

Made of serrated bone, a skin-working tool from Old Crow Flats in northern Yukon Territory, below, was used to deflesh the skin of barren-ground caribou. Bottom, hide-working stone from Lake Creek in Alaska's Koyukuk River region was used with other tools in preparing pelts and hides during the second millennium A.D.

fishes' skins and internal organs, from caribou lower leg skins cut away as a piece and head skins used as bottle-like vessels.

Hunting caribou at times other than the annual migration required much more effort. Samuel Hearne, one of the Hudson's Bay Company's first explorers, saw such a hunt take place in the 1770s. Chipewyans erected brush-and-pole human manikins twenty yards apart in lines as much as three miles long. They drove small herds of wintering caribou down these alleys into a mile-round brush enclosure surrounding a maze of brush barriers. Once the animals entered the trap, waiting hunters caught them in snares and killed them with spears and arrows.

While men engaged in their endless rounds of hunting, the women made clothing for all. Hide wardrobes included shirts, dresses and parkas with and without hoods. The Naskapi dehaired caribou skins and decorated them with painted designs. Athapaskans and Algonquians alike used beaver pelts for robes and fur hats. Athapaskans of the Shield made leather leggings with moccasins attached. Moccasins served well with snowshoes, which often enabled hunters to chase down big prey in winter's heavy snow drifts. Made with frames of spruce wood, they were laced with *babiche*—rawhide thongs. Thongs of the same material also served for fishlines and nets cunningly placed under lake ice in winter. Birch bark could be used to make canoes and boxes, saplings for construction of hide-covered shelters.

Although Edward S. Rogers of the Royal Ontario Museum and James G. E. Smith of New York's Heye Foundation were writing of historic Subarctic peoples, their comments probably apply equally well to the prehistoric: "Leadership was relatively diffuse…and depended upon personal qualities such as male hunting proficiency, generosity, demonstrated wisdom and judgment, and possession of supernatural powers. The dispersed population dictated by the environment…effectively prevented the development of coercive or complex political institutions. The leader was merely the 'first among equals,' and important group decisions were based upon consensus. In a climate of egalitarianism, excessive power was feared. Social control was maintained by enculturation, the prevalence of gossip, fear of supernatural sanctions and witchcraft, and the need for cooperative relationships. The value system emphasized generosity, sharing and hospitality among kinsmen and related groups, of evident value in the context of the uncertainties of life in the Subarctic. In their subsistence strategies, technology and social organization, the native people of the Shield Subarctic manifested effective adaptation buttressed and bound together by an ethic of generosity, sharing and mutual aid."

figures des montaignais

David pellet

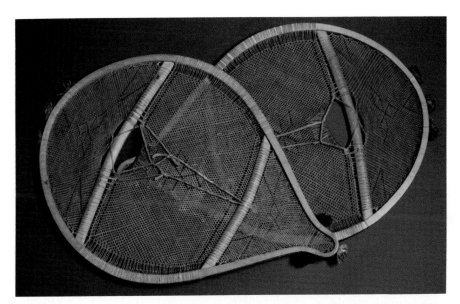

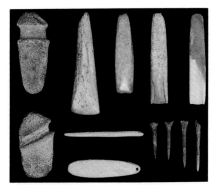

A Montagnais man, woman and child, opposite, are depicted on Samuel de Champlain's map of New France, 1613. The woman holds a decorated canoe paddle, the man a wooden shield and probably a ball-headed club. Left, these round-toed snowshoes may have been used by the northern Ojibwa for basic transportation during the fall, winter and early spring. Snowshoe types are usually distinguished by frame shape, with the more oval shapes typical of the east and the narrower shapes of the west. Above, a representation of the types of woodworking tools used by prehistoric peoples of Ontario includes drills, gouges, whetstones, adzes and axes.

To the west, in the region of the Great Slave and Great Bear lakes, McMaster University archaeologist William C. Noble begins the local chronology with sites representing Paleo-Indian traditions dating back to about 5000 B.C. The Acasta Lake culture complex, named for an area north of Great Slave Lake, comprises a dozen sites that have surrendered almost a thousand artifacts, among them weapons, butchering knives and tools used for working both wood and bone. At the Acasta Lake site, an area of 850 square feet, more than 100 hearths, many of them overlapping, indicated that these people returned repeatedly to a place they used as a "chipping station." Quarrying quartzite from a nearby outcrop, hunters baked the rock in their fires — an early example of heat-treating the stone to improve the way it fractures when worked by an expert toolmaker.

People seem to have entered the Shield — the eastern Subarctic — from the Plains long after the earliest Beringian migrants traveled down through western Canada and after the glaciers retreated. These were Plano peoples of the late Paleo-Indian period, who left projectile points of the Agate Basin style, dated elsewhere between 7500 and 6500 B.C. Northern Ontario and Labrador appear to have been occupied only after the onset of the Archaic period, which was under way by 4000 B.C. Dated between 1500 and 1000 B.C., some eastern sites contain a completely different tool kit, one associated with the Arctic peoples who evidently drifted down from the north in response to a worsening climate. By 300 B.C. pottery was introduced into the Laurel culture of Ontario, one

of the few changes in this region marking the transition from the Archaic period to the Woodland period of human habitation. Archaeologists still puzzle over where the pottery technology originated and use terms such as "stimulus diffusion" to describe possible southern influences.

In the western Subarctic, the Paleo-Arctic tool tradition—represented by minute cutting and engraving implements of stone—has been dated to about 8000 B.C. It seems to have strong links with Siberian technology of about the same time. This may have been shortly after some Na-Dene, ancestors of speakers of the modern Athapaskan language group, arrived from Siberia. Yet we have found no conclusive evidence. More certainly, this is later than the major migrations that gave rise to most other Indian populations, but probably before the migrations from Siberia of the racially distinct people who would become the Inuit.

If the genesis of the Athapaskans still awaits definition, their later lineage is more clear. (Members of the historical group all spoke closely related languages of the Athapaskan-Ayak phylum. Indeed, all spoke tongues of one branch; Ayak survived into modern times only in one small tribe on Alaska's Copper River.) By 5000 B.C., Athapaskans were expanding out of the western Subarctic to encounter earlier inhabitants of the Alaskan Plateau and Plains, from whom they borrowed new spear-point styles. Later, possibly because a Yukon volcano erupted about A.D. 750, some Athapaskans dispersed to settle the coasts of Alaska, British Columbia and California, giving rise to the ancestors of Pacific Northwest tribes such as the Haida, Tlingit and Hupa. Others moved east across central Canada north of the Great Plains. About the fifteenth century A.D., some Na-Dene appeared in the Southwest. As Navajo and Apache, their arrival caused some disruption among well-established south-western cultures about the time of first European contact.

Even with the arrival of the Europeans, the nature of the vast Subarctic lands retarded the rate of social and technological evolution. Fur traders and missionaries penetrated only so far—venturing little beyond the forts—and the Subarctic peoples shifted with little difficulty to a fur-trading economy. This life-style persists today. ✳

In the upper Northwest Territories, the Mackenzie River, opposite, curls past lakes and channels in a section of the river's delta region near the town of Inuvik. Flowing more than a thousand miles from Great Slave Lake to the Beaufort Sea, the Mackenzie has sustained native peoples for several thousand years. A fish effigy of bone, above left, possibly a fishing lure, is one of many prehistoric artifacts uncovered at the Klo-kut site in northern Yukon Territory. Above, a rock painting from Blindfold Lake, Ontario, may reflect an ancient shaman's vision.

THE NORTHEAST

Just as the great glaciers of the Northeast shaped the land, scouring a mountain range here, gouging a lake there, so the resulting complexities of the Northeast's landforms shaped the lives of their inhabitants. After the region recovered from the glaciers, Canada's Maritime Provinces and New England were rock-ribbed, clothed in spruce and birch. Farther south was a gentler land of sandy capes and beaches with many rivers reaching back across the Piedmont to the nearly impassable Appalachians and the Shenandoah Valley. Beyond the mountains were the deciduous forests and rich soils of the Upper Ohio and Mississippi river valleys and north the watery domain of the Great Lakes and St. Lawrence River. Revealed and made habitable by the melting glaciers, this land became home to Paleo-Indian caribou hunters about 12,000 years ago.

A number of Paleo-Indian sites have been unearthed across the Northeast. Camping places for the most part, they reveal the fluted projectile points characteristic of the early Paleo-Indian period in much of North America. Yet, some sites show evidence of long use. Near modern Pittsburgh, Meadowcroft Rockshelter offered convenient protection from the elements and access to a small river and game routes to the east. The University of Pittsburgh's James M. Adovasio has extensively excavated this shelter, frequented by Indians well into historic times. His work has uncovered eleven layers containing artifacts—including fragments of two human bones—perhaps dating as far back as 14,000 to 11,000 B.C. During this early postglacial period, however, it is extremely unlikely that bands of people penetrated the northerly reaches of the Northeast. Most Paleo-Indian sites appear in the southern areas: Pennsylvania, Maryland, Ohio and southern Indiana and Illinois.

As North America's climate grew warmer, a series of slow but ultimately dramatic environmental changes transformed the Northeast. Postglacial tundra was succeeded by grassland, then forest—coniferous in the north, mixed coniferous and deciduous in the southern regions. These changes, and perhaps human activity, brought about the extinction of the megafauna and other favored prey species, forcing Paleo-Indians to adopt new lifeways. Between 8000 and 6000 B.C., the older tool styles of the Paleo-Indian period gave way to newer traditions. Somewhat later, the peoples of the early Archaic period hunted caribou, deer, elk (*wapiti*), black bear, many smaller mammals, birds and other animals, fish and shellfish. Like the people before them, the early Archaic Indians consumed a wide selection of wild plant foods, including roots, nuts, berries and seeds. Some Archaic sites show evidence of seasonal use over long periods; middens sometimes contain grind stones and

Ever since glacial ice melted 12,000 years ago, Vermont, opposite, and the rest of the Northeast woodlands have been home to a wide variety of cultures. Above, long-nosed masks of bone were carved by the Mississippians of Illinois about A.D. 1000.

123

Mammoths feed at a site near Ann Arbor, Michigan, in this artist's evocation of a scene 10,800 years ago. Except for the coarse-haired pachyderms, this swamp of the last ice age resembles today's northern woodlands, where deciduous forests meet the great dark conifers. Moose and beaver have survived, but a changing climate and perhaps Paleo-Indian hunters drove the mammoths and their forest-browsing relatives, the mastodons, into extinction.

mortars, proof that nuts and seeds or wild grains were processed for food. In response to their changing environment and food sources, some Archaic Indians appear to have led more settled lives, wandering less widely than did their forebears.

In the upper Northeast, some seacoast dwellers adopted the practice of burying their dead in mounds accompanied by various kinds of artifacts. One very early mound grave, uncovered by James A. Tuck and Robert McGhee under the auspices of Memorial University of Newfoundland, proved astonishingly large and elaborate. At L'Anse-Amour on the Labrador coast by the Strait of Belle Isle, ancient gravediggers made a circular pit as deep as they were tall and more than thirty feet in diameter. There they placed the body of a child of twelve or thirteen years. They lit fires on either side of the body, which was covered with a flat rock and provided with knives or spear points of stone and polished bone; a cosmetic kit of red ochre, graphite paint stones and antler pestle to grind the paint; a walrus tusk; a bone pendant; a bird-bone whistle and a harpoon point. The grave was heaped with sand and then covered with three layers of boulders. Charcoal from the fires provided material for a radiocarbon date of approximately 5000 B.C.

During the next 4,500 years or so, which encompassed much of the Archaic period, the Northeast's coast changed with the climate and rising sea level, reaching its present outlines about 3,000 years ago. Throughout the region, mobile and semisedentary bands of Indians concentrated on one food resource or another as location, season and circumstance provided. Despite changes in tool styles, these lifeways persisted in most cases from the late Archaic into the next archaeological period, the Woodland, with little apparent variation. Indeed, in some parts of the Northeast, these hunting-gathering patterns would continue well into the historical period.

Toward the central midwest, as revealed by finds at the Koster site in Illinois, people lived by hunting, fishing and gathering from around 5000 to 3000 B.C. They manufactured slender projectile points and tools characteristic of the Helton culture. Settlement probably moved north from this area into the western Great Lakes region, where a long tradition emerged of native copper tools and ornaments. While copper tools and ornaments were not rare in prehistoric North America, the artifacts from the Great Lakes region certainly rank among the earliest.

Sometime around 1000 B.C., close to the end of the Archaic period or the beginning of the Woodland, agriculture and ceramics arrived in the upper midwest, undoubtedly via the Southeast. Probably the first domesticated plants in the region were squashes and gourds and other

125

Northeast

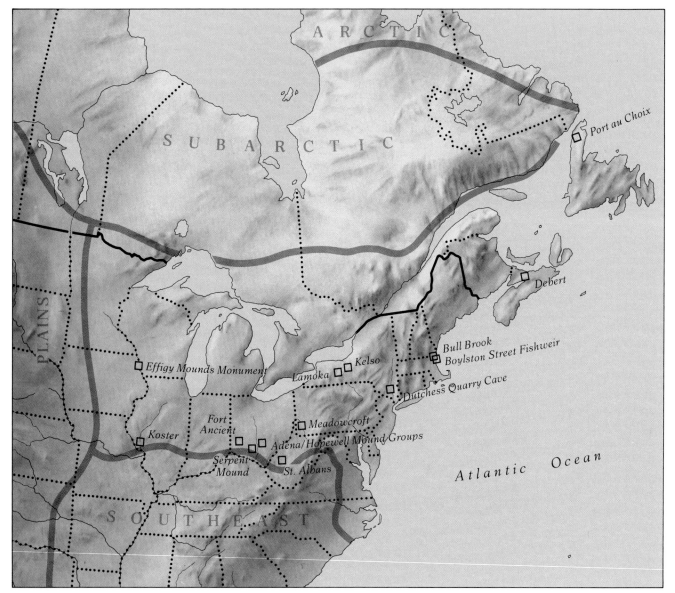

A 3,000-year-old cold-forged copper lance point and curved blade, above left, were crafted by artisans of the Old Copper culture of the Upper Great Lakes. Above, volunteers painstakingly excavate the Koster site in west central Illinois, a well-stratified site revealing an unusually complete record of nearly 9,000 years of human habitation.

seed-bearing plants such as sunflower, knotweed and goosefoot. Stone pots as well as clay ones have survived from this time.

Much later, after 1000 B.C., elaborate burials became widespread in much of the Northeast. The so-called Glacial Kame people buried their dead in natural mounds of gravel or earth—kames—deposited long before by the retreating glaciers. During this early Woodland period, peoples we have come to call Adena created a spectacular moundbuilding culture, centered in the valley of the Ohio River. The Adena phase, named for the landowner on whose property a variety of mounds was found, was characterized not only by burial mounds but by settled villages of circular post-and-wattle houses, increased agricultural activity and a variety of tool and ornament styles that reflected the Adena culture's ceremonialism. The goods found in Adena mounds include tubular tobacco pipes, sometimes in human form; copper beads; stone gorgets and projectile points.

While the core of its culture remained in Ohio, Adena's influence has been found at sites throughout the Northeast, even as far north as New Brunswick. During the middle Woodland period, however, from about 200 B.C. to A.D. 400 to 500 (a time that coincided with the increased importance of cultivated plants in the southern Northeast), a new influence arose in the same general midwestern area whence had come Adena. Known today as Hopewell, after the site of a huge Ohio mound excavated in the nineteenth century, this new cultural expression appears nearly to have supplanted Adena in a manner little understood today. It unquestionably became the dominant cultural force of the Northeast and part of the Southeast for hundreds of years.

Hopewell is no longer considered to be a "culture" by itself. Because it

Insouciant and unidentified, a cublike beast cavorts on a shell ornament called a gorget, made by artisans of the Glacial Kame tradition in the Great Lakes area about 1000 B.C. People associated with this culture buried their dead in the kames — gravel mounds left behind by melting glaciers.

influenced diverse peoples, archaeologists tend to refer to Hopewell as an "interaction sphere," a phenomenon somewhat akin to a cross-cultural religion in which linguistically and culturally distinct peoples share a set of beliefs or symbols, albeit sometimes imperfectly. Nor was Hopewell a political entity. Rather it is best interpreted as a kind of ideal, aspects of which—elaborate burial and moundbuilding, for instance—were attractive to many cultures.

The middle Woodland peoples lived in reasonably permanent villages. They evolved separate cultures, and their stylistic expressions in pottery and other works of artisanship and art reveal many local distinctions. Nonetheless, says David S. Brose, curator of archaeology at the Cleveland Museum of Natural History, these diverse peoples developed a web of reciprocal trade relationships.

Woodland period technology did not permit essential things, notably food, to be stored indefinitely. Every community doubtless experienced occasional shortages because of natural circumstances: the failing of an acorn crop one year out of three, a hard winter that killed off the deer, a local disappearance of fish. Because each locality was prone to such difficulties, the archaeological consensus holds that communities came to call upon each other for food in lean years, then for less essential goods in times of plenty. Individual leaders of each community would have served as agents in trading vital or desirable items. Such networks, which ethnographers have observed among subsistence-level agriculturalists in modern times, became the vehicles for the spread of exotic objects and intangible matters as well: ideas, tastes, habits. Eventually the Woodland peoples of the Hopewell sphere developed perhaps the widest trade network that existed in prehistoric North America.

This 3,000-year-old turkey-tail projectile point was flaked from Harrison County hornstone, a material coveted by flint-knappers and widely traded from its source in Indiana. The stem at the base makes the point unique; it may have assisted in hafting the piece to a spear shaft.

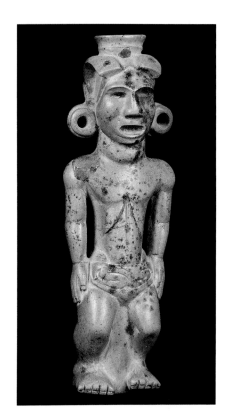

A t the height of their power in the Ohio Valley, peoples of the Adena culture filled their graves with goods held precious in life: left, the intricate figure on the carved-stone pipe may represent a dwarf; below, an animal effigy pipe suggests the Indians' delight with more humble items of personal value and adornment; above, the famous Wilmington Tablet was possibly coated with pigment in bear grease and stamped on bare skin.

Raw material for Hopewell trade goods came from all over the continent: copper from the upper Great Lakes, mica from the Appalachians, marine shells from the Gulf and Atlantic coasts, obsidian from the Rockies.

One of the most conspicuous manifestations of this middle Woodland period is the Great Serpent Mound in Adams County, Ohio, an earthen sculpture 1,254 feet long and still five feet high, even after farmers tried to plow it flat for many years. This icon, the largest in the world of its sort, appears to be a snake with an egg in its mouth overlooking a stream from a 100-foot cliff. Its purpose and meaning have yet to be explained.

Robert Silverberg wrote of Hopewell in *The Mound Builders*: "A single deposit from the Turner group in Hamilton County, Ohio, contained 12,000 unperforated pearls, 35,000 pearl beads, 20,000 shell beads, and nuggets of copper, meteoric iron, and silver,...copper and iron beads, and more....There is a stunning vigor about Ohio Hopewell, a flamboyant fondness for excess, that manifests itself not only in the intricate geometrical enclosures and the massive mounds but in these gaudy displays of conspicuous consumption. To envelop a corpse from head to feet in pearls, to weigh it down with many pounds of copper, to surround it with masterpieces of sculpture and pottery, and then to bury everything under tons of earth—this betokens a kind of cultural energy that numbs and awes those who follow after."

Nineteenth-century excavators of the Hopewell Mound complex measured its three-mile-long embankments and estimated that all its earthworks contained three million cubic feet of dirt. They reported finding coiled serpents carved in stone and enveloped in sheets of copper; fabric; bone needles and many more artifacts. The site was re-excavated in the late nineteenth century by Warren K. Moorehead of Harvard's Peabody Museum. Uncovering fifty burials in one mound, he found beads, pipes, copper jewelry and human jaws made into trophies. In the great central mound, which measured more than 500 feet across, he found 150 burials adorned with geometric figures, fish and bird effigies, serpent heads, axes, breastplates and balls made of copper, mica ornaments, ear spools, bear and panther teeth, stone tablets, terra-cotta rings, quartz crystals, flint knives and cloth. Before he was finished, he had found copper-covered deer antlers carved from wood, artfully carved human bones and ornaments made from marine turtle shells.

Late nineteenth-century archaeologist Henry C. Shetrone described the Hopewell grave of a young man and woman as "an imposing example of barbaric splendor....At the head, neck, hips and knees of the female and completely encircling the skeleton were thousands of pearl beads and buttons of wood and stone covered with copper; extending the full

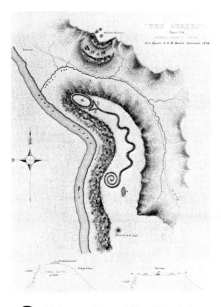

Ohio's great Serpent Effigy Mound, the Adena culture's most enigmatic production, is illustrated in a nineteenth-century map. The precise age and significance of the one-quarter-mile-long serpent has puzzled generations of archaeologists.

Art of the Hopewell culture incorporates bold design and mythic symbolism as seen in this ten-inch boatstone carving of a horned monster figure, at right. It is suggestive of the Indian legends of the water cougar, who hid in rivers and wrecked canoes.

length of the grave along one side was a row of copper ear ornaments; at the wrists of the female were copper bracelets; copper ear ornaments adorned the ears of both, and both wore necklaces of grizzly-bear canines and copper breastplates on the chest."

Archaeologists differ little over the reasons for the astonishing wealth contained within these Hopewellian graves. Ownership and disposal of valuable objects was a sign of power then, as it is now and has been all over the world. Powerful leaders conspicuously exhibited their influence through their material objects; their equally powerful families demonstrated their power by burying objects of great value with their deceased leaders. Some included human sacrifices in the tombs as examples of their great wealth and power.

However, David Brose offers an ingenious alternative to the commonly held hypothesis. He argues that burial removed potentially powerful and disruptive spiritual artifacts from public hands.

Nonindustrial peoples everywhere blur the distinctions that modern Western peoples make among matters of spirit, technology and art. Instead all may be understood as one, and a single object can embody all. In such a context objects contain power perilous by its very nature. In the hands of a master, the powerful entity—be it weapon, amulet or force like fire—can be controlled and used for good. But left to lesser folk, it can be a threat of the greatest magnitude. Brose borrows a term from our contemporary nuclear energy lexicon to suggest that in one respect a Hopewell burial mound was "a containment vessel." The obsidian cache, the sacred icon, the ceremonial axe, the chief huntsman's atlatl weighted

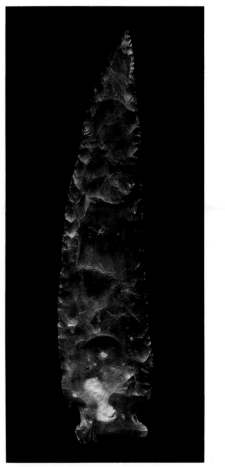

A startlingly vivid design from Ohio represents a bird's claw, at left, crafted from mica by Hopewellian artisans. Other mica figures such as human hands were also buried in mound graves. Above, a curved ceremonial blade of chipped stone may have belonged to a shaman from Wisconsin.

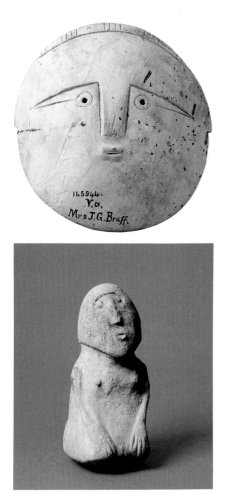

Curios from history's cache: the enigmatic effigy in shell, top, emerged from an archaeological dig in Virginia; above, a fourteen-inch-high Kentucky "idol" was presented to Thomas Jefferson in 1790. Both items reflect traditions of the southern Algonquian Woodland culture and artistic style.

with perfectly carved banner stones—all these have something in common with each other. While capable of providing great benefit, they can most easily cause immeasurable harm. Assuming the goods in a grave belonged to the mighty individual during life, Brose argues that they possessed such power that they could not safely be left around after their keeper's death nor even passed on to a successor. Perhaps the late leader needed such objects in the spirit world. They were therefore buried with ceremony lest their power wreak havoc among those still living.

In parts of eastern North America, the influence of some of these Hopewell traditions may have persisted little changed until historic times. As we discuss in *The Southeast* chapter, a new and even more spectacular moundbuilding culture overshadowed the Hopewell. Called the Mississippian because many of its hundreds of mound sites are clustered along the middle Mississippi River drainage, this group of related cultures would produce the most complex societies of prehistoric North America outside of Mexico, between A.D. 500 or 600 to 1000. But it is to the peoples of the Northeast's forests and coasts that we now turn.

For hundreds of years, the forests across the region of the Great Lakes, east to today's Maritime Provinces, Newfoundland and New England, south along the Atlantic Coast to the Carolinas and inland beyond the Appalachians, had been inhabited by various peoples who hunted, fished and gathered wild plant foods as had their ancestors for thousands of years. They led more or less settled existences, depending on local resources. Influences from the south wrought changes in their tool and pottery styles, and some in the more southern areas added agricultural products to their diets as they learned to grow squash, corn and other domesticated plants of the Southeast and Southwest. These trends perhaps accelerated during late prehistoric times, from about A.D. 1000 to 1600, when contact with Whites changed all native cultures profoundly and irrevocably.

The people of the coastal zone were the ancestors of those who would be called eastern Algonquians—speakers of tongues of the Algonquian language group, the tribes that would be known as the Micmac, Abenaki, Narragansett and Delaware, among others. These peoples had been among the first to populate these areas. They had adapted well to the region, making maximum use of its rich but varied resources. At one Massachusetts site, their food remains include beaver, dog, red and gray fox, black bear, mink, harbor seal, deer, loon, great blue heron, mallard, black duck, red-tailed hawk, bald eagle, great auk, snapping turtle, stingray, sturgeon, sea bass, sculpin, sea robin, scup, wolf fish, bay scallop, mussel, quahog, surf clam, long clam, moon snail, thick-lipped

The towne of Pomeiock and true forme of their howses covered
and enclosed some with matts, and some with barcks of trees. All compassed
abowt with smale poles stick thick together in stedd of a wall.

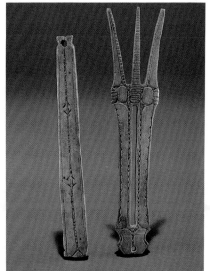

R are bone pendants collected in Newfoundland represent work of the mysterious Beothuk, exterminated by European settlers in the eighteenth century. Europeans called them "the Red Indians" because of their lavish use of a natural pigment to color their bodies. At left, longhouses and other structures of a southern Algonquian encampment appear inside a palisade of poles. The scene was recorded 400 years ago in North Carolina territory by British artist John White.

drill and channeled conch. The people lived in wigwams, domelike houses of sapling frames covered with slabs of bark and deerskin.

Separated from these coastal peoples by the Appalachians were the people of the St. Lawrence lowlands, an area including southern Ontario, upper New York State and the St. Lawrence and Susquehanna valleys. The term Iroquois refers to the five "nations" of New York—Mohawk, Oneida, Onondaga, Cayuga and Seneca. These Indians, along with others speaking tongues of the Iroquoian language phylum such as the Huron, Neutral and Erie, were characterized, according to Bruce G. Trigger of Montreal's McGill University, writing in the *Smithsonian Handbook of North American Indians*, by "large, often fortified villages, prisoner sacrifice, similar shamanistic rituals, and a matrilineal kinship system." The bark-covered longhouses they built were sometimes as long as 300 feet; their communities tended to be larger than the Algonquian settle-

Northeast, A.D. 1300

This artist's depiction of a spring afternoon in a pre-Iroquoian settlement is based on an archaeological map of the Kelso site near Syracuse, New York. Atop a low, flat-topped rise in a farmer's field, William Ritchie and Robert Funk from the New York State Museum discovered evidence of late prehistoric habitation. Their 1963 excavation uncovered two palisaded villages, each two acres in size. The task of reconstruction is especially difficult in the Northeast, where most traces of the structures have long since deteriorated. The evidence that does exist is in the form of post-mold patterns — slight discolorations in the soil produced by the rotting of wooden posts used in

the construction of palisades and longhouses. At the Kelso site, such patterns suggest that inhabitants built a double line of palisades to afford themselves greater protection from surprise raids by the other peoples. The longhouses in which the vast majority of the community lived were probably thatched with bark and might extend as long as 125 feet. In this reconstruction, Owascan hunters bring in white-tailed deer while women prepare corn soup, a staple of the daily meals. The Owasco might have occupied a locale such as the Kelso site for eight to ten years until their neighboring fields were no longer fertile and they were forced to move on.

ments to the east. Also during Woodland times, the Iroquois came to depend more heavily on agriculture than the Algonquians, often using slash-and-burn techniques — clearing and burning forest to create new planting areas when soil in old fields was exhausted.

The final general Northeast geographical area encompasses the rest of the region around the Great Lakes and south into Ohio, Kentucky and West Virginia. Its peoples were Algonquian- and Siouan-speaking and used agriculture to a lesser degree than the Iroquoian-speaking peoples of the St. Lawrence lowlands; their kinship system was patrilineal. The tribes included the Shawnee, Kickapoo, Miami, Winnebago and Fox.

All these people lived in villages of up to several hundred inhabitants linked by various kinship ties. All but the more northerly dwellers depended on some combination of hunting, fishing, gathering and agriculture for sustenance, fiber and fur. They were mobile, moving from their villages to favored fishing or bird-hunting spots at the appropriate seasons. Particularly in the fall, men went hunting, alone or in groups, seeking deer and black bear primarily, although they had uses for most of the animals that lived in the Northeastern forests.

Both archaeological and historical evidence suggests that these Indians

Iroquoians fashioned these "husk face" masks, opposite, from corn husks and wore them during midwinter festivals. Above, Frenchman Francis de Castelnau painted this scene of an Ottawa Indian fishing village on Lake Huron's Mackinac Island in the 1830s. Birch tree bark provided an important resource for the Ottawas, who used it to fashion tipis, canoes and other traditional handiwork.

139

I roquois women of northern New York State and Ontario shaped vessels out of clay and impressed designs on them before baking them. Heated stones might be placed in a scalloped-collar pot such as this one to heat food.

used fire both to clear fields and to control underbrush and create zones of varied vegetation. In this way they could have promoted mixed habitats capable of supporting not only a wide variety of plants and animals but also those that favored the particular kinds of plants and animals they most valued. In his landmark study of Indians, colonists and the environment of New England, *Changes in the Land*, Yale University historian Thomas Cronon argues that most European settlers failed utterly to comprehend the effects—or the importance—of the Indians' calculated use of fire as a tool in shaping their environment. Other scholars have countered that while the Northeast peoples undoubtedly used fire to clear fields for planting, its role in shaping the overall environment was more accidental than planned.

Once men had cleared trees and brush for fields, women did virtually all the farm work. They planted mixed crops of corn, beans, squash and pumpkins in hills. Cronon notes that no evidence exists to indicate that they fertilized the hills with alewives or other fish, despite the enduring Pilgrim myth. Although the nitrogen-fixing beans helped to extend the soil's life, corn inevitably exhausted the nutrients, whereupon the whole village would move to a new location. Relocation also shifted the population away from plagues of fleas and to new sources of firewood, vital for winter warmth.

Where coasts, rivers and lakes permitted, the Indians used canoes for fishing—paper birch canoes in the north, log canoes farther south—and traveled and traded fairly extensively. Travelers were always at risk from the constant small-scale warfare practiced by many Northeastern peoples.

Territorialism and perhaps other more complex and hotly debated social factors caused the late prehistoric Indians of the Northeast to war continually with one another. Conflict, particularly in the form of limited and sporadic skirmishes, was not at all uncommon in prehistoric North America. Groups waged war to consolidate their territories and to maintain substantial buffer zones. In the Northeast, the agricultural practices of many tribes required abundant land, yet suitable cropland remained relatively limited. However, the "reasons for [the Iroquois'] internecine warfare are unclear and probably will remain so," wrote James A. Tuck of Memorial University in the *Northeast* volume of the *Smithsonian Handbook of North American Indians*, "although a possible population increase related to the introduction of a horticultural subsistence base and resulting competition for land, local game supplies, and other resources has been suggested." Tuck's own suggestion is that "factors less directly related to the natural environment are probably more basic...." He finds merit in the thesis that as women became the dominant food producers,

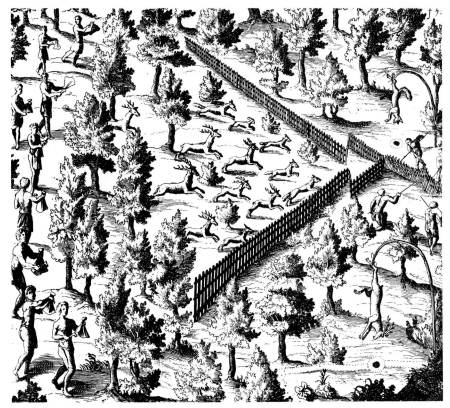

Top, the beauty and design of this ball-headed, maple war club reflects the importance of warfare in Iroquoian society. The figure on the handle probably represented the animal totem of the owner. Left, in 1615 Samuel de Champlain sketched a fanciful Huron hunt in which deer were driven into a fenced enclosure and killed with spears. Other deer were caught with snares.

the role of men as hunters declined and the killing of men increased.

Few peoples made war as much a part of life as did the Iroquois. By late prehistoric times their villages were designed for defense first and foremost, says William Finlayson, director of the Museum of Indian Archaeology in London, Ontario. They moved to natural promontories above rivers or streams, raised substantial palisades around villages and built mazes of earthworks and inner palisades within the stockades. Archaeological evidence also suggests that villages in some areas coalesced as their inhabitants sought safety in numbers.

Lacking the manpower to maintain anything like a standing army of full-time soldiers, Iroquois tribes became masters of the sporadic raid, attacking neighbors in their villages and laying ambushes in forests and corn fields. Their foes were both other Iroquois tribes and the Algonquian peoples who had occupied the region much longer and who had never depended on agriculture as fully as the newcomers. As Peter Farb argued in *Man's Rise to Civilization*, these warring tribes did not seek to subjugate others as vassals: "The best they could achieve was a succession of clashes by which they obtained captives, furs, and booty." Women and girl prisoners replaced wives and daughters lost in the continuing hostilities that often more closely resembled blood feuds than warfare in the European sense. But most grown men who had the misfortune to be captured were slowly and systematically tortured to death.

Evidence of frequent war is found in late Woodland cemeteries. More men's skeletons show broken arms and depressed skull fractures. Varied pottery styles turn up at specific village sites. Women made the pottery, and when one was captured by raiders and adopted into a new tribe, she brought her own way of making clay vessels with her.

Warring apparently reached a destructive peak among the Northeast's tribes between 1400 and 1600—certainly before direct contact with European explorers. Then a leader whom Senecas today remember as "The Peacemaker" persuaded the chiefs of the five Iroquois tribes to meet and call an intertribal truce.

The resulting confederacy, one of several that would be formed among Northeastern tribes, achieved its goal of ending the nearly systematic feuding between the member tribes. The Iroquois turned their aggressive attention to neighboring peoples, however, and peace did not come to the region as a whole.

The League made the Iroquois powerful enough to deal with the White invaders for almost 200 years. But in the end nothing availed them against the even better organized and far more numerous Europeans, nor against the devastating diseases they brought. ✳

Modern turtleshell rattles from the Iroquois of Canada are musical instruments used in religious dances, festivals and chanting. Traditional use of such rattles may go back to precontact times. Above, a bird totem of the Great Lakes Ojibwa may represent a hawk perhaps associated with a personal guardian spirit.

THE SOUTHEAST

 Nineteenth-century Americans regarded the prehistoric Southeast as the realm of the "moundbuilders," a mythic race of titans who had constructed the countless earthen mounds, some huge, that dotted a fourth of what is today the United States. More accurately, Spanish and French explorers of the region in the sixteenth and seventeenth centuries had described powerful chiefs who ruled large populations from ceremonial centers with mounds. As Vincas P. Steponaitis, archaeologist at the State University of New York at Binghamton and Southeastern scholar, has written of the chiefdoms the Europeans found in the Southeast, [though they] "were not as centralized or vast as those of the Aztecs or Incas, they nevertheless were the most complex societies to be found north of Mexico."

Who were these peoples? Where had they come from? Where did they go, to leave those nineteenth-century theoreticians guessing about the origins of the mounds?

The earliest date for human presence in the Southeast comes from a Paleo-Indian campsite discovered at Little Salt Springs in Florida. There archaeologists found the remains of several animals, including a giant tortoise killed with a wooden stake that has yielded a radiocarbon date of about 10,000 B.C. With the Clovis toolkit and its fluted spear points, the Paleo-Indians hunted many other kinds of animals as well, including such megafauna as mastodons, ground sloths and bison.

The end of the Paleo-Indian period faded into the beginning of the Archaic period around 8000 B.C. Some Archaic peoples harvested seed-bearing plants, among them sunflower, marsh elder, amaranth and goosefoot. But this casual horticulture was not farming. Wild plants supplemented the diet as Archaic Indians exploited the Southeast's resources, rich in fish, birds, deer, bear, small animals like rabbits and squirrels, seasonal plants, nuts and acorns and freshwater mussels whose discarded shells grew into huge riverside heaps of refuse known as "middens." Similar middens of shells grew at coastal sites where people gathered vast quantities of oysters and other mollusks as well as other marine creatures and plant foods native to the littoral.

For thousands of years during the Archaic period, people inhabited the Eva site on a channel of the Tennessee River, consuming vast quantities of mussels, deer and nuts. The site features scattered post holes indicating dwellings. Although their size and style cannot be read here, evidence at other similar sites indicates that these houses probably measured seven to ten feet in diameter, with walls of upright poles set in the ground and packed clay floors. Some floors reveal several layers, suggesting that the dwellings were used over and over. The Eva people's

From Key Marco, an island off Florida's southwestern coast, this wooden creature has been interpreted variously as a cougar god or a human disguised as a cat. The six-inch feline figurine, discovered on a famous Smithsonian dig, resides at the National Museum of Natural History. Above, a vase embellished with avian heads reflects burial art techniques and themes of the Weeden Island culture, which influenced the peoples of western Florida and surrounding areas from A.D. 200 to 1200.

Spiritual guardians of the dead, magnificent totem creatures rise in an artist's recreation, right, much as they did twenty centuries ago. Their many wooden poles lift the charnel house high above waters of an artificial pond north of Lake Okeechobee and the Everglades. On top of the platform are the bundled remains of the dead. Opposite, one of the supports in the form of an eagle was preserved in the sediment at the pond's bottom. A great horned owl, above, sculpted half a millennium ago from a Florida yellow pine log, was discovered at the St. Johns River near Cape Canaveral in 1955. The effigy originally stood at the water's edge.

tools included bone fishhooks, awls, needles, drills, gorgets for personal adornment and tubular smoking pipes. At Indian Knoll, Kentucky, more than 1,200 graves have been found, a third containing such artifacts as projectile points, pestles, stone slabs with marked indentations for holding nuts to be cracked ("nutting stones"), stone axes with painstakingly pecked grooves for wooden hafts, bone fishhooks and atlatls. A tiny fraction of the graves contained exotic imports like copper and engraved seashells, evidence that far-flung trade had begun.

Around 4000 B.C., the region's population began to increase markedly, and a number of other momentous changes are revealed in the archaeological record. Agriculture reached the area, perhaps through today's Missouri, where remains of squash have been found that may date back to almost 5000 B.C. And vessels of stone and pottery appeared. These innovations seem to have been accompanied by the adoption of more sedentary living habits, a change suggested by the increased use of pits for storage of seeds and other dry foods. A sedentary life-style often required increased social order if groups were to survive local shortages, during which, for instance, oak trees might produce fewer acorns than in other years, or the deer or rabbit populations might crash after extremely severe winters.

These developments also suggest that goods, including foodstuffs, may have been traded. Indeed, exotic materials such as marine shells from the Gulf Coast, copper from the Great Lakes area, fine horn-stone from Indiana and mica from the Appalachians were increasingly exchanged throughout the Southeast as Indians plied the great river systems in dugout canoes.

Much later, perhaps around A.D. 1000, many Indian societies in the Southeast came to depend on farming for most of their food. Population density continued to increase; according to physical anthropologist Douglas H. Ubelaker of the Smithsonian Institution, estimates of the region's population at the end of the fifteenth century A.D. range from 155,000 to 286,000. Most of the societies were hierarchical; the special status of leaders and others of the elite class is indicated by the richness of artifacts buried with them in their graves. Beautifully made and decorated objects often found in graves and other sites suggest elaborate ceremony and religion, even warrior traditions. But far overshadowing all other archaeological evidence from the Woodland and Mississippian periods are the mounds.

While not all of the Southeast's inhabitants built mounds, these earthen structures constitute the region's chief characteristic, archaeologically speaking. All over the East, from Maryland and New York to Florida and Texas and west to Missouri and Illinois, uncounted thousands of mounds still dot the countryside. The earliest substantial mounds in the Southeast seem to have been made by people at the site known as Poverty Point in northeastern Louisiana about 1500 B.C.

A number of different kinds of mounds were built at various times and places and for diverse purposes. Burial mounds were raised over the bodies of the elite. So-called temple mounds served as religious sanctuaries. Platform mounds raised the homes of nobles above the common throng. Some more mundane embankments may have been part of defensive earthworks.

That much said, let us take a closer look at some of the Southeast's outstanding archaeological sites. One hundred years ago, Smithsonian

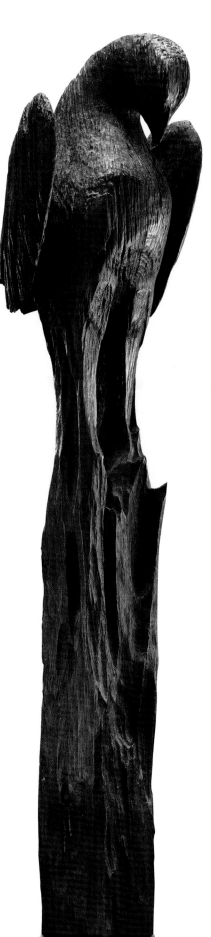

147

Southeast

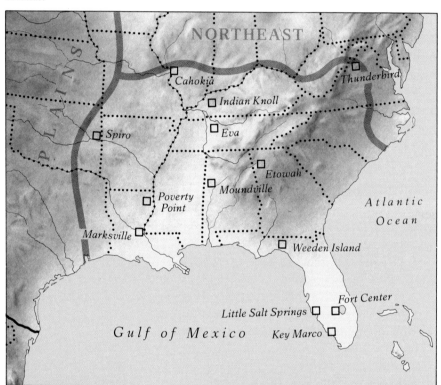

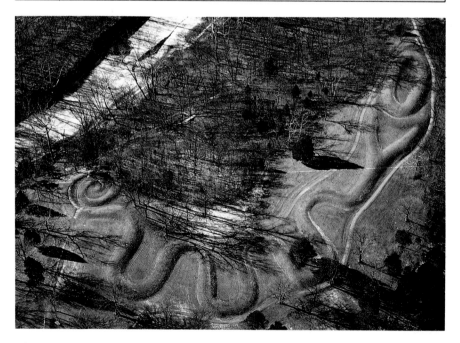

North America's most elaborate effigy
mound: a serpent swallows an egg or,
perhaps, the sun. The quarter-mile-long
mound, built more than two millennia
ago during the Northeast's middle Woodland
period, still uncoils on a creek bluff near
Cincinnati, Ohio.

148

ethnologist and archaeologist Frank Cushing unearthed a treasure trove of artifacts at Key Marco in the swamps of southwestern Florida. Included in his find were animal effigies and a wide variety of other intricately carved wooden artifacts. Archaeologists usually faced with working with nonorganic artifacts—projectile points and the like—suddenly had ancient organic objects to study, remarkably preserved by the mud of pond bottoms and river beds.

In the twentieth century, a half-dozen more of these so-called wet sites have been excavated, revealing the remains of large ceremonial centers. Evidence from these discoveries has forced archaeologists to rethink old notions about the Archaic peoples of the region. Working from a limited selection of durable goods (pottery and stone tools), some archaeologists had imagined impoverished societies. The wet-site wooden artifacts reveal flourishing, complex cultures.

William H. Sears of Florida Atlantic University found such a culture at the Fort Center site near Lake Okeechobee in Florida's southern interior. Between 1000 and 500 B.C., peoples living along Fisheating Creek built linear earthworks perhaps designed to raise living quarters above floodwaters.

Around the time of Christ, these earthworks took the form of circular mounds. Two of these mounds, Sears surmises, were the scenes of an elaborate burial ritual. Low earthworks were built around the edges and

A delicate enclosure of earth rings so-called Mound City, a Hopewell site less than four miles north of Chillicothe, Ohio. The artwork appeared in 1858 in *Sketches of Monuments and Antiques: Found in the Mounds, Tombs and Ancient Cities of America*, by Edwin Hamilton Davis. He and E.G. Squier unearthed hundreds of stunning artifacts from the small, rounded burial mounds.

A high-flying aircraft took this digitally processed, artificially colored mosaic image of Poverty Point, a major archaeological site in Louisiana dating from 1500 B.C. The pink concentric ridges enclosing a central plaza may have been constructed as platforms for dwellings as shown in the drawing, opposite. Satellite imagery and aerial photography have become increasingly important archaeological tools.

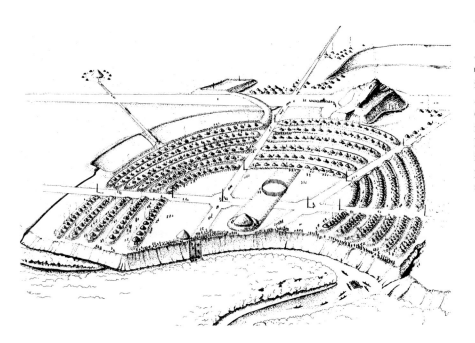

Near the confluence of the Arkansas and Mississippi rivers, Poverty Point thrived for 300 years on trade and fine lapidary work. The one-square-mile complex includes six miles of these artificial ridges. Archaeologists estimate that thirty million loads of soil were carried by hand in fifty-pound increments to build the settlement. While the Poverty Point culture may have benefited from indirect contact with Mesoamerican cultures, no prehistoric site in the Southeast has yielded a single Mexican relic.

water added to form an artificial pond. On a raised wooden bier in the pond were placed the bundled remains of the dead. Each of ten poles supporting the structure was decorated with effigies of the eagle, bobcat, otter and duck; more than thirty such animal clan symbols have been identified. Preservation was so complete at Little Salt Springs, to the northwest of Fort Center, that the investigators could describe in detail how bodies were prepared for burial.

To the west in northeastern Louisiana lies the enigmatic Poverty Point site. From the top of a steep bluff carved by the bayou several million years ago, Poverty Point's Macon Ridge looks flat save for a series of almost imperceptible rises that were plowed nearly level in the course of the last century. But in nearby woods, these earthworks reveal their ancient size: ten feet high, seventy-five feet wide and 100 to 150 feet apart. Six concentric crescent ridges broken by four spokelike aisles form a "C" some 3,950 feet in diameter surrounding a thirty-seven-acre plaza. Just beyond the central group of ridges opposite the bayou rises a towering, seventy-foot-high mound spanning 640 feet in one direction and 710 in the other. Three other earthworks stand nearby, and about a mile and a half north and south are two other mounds. Layers of debris, postmolds and hearths have been found near the outlying mounds, along the bluff to the north of the ridges and atop most of the ridges themselves, suggesting that people inhabited all these areas.

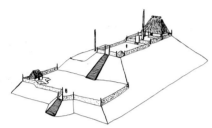

One-hundred-foot-high Monk's Mound, top, at a great North American Indian metropolis called Cahokia, covers sixteen acres — three acres more than the Great Pyramid of Giza. Above, a Mississippian culture effigy pipe in the shape of a frog served its owner at council ceremonies and also for personal use. Indians smoked the leaf of a strong tobacco species native to the Andes, *Nicotiana rustica*. Opposite, this ceramic of a serene mother and nursing child came to light at the Cahokia metropolis, which may have been inhabited by 30,000 people at its zenith.

The culture whose people erected this massive center began to appear as early as 3000 B.C., according to Jon L. Gibson of the University of Southwestern Louisiana, who has conducted most of the recent studies. It became a distinct culture by 2000 B.C., stretching 300 miles from the Gulf Coast to the junction of the Mississippi and Arkansas rivers above present-day Greenville, Mississippi, and reached its height from 1500 to 700 B.C. Many aspects of the Poverty Point culture remain mysterious. But one thing is certain: to build Poverty Point required substantial leadership and social organization. As Smithsonian archaeologist Bruce D. Smith has written, "When combined with adjacent mounds, the largest two of which measure 6.6 meters (22 feet) and 21.3 meters (70 feet) in height, these habitation ridges provide massive supporting evidence of both extensive occupation [more than 200,000 cubic meters (266,000 cubic yards) of habitation debris] and organized corporate labor efforts [more than 350,000 cubic meters (466,000 cubic yards) of basket loaded dirt] that would not be approached anywhere north of Mexico for another thousand years."

Poverty Point was built before the rise of intensive agriculture. Arkansas archaeologist Ed Jackson investigated the nearby Copes site in search of clues to the plants and animals that Poverty Point people used. He uncovered the remains of such wild fruits as persimmon and plum, nuts such as acorns and pecans and seeds such as goosefoot and marsh elder, with typical artifacts: lance points, a slate awl and the earthen "cooking balls" that are characteristic of Poverty Point. (These baked lumps of clay presumably served the same purpose as did cooking stones in places where rock was common: heated in a fire, they were then placed in containers to warm soups and stews.) The only traces of domestic plants that Jackson found were squash seeds, which may have produced bottle gourds for containers or the edible squash. The site, dated between 1400 and 1100 B.C., was rich in the remains of fish, deer, birds, reptiles and small mammals.

While it has been proposed that Poverty Point culture was the result of trading connections and influence from Mesoamerican cultures, particularly the Olmec of Mexico, many archaeologists believe that Poverty Point was the center of a culture that arose locally. Its influence, reaching as far as Florida, Tennessee and Missouri, has been traced through its characteristic artifacts: the cooking balls, stone plummets (possibly used for the string-and-ball weapons called bolas or for fishing weights), stone beads, beautifully wrought miniature jasper owls and hundreds of stone forms whose purpose remains unknown. In turn, Poverty Point received goods — typically choice stone and other minerals — from as far

as 1,000 miles away. Ed Jackson has discovered wing bones of roseate spoonbills and brown pelicans, birds not normally found here in prehistoric times. Perhaps, he surmises, since only wing bones appear, bird wings may have been imported for their plumage. Clearly this area was a center for trade, probably carried out via the waterways that connected with the nearby Mississippi and thence up its tributary rivers. And if it was a trading center, it follows that settlements of this magnitude must have played a central role in government and religion.

By about 500 B.C. Poverty Point culture and its influence had waned. The site itself still raises more questions than it has answered, and it will unquestionably remain a fertile place for excavation and hypothesis for years to come.

Lifeways of the Southeastern late Archaic period continued into the early and middle Woodland periods (from about 700 B.C. to A.D. 600). Agricultural products supplemented diets that were still largely based on hunting and gathering of animals—particularly deer, raccoons and turkeys—of the region, shellfish and mollusks along the coast, and abundant acorns, hickory nuts and other wild plants. Plants such as sunflower, goosefoot and knotweed were both harvested from the wild and cultivated for their seeds, and significantly, corn cultivation made its appearance late in the middle Woodland period, although it does not seem to have contributed much to peoples' diets at that time.

Elaborate rituals surrounding the disposition of the dead became much more common during the Woodland period, and mounds related to burial ceremonies appeared throughout the region. These mounds usually consisted of a low platform used in mortuary rituals. The dead were either buried under the floor of the platform or placed on it. After some period of use, the platform would be sealed or capped with a mound of rock or clay and closed to further use.

One example of the mortuary mound tradition can be seen at the McKeithen Weeden Island site, excavated in the late 1970s by Jerald T. Milanich and his colleagues from Florida State Museum, the University of Alabama and Washington State University. Located in northern Florida about halfway between Jacksonville and Tallahassee, the site was named for both Leon A. McKeithen, owner of the property on which the site was found (and a highly regarded amateur archaeologist), and the Weeden Island culture. Characterized by its mortuary traditions and its stunning pottery, the Weeden Island culture influenced much of northeastern Florida, southwestern Georgia and southeastern Alabama during the middle and late Woodland periods, about A.D. 200 to 900.

The McKeithen Weeden Island site consists of three mounds, a village

Students from Columbia, Illinois, gain firsthand archaeological experience at the Range site, a satellite village of the great Cahokia site located in modern-day East St. Louis. Archaeologist Ann Stahl, in a white anorak, removes earth by trowel, then passes it through a sieve to catch any small pieces. Visiting fourth to sixth graders have the chance to step briefly into the excavations, conducted before a highway was built over the site. Sheets of plastic keep soon-to-be-dug areas dry, preventing rain from turning the dig into a muddy pool.

M ost prehistoric Indians of the Southeast never beheld the Atlantic or walked the beaches of the Gulf of Mexico, but traders carried bits of the shore deep into the continent in the form of shells for craftwork. In Mississippian times, not long before the arrival of the Europeans, shell carvings held an especially strong appeal for a culture in what is now Oklahoma, near today's town of Spiro. There the Craig burial mound yielded bushels of such carvings, including the items on these pages. Below, the large end of a shell forms a cup inscribed with a male figure. At right, a broken gorget shows a man in fancy dress wearing a gorget of his own, a necklace and a woven fiber band or belt with diamond design and flowing garments at the side. Opposite top, hands display the cross design, associated in old Indian lore with the cardinal directions of the rising and setting sun at the summer and winter solstices, a theme also reflected in a disk, below center, with five faces in relief. The shell disk, below right, holds a rough cameo image of a man. Opposite below, a whole shell bears a treelike shape.

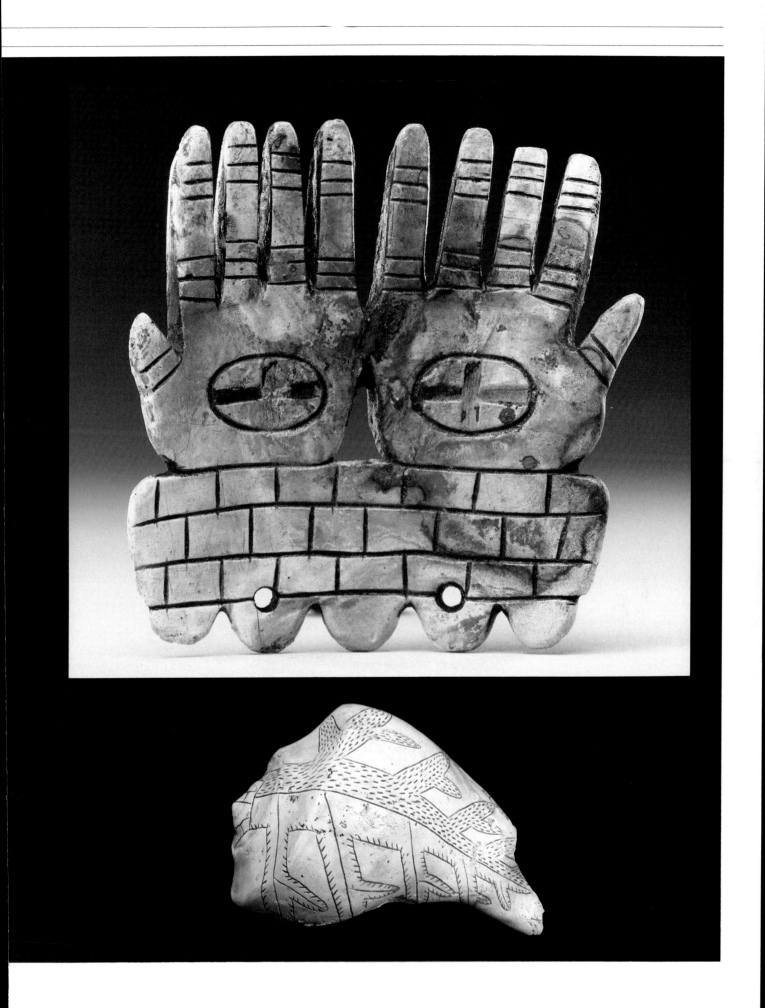

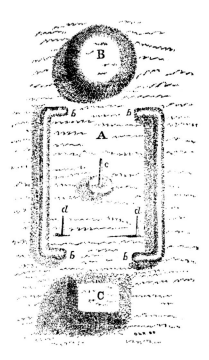

and its middens or dumps. The horseshoe-shaped, forty-seven-acre village was located on a low sandy ridge in forest-and-brush country that provided an excellent habitat for the animals and plants upon which the hunting-gathering people depended. Judging from animal and plant remains found at other sites in northern Florida, the people of the McKeithen village probably ate nearly everything edible, including the usual deer and other mammals, fish, toads, frogs, newts, salamanders, turtles, snakes, birds of many species, clams and snails, in addition to nuts and other wild plant foods.

Radiocarbon dates show that the village was settled about A.D. 200 and existed as a dwelling site until about 750. Milanich and his colleagues estimate the peak population at a little over 100, although a maximum of 350 people could have lived there. Few remains of houses, such as postmolds, have been discovered. Those found suggest small oval or rectangular residences of posts set in the ground, possibly covered with daub. The middens contain vast quantities of broken pottery and stone tools.

Located within the village are three mounds: A, B and C. They were sited on three natural prominences, so that their builders had only to construct a platform perhaps one-and-a-half to three feet high to create the illusion of a mound up to ten feet high.

The three mounds form a nearly equilateral triangle about 900 feet on a side. The excavators believe that the mounds served as a "mortuary complex for the disposal of the dead." The largest, Mound A, contained no structure but was apparently used for burials and exhumations. Mound C was surmounted by what may have been a charnel house, wherein cleaned bones, treated with red ochre, were stored. Mound B seems to have served as a residence or religious edifice occupied by a

158

N orth American peoples of many regions played the hoop-and-stick game; the most popular Southeastern variation was *chunkee,* played with a stone disk such as the one at right. The object of the game was to toss a pole as close as possible to the spot that a player's rolling disk would eventually stop. Creek men played the game at their village ceremonial center, opposite left, on a field (A) between mounds B and C. Mandans of the Missouri River region also enjoyed the game. Opposite right, Mandans are pictured in a heated chunkee match by artist George Catlin in 1832. They employ a chunkee stone, seemingly similar to the one shown on a shell pendant uncovered in Kentucky, above.

Sixteen flintwork masterpieces from Tennessee comprise less than half of the magnificent archaeological find known as the Duck River Cache. The entire array of finely flaked objects may represent the work of a single consummate craftsman. Never used, they were recovered in a carefully wrapped bundle from an Indian cemetery dating from before A.D. 1500. Representative of toolmaking traditions of the Mississippian culture, the large repertoire of shapes suggests the high level of skill achieved by Southeastern artisans who worked the local chert.

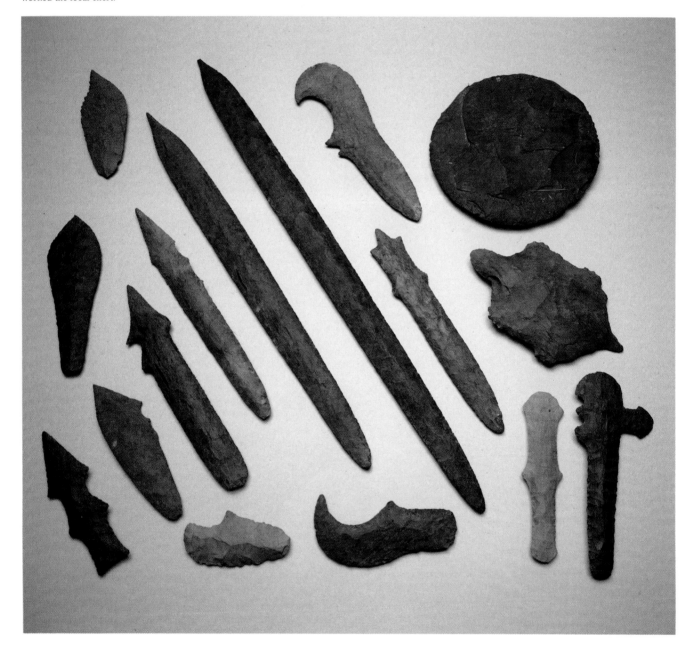

"religious specialist." Found throughout the mounds were large numbers of ceramic shards representing vessels of the type associated with the elite in the Weeden Island culture. Also unearthed were parts of bones from deer and other animals, perhaps offerings. These mounds were built some time after A.D. 350 and sealed or capped around 475. Therein lies a tale.

Under the floor of Mound B, the excavators found the skeleton of a man who had been buried with some ceremony, accompanied by Weeden Island ceramics, including an extraordinary ceramic representation of a turkey vulture's head, several plates and dishes decorated with birds, and the leg bone of an anhinga or snake bird, a bird indigenous to Florida. Embedded in one of the man's hip bones, as if it had struck him from the back, was a small stone projectile point of a type found elsewhere on the site. Examination of the bone showed that the wound had healed, perhaps completely, before the man's death.

Shortly after this individual's burial, the structures on Mounds B and C were burned and scattered and all three mounds were sealed with soil, never to be used again. Is it possible, the excavators asked, that the entire existence of these three mounds, their creation, use and capping, was the result of the influence of one individual, a powerful "religious specialist"—the individual buried in Mound B?

While the McKeithen village declined and was abandoned, the trends that had been slowly transforming the life-styles of Southeastern peoples throughout the Woodland period—population growth, the increasing importance of agriculture and the growing tendency toward centralized government—suddenly and dramatically accelerated. One of the late Woodland cultures, the Coles Creek culture that emerged around A.D. 700 in the Lower Mississippi Valley, was characterized by scattered ceremonial centers with small groups of mounds that may have been used for mortuary rituals and burials or as platforms for residences of an elite class, in some cases for hundreds of years. Such longevity of use suggests that a new kind of elite status had evolved that could carry over from generation to generation.

Evidence of the importance of corn cultivation in the Coles Creek area has been variously interpreted to indicate both heavy and light reliance on corn. It is clear, however, that agriculture involving corn as well as other crops assumed greater significance in many parts of the Southeast between A.D. 750 and 950, the time just before the beginning of the last prehistoric period, the Mississippian.

During the Mississippian period, from about 1000 to 1700, all the trends of the earlier epochs reached a peak. Inhabiting the fertile river

A ceremonial ax bears testament to the superb control of tool and stone of the unknown Duck River master of Tennessee. Axes found elsewhere were nearly all made of a softer stone that was ground into form rather than flaked as was the chert used by this Tennessee artisan.

Southeast, A.D. 1300

The large Mississippian town of Moundville served for three centuries as a religious, political and economic center for much of western Alabama after A.D. 1200. The vast majority of the town's population lived beyond the complex in small, agricultural satellites, visiting only during special occasions. Nobles lived in wattle-and-daub houses atop the small mounds describing the perimeter of a great plaza. In the middle was a temple mound where much of the community's civil and religious activities probably took place. This mound is a tribute to the social organization of Moundville since more than four million cubic feet of earth were needed to complete its construction. The

people in the outlying settlements probably provided food tribute in addition to labor. Floodwater of the Black Warrior River regularly enriched the soil, enabling the residents to practice an intensive bottomland horticulture in which maize was the staple and beans, squash and pumpkin were also grown. In addition, the deciduous woodlands contained a wealth of white-tailed deer, raccoon and turkey; the river yielded a variety of fish that were often trapped in weirs.

Ritual objects from Moundville, a site in west central Alabama, are decorated with a hand-and-eye symbol, horned rattlesnakes, above right, and a cross within a circle, which often stands for the sun. Past researchers and observers, who knew little of what the symbols signified, often attributed their forms to Mexican or even Egyptian influences.

valleys, peoples all over the Southeast came to depend to a large extent on agriculture to feed their burgeoning populations. Great ceremonial centers arose, such as at Etowah, in northwestern Georgia; Spiro, in Oklahoma just across the state line from Arkansas; Moundville, in northwestern Alabama; and greatest of them all, Cahokia, whose mighty Monk's Mound looms over the Mississippi River just across from St. Louis, Missouri.

These centers were supported by networks of palisaded villages and small farmsteads scattered throughout the areas dominated by each center. Here people farmed, fished, hunted and gathered. Fields for crops were cleared of trees, probably by fire, and then planted year after year until the soil was exhausted and the forest began to reclaim the land. The farmers then simply cleared another patch and repeated the process.

Their labors supported high-status families, including that of the chief of each center and its surrounding area. Smithsonian archaeologist Bruce D. Smith has described these elite groups and their social order in general terms: "These Indian groups had...attained a sophisti-

cated chiefdom level of socio-political organization. Such chiefdoms are characterized by the existence of a family or kin grouping enjoying elite social and political status. At the top of the hierarchy was the chief, who, along with a small group of closely related kinsmen, made many of the important decisions that faced the society. The elite kin group, the family of the chief, was set apart from the rest of the population in a number of important respects."

These members of the high-status class lived in residences raised above the plazas of the centers on mounds. Dominating everything were the large temple mounds, where the elite conducted the ceremonies and rituals that regulated the lives of all inhabitants. Members of the elite groups wore clothing and jewelry denoting their elevated status and carried other badges of rank, including batons and axes. Those with high status ate more and better food, particularly meat, than did the common folk, using vessels reserved for the use of the elite. When they died they were buried in public buildings on mounds, sometimes even in their own mounds, instead of in cemeteries or lonely graves, as were ordinary people. Items interred with them were the valuables of their

The Emerald Mound complex near Natchez, Mississippi, contained an active population at the time of Hernando de Soto's expedition in the early 1540s. Perhaps the last major chiefdom of the Mississippian culture, its extinction in the early eighteenth century is attributed to European diseases and to warfare with the French.

society: shell beads and jewelry, headdresses of copper, and ceremonial weapons, among other things.

Of all of these extraordinary chiefdoms, the great center at Moundville in west central Alabama was one of the largest. It began as a village on a bluff overlooking the Black Warrior River near modern-day Tuscaloosa about A.D. 1000, at the beginning of the Mississippian period. It grew into a small ceremonial center, then a major one, reaching its zenith sometime between 1250 and 1400. At the height of its magnificence it sprawled over 370 acres, more than half a square mile, and included twenty mounds, the largest of which rose sixty feet and covered an acre and a quarter. Some of the mounds were actually platforms for elite residences; others were devoted to ceremonies and rituals, including all of those associated with death, preparation of bodies for burials, and other public functions.

According to Christopher S. Peebles of Indiana University, various excavations and studies have established that Moundville was occupied by two distinct social classes: an elite group comprising five percent of the population and probably hereditary in nature, and the rest of the population. Moundville was divided into distinct areas for settlements, mounds and areas where crafts were practiced. Some space was set aside for *chunkee,* a game played with a stone disc.

About fourteen percent of the ceramics found at Moundville came from elsewhere, suggesting a fair amount of trade. Indeed, the large number of shell beads, the tools for their manufacture and the amount of shell debris found at many Southeastern sites suggest that beads, beaded clothing and other beaded items might have become important symbols of trade and interchange during the Mississippian period.

In the early 1540s, Hernando de Soto's expedition recorded one chiefdom, Coosa, that spanned 300 miles from central Alabama to northeast Tennessee. But by that time, the power of the chiefdoms was waning. Despite their magnificence and apparent power, they were probably fragile entities, easily made lesser or greater by the shifting tides of alliance and war.

The Mississippian culture and its way of life continued into the seventeenth century. French adventurers encountered remnants of the chiefdoms' former glory in the Natchez Indians. But, inevitably, disease struck and, weakened by social disruption caused by other aspects of White-Indian contact, most hierarchical societies of the Mississippian were gone by 1700. By the time European settlers began moving in, it was easy for them to overlook the native origins of the mounds and to create their own cultural myths. ✳

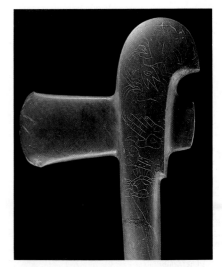

At the Etowah site in the Cumberland Highlands of Georgia, war parties of several Indian nations met. Opposite, a warrior in copper repoussé wears the guise of a falcon, a universal symbol of power. A war club appears in one hand and perhaps a severed head in the other. Above, a monolithic ax was reserved for ritual purposes. The incised design includes two heads and a hand (perhaps severed), a long bone and a hoop decorated with a scalp lock.

THE PLAINS

 "The prairie is not congenial to the Indian, and is only made tolerable to him by possession of the horse and the rifle." So wrote Lewis Henry Morgan, otherwise an insightful pioneer of American Indian studies, in 1859. According to Morgan, the grassland fastness was prehistorically uninhabitable from the Mississippi's margins to the Rockies and from central Texas to the Canadian subarctic.

His statement's error was matched only by the universality of its acceptance by anthropologists, which in turn was exceeded by its popularity among the general public. The Smithsonian's Waldo R. Wedel, the dean of Plains archaeology at the Smithsonian, remembers being taught that the Plains must be barren of ancient artifacts. The reasoning went as follows: The only game capable of sustaining a native economy on the Plains was the bison, which was so big, gregarious and intractable, so elusive and mobile, that it could only be hunted on horseback. (Bison, commonly called buffalo, are American and European animals of the genus *Bison*; true buffalo [genus *Syncerus* and *Bubalus*] inhabit Africa and Asia.) Indians afoot, whether armed with bow and arrow or spear and atlatl, simply could not have taken this beast in any numbers, said the savants; thus they could not have inhabited the Plains until the Whites arrived with their horses and guns.

Nothing could be further from the truth. No other single prehistoric region has been misunderstood by so many for so long. Native Americans inhabited the Plains for millennia; many lived in large, settled villages and planted crops. And particularly in the western part of the region, the bison did provide many necessities and amenities: food in its meat, viscera and marrow; shelter in its dehaired hides; clothing and blankets in hides cured with the hair on; fuel in its excreta (the ubiquitous "buffalo chips"); tools in its broken or worked bones; and beneficent spirits in its very image.

As the evidence accumulated, it appeared that the bison provided virtually everything that most Plains populations could want or need. This in turn led archaeologists to assume that these prehistoric peoples had a monospecific economy—that they harvested only this single beast. Yet even this idea would be modified as investigators began studying the vast Plains culture area in depth. More subtle and complete recent digs reveal that Plains Indians used a constellation of other animals and cultivated plants as well. Bison may have been the mainstay for many Plains peoples, but they were by no means the only source of food and materials. Like every other group, Plains Indians found the key to survival in resourcefulness and adaptation to the region they inhabited.

Pronghorn antelope of the Dakota Badlands roam beneath a stormy sky in the upper Plains, opposite. In search of bison and other prey including pronghorns, Plains Indians made seasonal migrations but usually returned to permanent winter lodges. Above, a figurine from A.D. 1100 came to light during excavation of such an earth lodge site in Iowa.

169

Plains

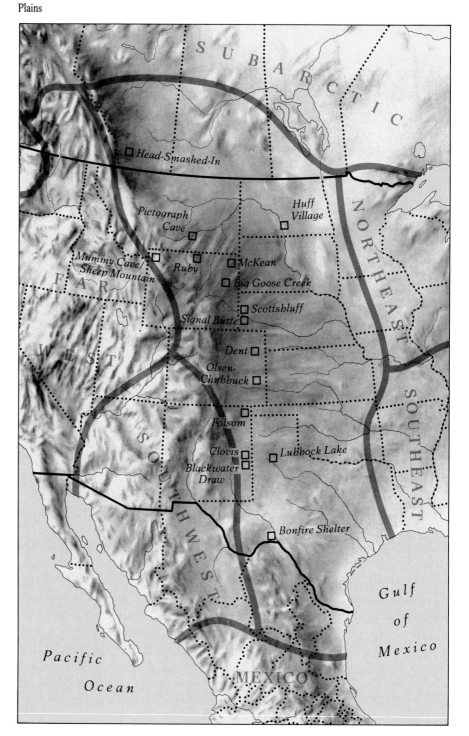

Wyoming's Mummy Cave, near Yellowstone, yielded 1,300-year-old agate projectile points, above, from one of the uppermost of its thirty-eight layers of artifacts and other evidence of human habitation. Named for the naturally mummified remains of a man who died in the cave about A.D. 1300, the cave has preserved a 5,000-year record of human activity.

Of all North America's regions, few have boundaries as easily defined as the Plains. To the east, where nineteenth-century painter George Catlin found meadows stretching "as far as the eye can see and thought can travel," they fade into well-watered lands along the Mississippi River. To the west, they reach into the Rocky Mountains. From Texas, where grasslands merge with the southwestern desert, to the limits of Canada's boreal forest, they cover twenty degrees of latitude.

Given the size of this expanse, it contains many kinds of habitat: flatlands, tablelands, dunes, hills, stream valleys and mountains. Lying in the Rockies' rain shadow, it is a largely dry region; thus it generally lacks trees except along rivers and streams. Instead, the nutritious short buffalo grass in western areas and mixed tall grasses in the moister eastern realm predominate. Before Whites arrived, this barrier-free expanse sustained a variety of animals—bison above all, and white-tailed and mule deer, pronghorn antelope, mountain goat, bighorn sheep, elk or wapiti, the occasional moose, wolves, black and grizzly bears, birds from meadowlarks to eagles and a host of small animals.

Into this vast realm came people who hunted mammoths and a now-extinct species of bison at the end of the ice ages, as famous archaeological finds at Clovis and Folsom, New Mexico, have shown. The Plains have been occupied ever since, and archaeologists have developed

University of Texas archaeologists excavate bone-littered deposits below the immense limestone bluff of Bonfire Shelter near the Rio Grande and Pecos rivers. Here Paleo-Indians and later peoples stampeded bison and other large mammals over the edge to their deaths.

Flames creep up prairie bluffs in artwork by George Catlin. For 10,000 years, Plains Indians employed fire as a tool in hunting and warfare and perhaps even to manage the prairie environment. In an 1820s depiction by Swiss artist Peter Rindisbacher, right, Cree hunters of the Canadian Plains snowshoe briskly after bison slowed by deep snowdrifts.

basic chronologies to provide a general framework of Plains prehistory. According to Wedel, the Paleo-Indian period faded into the Archaic by about 5000 B.C.; the Archaic overlapped the Plains Woodland period, which began about 250 B.C. and lasted until A.D. 950. Shortly before that tradition's end, the Plains Village tradition arose, particularly on the eastern Plains where it lasted until well into the historic period.

In the Plains region as elsewhere throughout the continent, Paleo-Indians displayed remarkably uniform habits. Wherever their traces have been found in association with the remains of animals, it appears that these early descendants of the Beringian immigrants followed the ice-age game they had pursued all through their multigenerational trek across North America. When the glaciers retreated and the climate warmed, the megafauna declined or became extinct. By about 5000 B.C., North Americans pursued a wider variety of mixed game and collected wild plants as well; thus arose the hunting-gathering lifeway of the Archaic period.

During the Archaic period, the peoples of the northwestern Plains traveled frequently, perhaps with their dogs in traces dragging travois— the simple arrangement of two crossed poles holding a load of goods, ends dragging on the ground. George Frison believes they moved as often as 100 times a year—every day or two in summer, and much less in winter when snow and cold made travel unwise, uncomfortable and sometimes impossible. Using the light and serviceable hide-covered tipi, which could be pitched by a woman in an hour, they made camp in almost every kind of location (judging by the nearly ubiquitous surviving circles of stones that held tipi skirts to the ground). Returning to the same camps again and again, they favored streamside sites near the sheltered areas where bison wintered and might be stalked by small hunting parties. Yet they also frequented exposed hilltops and buttes, quite possibly because these seemingly inhospitable sites were ideal places for air-drying meat quickly (and escaping swarms of mosquitoes).

Unlike their neighbors elsewhere in the Plains, the prehistoric peoples of the northwest part of the region—today's Wyoming, Montana and Alberta—never settled in villages, raised crops nor even adopted ceramics until quite late in prehistoric times. As European settlers later learned, the environment of the High Plains discourages most crops except those related to the grasses, such as wheat.

The bow and arrow probably came to the Plains dwellers via the Na-Dene, Athapaskan speakers who migrated south out of the Asia-Alaska region into western Canada and the Plains. The people of Wyoming's High Plains adopted the bow quickly, Frison believes, because

A diorama at the Montana Historical Society in Helena illustrates a typical bison jump, a controlled stampede known as the *pishkun*. Here Blackfoot Indians channeled a herd toward the cliff. The bison either died where they fell or were dispatched by waiting hunters.

173

High in Wyoming's Rockies, Bighorn Medicine Wheel remains a testimony to the Plains peoples' keen interest in practical and ceremonial astronomy. The circle's diameter is seventy-five feet; spokes point to solar and stellar alignments. Dawn at the summer solstice appears above. Many much smaller stone circles mark the High Prairie near the Great Divide, but they are tipi circles, made of rocks that held down the hide fringes of Plains travelers' bison skin dwellings. The great tipi of fourteen bison skins, right, was acquired by the Smithsonian in 1874 and is believed to be the oldest complete tipi in existence.

it has important advantages over the atlatl and spear. While the atlatl extended the range of the hand-held spear, the hunter who used it had to stand up and take an obvious stride or two in order to throw, and then to fit another awkwardly long spear to the atlatl and throw again if all the game in sight had not already fled. (Spears used with atlatls must measure six feet long or so for best results; as with javelins, length combined with flexibility augments their flight and accuracy.) By contrast, a Plains archer armed with a short bow could shoot from hiding behind a bush or rock cairn, then fit another short arrow from the bunch held in his left hand and silently fire again without revealing his presence to the quarry. Bow and spear-thrower imparted roughly equal velocity to stone-tipped missiles, but the bow could be fired faster and more secretly — and most important, far more accurately.

The Plains peoples quarried suitable stone for their stone-tipped weapons in prodigious quantities. The Spanish Diggings, in southeastern Wyoming, originally investigated by Smithsonian archaeologist W. H. Holmes in the early twentieth century, is but one example. Here the Indians used elk antler picks, bison ribs and stone mauls to mine quartzite for use in making tools.

Nor were these projectiles the early High Plains hunters' only weapons; a recent find at Sheep Mountain in north central Wyoming's Absaroka range indicates they netted game — probably mountain goats and deer, perhaps rabbits — as long ago as 7000 B.C. The evidence, preserved in a remote cave, is a hunting net about 200 feet long and 6 feet high. This implement clearly represented a major investment in time for Paleo-Indian hunters, since it required a mile and a quarter of two-ply cord twisted by hand from juniper bark fibers. (The net was stored folded for quick deployment; as a result, its dimensions can only be estimated, since the material is too brittle to be unfolded.)

The hunters who made the Sheep Mountain net probably used it by stringing it across a game trail in the rugged mountains and waiting for animals to pass, or by hanging it across a natural bottleneck and driving game into it. Once an animal was snared, the hunters probably leapt from hiding and dispatched it with a club — a presumption based on practices observed hundreds of years later.

Various sites in the High Plains reveal the remains of sheep, deer, wood rat, rabbit, bobcat, badger, bear and coyote, in addition to bison. Traces of nearly 100 species of plants from human living sites have also been recovered. Of these more than one-third were berries and fruit gathered from late spring to early fall, depending on elevation; roots and bulbs in springtime; and grasses and seeds in late summer. These peoples'

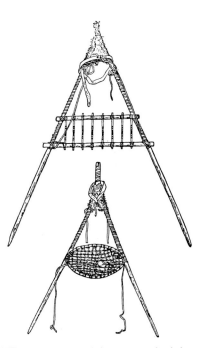

Before Spanish horses reached the Plains and sparked a revolution in the lifeways of many of its societies, dogs may have pulled children and goods on a V-shaped frame called the *travois*. The larger of the historic Blackfoot travois, above, was pulled by a horse, the smaller by a dog.

175

Late Paleo-Indian to Middle Archaic Plains peoples used the Cherokee Sewer site to kill bison and other large mammals from about 6500 to 3500 B.C. The curious site name derives from the local town's name of Cherokee and has nothing to do with the Cherokee Indians themselves. The spot came to light during expansion of the town's sanitary wastewater disposal system.

diet also included arrowroot, bee plant, goosefoot, sego lily, buffalo berry, gooseberry, yucca fruit, Indian ricegrass, wild rye, rosehips and saltbush seed. Grinding stones were doubtless used to husk small seeds.

For cooking, the Plains Indians used earth ovens. They heated stones in a fire and then cleaned out the hearth or more likely removed the hot stones to another pit. Food was wrapped in an untanned hide or placed in fiber bags, which were then covered with earth and left to bake with little threat of charring or sullying by ashes.

Perhaps the most ambitious way of obtaining food was the bison drive, an event that occurred throughout the Plains from Paleo-Indian times onward whenever and wherever bison were plentiful. Even the most sedentary of Plains villagers practiced the communal hunt in summer and winter; it assumed ritual as well as dietary importance. The community bison hunt required as much planning and cooperation as any event in the repertoire of the world's hunting-and-gathering peoples. At Alberta's Head-Smashed-In kill site, which has been listed on UNESCO's roster of World Heritage Sites, University of Calgary

176

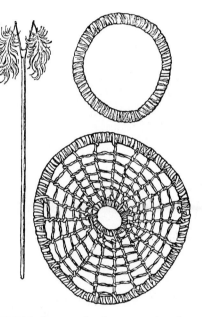

The hoop-and-pole game enjoyed popularity in both summer and wintertime along the Canadian and United States border. At left, Hidatsa men toss pointed spears at the rolling target during a cold-weather game. Hits in or on a ring or netted hoop won points. Crow artisans made the game equipment sketched above.

archaeologist B. O. K. Reeves found evidence of regular prehistoric use for uncounted generations. "The Piegan Indians of historical times and their predecessors have been stampeding buffalo to their death over a cliff for at least 5,600 years and possibly as long as 9,000," he wrote.

The cliff, now more than thirty feet high but twice as high 2,000 years ago, marks the edge of a shallow basin covering fourteen square miles. As at other sites, the hunters chose their topography carefully. The jump was high enough to kill or disable bison, but not so high that they would be smashed by the fall. The people must have gathered in sizable numbers—probably in the autumn, since remains show that nursery herds comprising three calves for every cow were most common. Then the Indians must have spent considerable time raising or repairing lines of stone cairns that served as blinds to channel the buffalo toward a bottleneck. Choosing a day when the wind was right—bison have poor eyesight but a keen sense of smell—the hunters, and perhaps their whole families, dispersed, many hiding behind the cairns. Keeping their distance so as not to alarm the bison, the drivers slowly forced the animals into

I n winter, Mandans and other tribes of the northern Plains lived in villages in massive earth lodges of sod and wooden beams. A long entrance hall or vestibule with doors of skins helped to keep out the cold, while the sod covering provided effective insulation and a smoke hole permitted some ventilation. Ceremonial lodges might measure as much as sixty feet in diameter, and even those that were smaller could accommodate several families.

the bottleneck until at a chosen moment people leapt from hiding to start the stampede, which, once under way, could end only at the cliff. The final stretch approached the actual jump obliquely, then turned abruptly to force the lead bison toward the cliff, with no room to maneuver.

Curiously, bison remains are scarce from the archaeological record at a number of Plains sites, at stratigraphic levels representing two periods. These may be archaeological rather than real absences. The earlier period, from about 5000 to 2500 B.C., roughly corresponds to the time of the Altithermal, the name given by climatologists to a hot, dry episode that began on the Plains about 7,000 years ago. Possibly, during this period and the later one, which lasted from about A.D. 500 to 1200, climatic changes forced the bison herds to move to other areas. Their hunters either moved with them or sought other prey. It is equally possible that the climatic stringencies eliminated the evidence. During the Altithermal, lake levels fell by as much as sixty feet. People may have been forced by the severe drought to inhabit sites that are now covered again by the lakes; their middens, perhaps including bison bones, may be accessible only to scuba-diving archaeologists. Other drier sites may have been eradicated by wind erosion — or may simply not have been found yet.

Brian Reeves believes that while the Altithermal was an extremely

stressful time, people adapted to the conditions, as did the plants and animals, including bison. Nonetheless, only the Hawken sites in the Black Hills of Wyoming have provided evidence of bison kills during the Altithermal period. It is worth noting that at sites in the northern Plains areas of southern Canada, bison remains seem to be common throughout the two periods, indicating that perhaps the northern regions were not affected by drought or whatever else it was that may have reduced the number of bison kills in the south.

While all Plains Indians probably hunted bison at one time or another, all did not share the same living styles. The inhabitants of the western Plains and High Plains tended to live in tipis or other easily transportable dwellings and to travel a great deal. Eastern Plains peoples, living closer to major rivers and to the more agricultural tribes of the Northeast and Southeast, often created permanent villages composed of substantial houses. These patterns probably began to develop as the Plains Archaic period ended about 250 B.C. In the eastern part of the region, a new tradition arose, called by archaeologists the Plains Woodland.

For some decades, the appearance of Woodland culture in the eastern Plains was regarded by archaeologists as the result of a migration of Woodland peoples from east of the Mississippi up its western tributaries and the Missouri. A newer hypothesis, however, raises the possibility that

Mandan women paddle bullboats—bison skins lashed to willow frames—at the site of Mih-Tutta-Hang-Kusch village on the Missouri River. Plains people lived in such bluffside lodges during pleasant winter spells, retreating to tree-protected lowland lodges when blizzards or sub-zero weather hit.

the Plains Woodland tradition was a spontaneous local phenomenon—that the Plains Woodland lifeways developed for the same reasons that Woodland cultures did in the East. Of course, squash and corn agriculture and pottery might have been imported or transplanted.

Cultures with distinctly subregional characteristics began to develop in areas such as Oklahoma, Texas, North Dakota and Canada's Prairie Provinces. Mound burials in stone-lined chambers occurred as far west as Manitoba; squash agriculture reached Nebraska; a mound complex much like that found in the eastern Midwest arose near Kansas City. Throughout the Plains (save for the High Plains of the northwest) arrays of artifacts have been found resembling those of the eastern Hopewell culture, or in recent archaeological parlance the "Hopewellian Interaction Sphere." This mouthful suggests what the Hopewell phenomenon more likely was: not a single culture that grew until it stretched from the St. Lawrence Estuary to the Grand Tetons, but instead a loose network of

independent peoples who exchanged goods and ideas across two-thirds of the continent.

By about A.D. 900 the Plains Village tradition arose, taking on some of the markedly stratified hierarchies and ceremonialism of the Southeast's Mississippian tradition. While peoples in the western Plains continued to be nomadic, the eastern Plains saw the establishment of permanent settlements with fixed multifamily earth lodges—dwelling forms that would survive and be mimicked by White settlers well into the nineteenth century. Many of these villages featured protective stockades or dry moats, suggesting the need for defense (except, curiously, in the central Plains).

The Plains Villagers were farmers, too. Cultivating their fields with hoes made of bison shoulder blades, they raised squash, corn, beans, sunflowers and amaranth, all of which they stored for the winter in pits in the floors of their houses. Trade with the Mississippian peoples to the south and east brought them pots and shell beads. Riverside dwellers

Though carved from catlinite during the historic era, the Sioux tobacco pipe, above, retains a pre-contact style. Top, Smithsonian archaeologists reconstructed this five-inch-tall earthenware pot from a piece including the rim and handle section found in northern South Dakota.

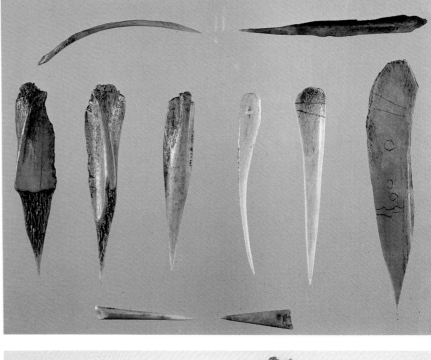

Bone sewing awls, above right, came from the same 1,300-year-old layer in Mummy Cave as the agate projectile points on page 170. Right, this "high top" moccasin was one of a pair found in the same Wyoming cave. Made of bighorn sheepskin, fleece side in for winter wear, the moccasins have been dated at about A.D. 1300 and are the oldest examples of such footwear yet found. Artist George Catlin bought a Sioux cradleboard, above, decorated with porcupine quill designs, during an expedition to the Plains in the mid-1830s. The art of porcupine quill work was almost lost when traders' colored glass beads became common and cheap enough to replace dyed and undyed quills.

From Iowa, a freshwater shell gorget, left, of about A.D. 1000 represents a fabulous beast—part mammal, part serpent. Above, soon after contact, officers of Blackfoot warrior societies, or "bear men," wore shirts of thin hide with many small holes decorated with beads. A necklace of eagle talons, top, came from South Dakota. Plains Indians hunted both golden and bald eagles for their feathers and claws.

Population pressures and environmental stress may have prompted an attack during A.D. 1325 that left the bones of 500 men, women and children at the Crow Creek village site on the Missouri River in South Dakota. After overwhelming and burning the partially palisaded village, the attackers scalped and dismembered the dead, apparently carrying away hands and feet as trophies. Scarce remains of young women and children suggest that the aggressors spared some to strengthen their own ranks. Later, survivors must have buried the bodies in a mass grave, where they were discovered in 1978. The massacre appears to have been an exception to the usual form of Plains warfare: small ambushes and formal battles in which few were killed.

traded with others traveling the waterways. Pottery styles became varied, and the range of artifacts expanded to include clay and pipestone pipes and many other items made of stone, bone, horn, copper and exotic shell imported from the Gulf of Mexico and the Atlantic and even Pacific coasts.

This period witnessed the consolidation of some groups as they influenced each other and responded to various outside influences. Siouan-speaking Mandan and Hidatsa and Caddoan-speaking Arikara maintained their distinct languages but became what one archaeologist calls "culturally almost identical." By the sixteenth century, Dean Snow writes, "The high Plains had reverted to the foot nomads such as the Kiowa who had been there for millennia, and to newcomers such as the Apache. The Arikara had found their niche alongside the Mandan and Hidatsa. The Pawnee had pulled back to their compact villages nearer the Mississippi, as had the Ponca and Omaha [except when on the hunt]. The north-western branch of the Mississippian tradition that we have called 'Oneota' gradually became the historical Iowa, Missouri, Oto and Winnebago tribes. To the south the Kansa and Osage, late arrivals from the eastern forests, joined the others on the Prairie fringe. Still farther south, another Plains culture was established by the people we know as the Wichita."

Regardless of Hopewellian or Mississippian influences, the settled peoples of the Great Plains, like their wandering contemporaries to the west and northwest, continued to set out for bison after spring planting and again after the harvest of autumn crops, which now included the hardier strains of corn and beans. Though they now lived in permanent earth lodges beneath sod roofs supported by stout beams, they did not abandon the bison hunt, a central part of their heritage: entire villages would embark en masse for weeks of adventure and ceremony.

Sadly, their village life-style would make them particularly vulnerable to diseases carried by the Whites. Before they were stricken, however, many Plains peoples would adopt the horse, brought back by Europeans to the continent where it had originally evolved. For a few score years, the Plains tribes would reign as peerless sovereigns of their prairie domain.

For many reasons, mostly born of White legend, they would become the best-known of all native Americans. Presidents and princes, artists and adventurers would visit their territories to witness their lives first-hand. But they would eventually suffer the fate of most North American Indians; disease and displacement would disrupt their cultures. A century after United States military might put an end to the freedom of the Plains peoples, they would still be recovering from their calamitous decline. ✴

Deftly fashioned of elkhorn, a war club from the Sioux resembles a water bird, enhanced by the addition of two copper disks for eyes. It was collected by artist George Catlin before 1840 on one of his trips to visit tribes of the Great Plains.

THE FAR WEST

 The spine of the Rocky Mountains physically and climatically separates the area of the Far West—California, the Great Basin of Utah and Nevada, and the Columbia-Fraser Plateau comprising parts of Oregon, Washington, Idaho and Canada —from the rest of the continent. No other North American region, with the exception of the Arctic, presents as difficult a challenge for human habitation as do parts of this vast area.

The Cascade-Sierra mountain chains bordering the Great Basin to the west rob the Pacific winds of moisture, creating arid, desertlike ranges. Yet the same winds that blow over different topography in California have created one of the most fertile areas in North America. The semiarid intermontane environment in which denser vegetation is found on the mountainsides and near rare watercourses has shaped a common basic history throughout the Far West, making it one general environmental area.

Many scholars have argued that the numerous but isolated tribes of California, the nomads of the Great Basin and the riverbank dwellers of the Columbia-Fraser Plateau have shared similar life-styles of great longevity and stability. According to these theorists, although the peoples of the Far West relied more on gathering than on hunting as a means of subsistence, their social organizations and hunter-gatherer lifeways resembled those of the Subarctic. Julian H. Steward of the University of Illinois observed of Great Basin peoples that they ate more small game, including insects and rodents, than large game. Hunting and fishing were unquestionably vital—the Plateau peoples, for instance, depended heavily on salmon—but the primary means of subsistence revolved around gathering: wild seeds in the Basin, acorns and shellfish in California and roots in the Plateau. The archaeological record and linguistic patterns seem to these scholars to point toward common origins for many ancient peoples of this macroregion. Similar basketry, building techniques, puberty rites, folktale motifs and other traits shared by historic era cultures in California, the Basin and the Plateau suggest "that a common ancient tradition, from which Basin culture had departed the least, must once have characterized all three areas," according to C. Melvin Aikens of the University of Oregon.

Others, however, among them Claude Warren of the University of Nevada-Las Vegas, counter that seeming similarities in cultural practices do not necessarily imply great longevity and stability in these cultures, or a common origin. Rather, these scholars argue, the similarities may be quite recent—may be, in fact, artifacts of contact with the Whites in the nineteenth century. As White settlement of the Far Western regions

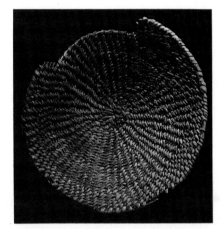

P rized ornaments of carved bone, perhaps fragments of combs, were buried with their owners near Oregon's The Dalles. Here near the junction of the Columbia and Deschutes rivers, people of many tribes gathered to trade, fish for salmon and gamble. Above, fragment of a utility basket came to light at Hogup Cave in Utah near the Great Salt Lake. Throughout the Far West, many domestic tasks involved the use of basketry, usually woven from plant fibers and in many instances used instead of pottery—even in cooking, in which hot stones were lowered into watertight baskets to boil porridge or stew.

Far West

Enigmatic figure of clay from Utah's Fremont culture holds a mystery. After thriving for 700 years, until A.D. 1300, these cultivators of maize, beans and squash disappeared. Scholars can only surmise that perhaps drought and migration or assimilation caused their culture to disappear.

displaced these peoples, and disease and loss of access to important food-gathering locales disrupted their lives, their old and possibly distinctive lifeways no longer answered their needs. Facing new problems of survival, the various peoples adopted new cultural practices better suited to their changing situation. More frequent contacts among the native peoples, perhaps caused by White displacement, may have aided the spread of shared cultural practices and ideas, so that when Whites began to study the Far Western peoples, their cultures seemed to exhibit

a remarkable degree of homogeneity. The controversy continues and will probably only be resolved by extensive reexamination of the archaeological and historical evidence.

There is, however, little argument that during the late Pleistocene, bands of Paleo-Indians spread across the Far West region. Seemingly alone among all the Paleo-Indians of North America, those of the Plateau did not use Clovis projectile points; at least none have yet been found in the region. At the Lind Coulee site in southeastern Washington, projectile points as old as Clovis points have been found, but they lack the characteristic flutes or chips of stone removed from the flat sides of the Clovis points.

As the climate changed, these people became Archaic-period hunter-gatherers pursuing a widening variety of smaller animals and supplementing their intake of meat with wild grains and other vegetable foods. Their cultures might have displayed more similarities than dissimilarities —or the reverse—throughout their various locations, but changing climate combined with topography to create different conditions in the three principal areas.

Within the Great Basin, melting glaciers created two enormous inland seas, Lakes Lahontan and Bonneville. With no outlets to the ocean, they

Many peaks and parched valley floors characterize North America's Great Basin, the high plateau land of over 100 basins and ranges between the Rocky Mountains and the High Sierra. The territory above lies near the Great Salt Desert shared by Utah and Nevada. As North America's last ice cap melted, freshwater lakes occupied much of the area that is now dry land. As the water disappeared through evaporation, Indians ventured into the formerly flooded territory, a process that continued over nearly ten millennia.

Carrying a basket of 2,000-year-old duck decoys, archaeologist L.L. Loud, of the University of California at Berkeley, emerges from Lovelock Cave in north-western Nevada (see details opposite). The 1924 discovery illustrates just one of the masterful adaptations of Great Basin Indians to a landscape that grew increasingly arid until it became one of the continent's harshest environments, in some ways less inviting that the Artic.

grew larger as long as annual rainfall and ice melt exceeded evaporation. Then, during the warm, dry climatic episode known as the Altithermal, which lasted about 2,000 years beginning around 5000 B.C., the lakes shrank. Once 1,100 feet deep and covering 20,000 square miles, Bonneville dropped to 200 feet and became the Great Salt Lake, while Lahontan exists today as Nevada's Pyramid Lake.

The historical Shoshones, Utes and Paiutes who inherited the Great Basin survived with less in the way of worldly goods than many other native Americans. It appears that they were the latest in a succession of Basin peoples who contrived ways to live involving material simplicity. Survival in this singularly rugged realm dictated that they limit their physical possessions to a minimal array of weapons, tools, utensils and portable shelters—the better to lighten the load when moving from place to place to harvest scattered resources. Traveling in small bands, they took what the land provided.

The University of Utah's Jesse Jennings found what he believed to be convincing evidence of the Basin peoples' unchanging lifeways during his excavation of Danger Cave, near the Great Salt Lake. The dry rock shelter preserved most of the objects dropped there for 10,000 years, providing an excellent record of the artifact styles and dietary habits of generations of inhabitants. Jennings unearthed 2,500 stone tools, more than 1,000 grinding stones or manos and the remains of sixty-five species of food plants. In addition, this cultural cache included a priceless trove of rarely preserved wooden implements: arrow shafts, traps and stick figures made of twigs to resemble game animals. There were even moccasins fashioned from the lower-leg hides of deer. The material evidence suggested to Jennings that while Basin technology had grown more sophisticated through time, the general hunter-gatherer lifeway had not deviated for ten millennia.

The notion of a uniform pattern for all Basin peoples throughout prehistory has been subject to recent criticism. For example, while it was once assumed that they always lived in portable shelters or natural caves, recent discoveries of open sites reveal that the Basin peoples constructed a variety of earth lodges and pit houses. Another change was the gradual replacement of the atlatl by the bow and arrow. Bows and arrows found in northern Nevada's Lovelock Cave have been dated between 500 B.C. and the birth of Christ. The more efficient weapon must have significantly altered hunting styles of the early hunter-gatherers.

These peoples survived through the most subtle adjustments from season to season and year to year. "The principal importance of Great Basin archaeology lies in the glimpses it affords of cultural adaptation

190

Ancient hunters near Lovelock Cave fashioned these duck shapes from buoyant tule rushes and often covered them with feathered bird skins to create lifelike decoys. Just how they hunted with these handiworks is not clear, though they may have entered the water, decoy on head, and carefully moved among the paddling ducks. Then they pulled one after another underwater by their feet to drown.

to a demanding environment, surely one of the most rigorous in native North America," according to Aikens. The Basin peoples were masters of adjusting to "nuances of environmental variation."

Their adaptability is well illustrated by the excavations at Lovelock Cave. Here existed an oasis, a sequence of three brackish lakes supporting a wide variety of water birds and plant life. Extremely well-preserved artifacts found in the dry cave reveal the degree to which the people of this area exploited the available resources. The roots and seeds of tule, a reed that grows along shorelines and in the shallows, were eaten and the reeds themselves were used to make baskets, cord, sandals and clothing. Hunters used tule reeds to make duck decoys, which were then covered with duck skins to make them even more lifelike. Water birds, fish and small game were caught and eaten.

Like other hunter-gatherers the world over, the Basin peoples knew their territory intimately. Their "wanderings" were carefully orchestrated, adjusted to the seasonal availability and abundances of food. They were nomads not only along the horizontal plane but also in the vertical, taking advantage of the mountains' various ecological zones. Piñon pine nuts collected in large quantities grew at about 5,000 to 6,000 feet.

The land's low carrying capacity required the Basin peoples to live in family bands most of the year. The families gathered together at times and places where substantial food surpluses were available or to partici-

A charming bear in basalt — a volcanic rock that solidified around small bubbles of gas — originated with artisans in Oregon's northern plateau country near The Dalles — a site where many cultures met. The effigy expresses a common concern of many prehistoric peoples with wild creation and suggests a belief in a spirit world parallel to the everyday physical experience of human beings.

pate in activities that required a considerable number of people. One such activity was the annual rabbit hunt, witnessed in historic times. It was a well-organized affair involving at least several family bands. Part of the typical family's tool kit was a net made of fiber cordage. When several families gathered, they pieced their nets into a single trap that stretched perhaps several hundred yards. While some stood by with spears and clubs, the rest of the people beat the sagebrush over a wide area and drove the rabbits — thousands of them in a good hunt — toward the net. As soon as a rabbit got entangled, it was dispatched lest it damage the valuable net. After the hunt the catch was divided among the families.

A time for communal cooperation, the rabbit hunt was also a social event, an occasion for revelry, feasting, sharing information and matchmaking. When the hunt was over, the families dispersed to go their separate ways so as not to tax the land's resources.

While most Basin peoples appear to have been gatherers, a farming culture emerged in Utah about A.D. 500 and survived for 700 years. The people of the Fremont culture, whose lifeways were in some ways similar to those of Southwestern Pueblo dwellers, lived in small settlements of adobe or stone pit houses, raised corn in addition to hunting and gathering, made pottery and left characteristic small clay figurines. The culture seems to have perished from a combination of drought and perhaps other, unknown factors; there is no consensus on what became of its survivors. In any case, the Fremont culture overlapped the arrival of native newcomers about 1,000 years ago. The heirs of these new arrivals spread from as far west as California to the northwestern Plains. It was evidently these peoples' descendants who survived into historic times as the Great Basin tribes: Shoshone, Paiute, Ute and Gosiute.

Almost as dry as the Great Basin, the Plateau region differs principally in that it has two great rivers, the Columbia and the Fraser, that flow into the Pacific Ocean. Before dams, these drew upstream from the Pacific huge quantities of ocean-dwelling fish, notably salmon, which sought inland freshwater shallows as spawning grounds. The annual return of the spawning fish provided a significant part of the native economy of the region.

By 8500 B.C. stone workers of the Plateau were making tools similar to artifacts found as far away as southern California and around Great Basin Pleistocene lake sites. For 3,000 years, people using a single rock shelter near Washington's Snake River hunted deer, elk, antelope, rabbit and beaver without changing tool styles. These early inhabitants not only worked with large stone blades but fitted their atlatls with polished weights and evidently sewed fine seams, so small were their bone needles.

To vary their diet they collected freshwater mussels; to vary their goods they acquired marine shell beads from the Pacific.

By 5000 B.C. people on the Plateau were making grinding stones—their diet now included processed seeds—while they dwelt in pit houses and caught salmon. Some archaeologists have argued that the salmon-based culture started after the Altithermal dry period; others that it began around the start of the Christian era. Evidence suggests, however, that along the Columbia River salmon fishing may have started as early as 9000 B.C. Fishing gear of many kinds was swiftly deployed. Archaeological findings show that Plateau fishermen used bone hook and line, gorge, trotline, dip net, gill net, seine and funnel net, barbed spear and three-pronged leister, simple and toggled harpoon, noose, snare, weir, trap, torchlight and poison.

Since salmon fishing is a seasonal business, the Plateau people doubtless hunted through most of the year while gathering a variety of plants, especially roots and bulbs, as well. With bolas they captured and ate birds along the riverbanks: cormorants, condors, vultures, bald eagles and gulls. Yet as much as half their diet may have been supplied by the salmon runs, not only because of the fish's abundance but also because it can be dried and stored. Fishing was so crucial, the University of Oregon's Luther Cressman argues, that the various Plateau peoples contrived ways to assure access for all to the limited and unequally productive riverside sites. This goal was achieved by intermarriage and trading relationships. At a site near The Dalles in Oregon, where the Columbia River plunges over waterfalls and down rapids, diverse Indian groups may have fished annually for 11,000 years.

California contains a mosaic of environmental zones: seacoast, central valley and mountainous sierra. So it comes as no surprise that the California region nurtured an array of cultures as astonishingly complex as within any other single area. Descendants of the same immigrants who peopled the Plateau and Basin—and latecomers as well—developed a unique complex of communities. At the time of Spanish contact in the seventeenth and eighteenth centuries, as many as 350,000 natives may have been living in California, speaking 100 or more languages of six or seven linguistic stocks and representing 500 ethnic groups.

"Aboriginal California was biotically rich, densely populated and culturally diverse, more so than any comparable area of North America," writes Aikens. The state also featured more diverse ecological zones than most. Some of California's regions resembled those adjacent to the north and west, while others were unique. Central California shared some customs and technologies such as basketry with Basin peoples.

The effigy of a human female—others show faces—came from the same highland region by the Columbia River that produced the bear, opposite. It has been termed a fetish, though its true meaning and function are lost forever to modern observers, as are those of so many other prehistoric artifacts.

A land of three major areas—the High Sierra, the Great Valley, and the coast and its ranges and canyons—California offered widely varying habitats to its prehistoric peoples. Cloaked in snow, Half Dome at Yosemite evokes a sense of the separate and special domain of mountain California. Northern forests yielded acorns, the staple of many tribes. Above, depressions in rocks called nutting stones were pecked out to hold acorns for processing into acorn meal. At center, men gather in a *temescal*, or hot-air bath, a male social institution among many tribes of Upper California. Here, people moved with the seasons of a land of forests, clear streams and rivers and a cool and misty climate. Great slabs of redwood and sequoia bark provided sides and shingles for their lodges.

Northwest California cultures were allied with the peoples of the North-west Coast. Southern California's pottery and sand painting linked the region with the Pueblos. "These similarities suggest the historical origins and contacts of the native Californians," according to Aikens, who sees further links in language patterns. Northwestern California was domi-nated by Athapaskan and Algonquian speakers, central California by Penutian speakers, southern California by Shoshonean and Yuman speakers. As for the scattered groups who spoke Hokan tongues, they may have been survivors of the most ancient inhabitants, "perhaps the original Californians" who were displaced by later arrivals.

Again, other scholars disagree, pointing out that cultural similarities among California tribes and others including Great Basin peoples may be the result of White displacement and disruption, and therefore quite recent phenomena.

Following the Paleo-Indian period, Archaic cultures were established by 5500 B.C. in the south, where people of the Encinitas tradition left numerous milling stones—proof of the use of plants—and shellfish remains. Near San Diego this lifeway lasted until A.D. 1000, while around Santa Barbara it lapsed 4,000 years earlier, perhaps altered by external influences from migratory peoples. The succeeding peoples of the Campbell culture made a variety of points, large knives and scrapers and relished deer, rabbits and other game along with bears, seals and fish. This complex and wealthy tradition seems to have evolved into the Chumash of modern times.

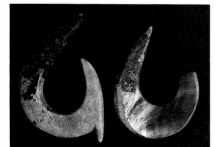

Bounty of California's Pacific rim, embodied in an emerald tide pool on Santa Cruz Island, helped feed Indians dwelling at the site of modern Los Angeles. Fishhooks, one in bone and the other in colorful mother-of-pearl, were found on the island of Santa Cruz: mainlanders of southwestern California traveled across the twenty miles of ocean to hunt sea mammals, fish and collect abalone, lobsters and scallops.

During the middle Archaic, from 6000 to 4000 B.C., people in California's northeast lived in semisubterranean pit houses and seem to have been sedentary most of the year; they relied primarily on acorns as suggested by the many mortars and pestles used to process them. Deft toolmakers, they had sophisticated kits complete with bone and antler implements. Others of the period had adapted to the brush, littoral, deserts and lakeshores. As time went on, some refined their lifeways to enter the coastal and interior valleys as well.

In the central California region, large cemeteries suggest that people lived in waterside villages perhaps as early as 3000 B.C. Tools at the

196

A dramatic dagger from a site near coastal Santa Barbara consists of a stone blade hafted in wood. Delicate shell inlay provides decoration, as does the translucent tip of the splendidly flaked tool. The work of a consummate craftsman, the object surely affirmed the social status of its owner.

earliest Windmiller sites reveal a people who lived by hunting and gathering and buried their dead intact with ritual goods, including marine shell beads. Their successors added fishing to the repertoire and made acorns a staple as well. Some of them summered along riversides east of San Francisco Bay and wintered in the Sierra foothills. Abalone beads, ornaments, coyote teeth, bear claws and a variety of charms numbered among their amenities. Around A.D. 500, the Hotchkiss people became widespread and active in central California. They processed acorns, while also fishing, hunting and capturing birds. They wove baskets and traded a rich array of shell, raw iron and soapstone ornaments. This

cultural tradition was succeeded by the historic Wintun, Miwok and Yokuts peoples.

Pottery was never particularly important in California, according to Joseph and Kerry Chartkoff of Michigan State University. Instead, Indians here developed basketry to "technical and artistic levels unsurpassed in the New World." In central and northern California, the natives formed long ceremonial knives by chipping pieces of obsidian. A variety of ground and polished stone tools were made, perhaps in response to these peoples' dependence on seeds and other vegetable matter. Clothing was minimal in much of prehistoric California. The women had simple aprons; in winter men wore shirtlike garments, in summer little more than thongs around the waist, which served as belts to carry tools. In social terms, Archaic groups operated as bands of several families, each of which tended to be self-sufficient within the band. As the groups grew, each was probably led by a headman and greatly influenced by a shaman chosen for spiritual and medical gifts.

In their lucid synthesis of California prehistory, the Chartkoffs call the period of cultural efflorescence following the Archaic period "the Pacific," an analogue to the Woodland period in the East. Stability increased, as did security from hunger. People concentrated on a few well-known food sources: mesquite and screw beans in the desert; acorns, deer and seeds in the central valleys; sea mammals, fish, shellfish, seeds and acorns along the coast; pine nuts and deer in the mountains. Recently, some archaeologists and ethnologists have proposed that peoples in various parts of California cultivated certain plants. They believe that central California natives planted acorn oaks in orchards convenient to their villages, while southern California peoples planted prickly-pear cactus hedges around their villages, for protection and for the seasonal fruits. The Channel Islands had long since been inhabited by Archaic people using boats; now their successors were venturing offshore for fish and sea mammals. During this Pacific period, boats also enabled the rivers to become arteries of transportation and trade.

More efficient use of resources led to larger communities—at least a dozen numbered well over 1,000. Yet full-fledged tribal organization was the exception. California remained a mosaic of small communities, each one a self-contained cluster of related communities. For reasons that remain obscure, invasions and intrusions apparently did not prompt endless rounds of warfare, though conflicts occurred. Generally speaking, the neighboring groups throughout California seem to have lived peacefully until the historic era. ✳

Opposite, some of the world's most beautiful basketry originated with the Pomo, a people who lived north of San Francisco Bay. Feathers from wild birds brighten two small baskets in the foreground and the large one at far right. Deer bone awls helped Pomo women artisans fashion such sophisticated containers. Above, a Pomo woman paddles a bush, dislodging ripe seeds into her burden basket. Along with acorns, smaller wild seeds were an important ingredient in the diet of Far West peoples.

THE NORTHWEST COAST

 Anthropologists employ the term "subsistence" without meaning to imply an impoverished existence. Applied to a modern culture, the word might embrace all the goods supplied by the postindustrial complex of institutions from agribusiness farms to supermarkets and department stores. When used to describe the basis of the native life-style along the Northwest Coast, the term "subsistence" again refers to resource-rich rather than impoverished societies, for, as Gordon Willey of Harvard's Peabody Museum wrote, "there are few places in the world where land and sea combine to offer such a rich and regular bounty for human consumption, and the Indians of the Northwest Coast...exploited it to the full."

This spectacularly endowed habitat and its opportunity for wealth were accidents of geography. Though 1,500 miles long, the region is no more than 200 miles wide; its mountainous eastern boundary presents a formidable barrier to travel or migration. Thickly forested, the Cascade and Coast ranges of the Pacific Northwest remain a fastness even today, some regions still virtually unpeopled and barely explored. These coastal ranges block the prevailing westerly winds saturated with moisture from the warm Japan current. Masses of air blowing off the ocean hit the mountains and drop their burden as rain (snow in the higher elevations) to create a worldwide rarity, a temperate rain forest of gigantic redwoods, cedar and firs. Rainfall averaging up to 160 inches a year and temperatures that rarely fall below freezing nurture abundant plants of every sort, which in turn sustain a menagerie of birds and mammals from rodents to deer, elk and bear.

The sea offered native Americans its seals, whales and sea otters, to say nothing of shoals of oysters, mussels and abalone. There were schools of candlefish—fish so oily they could be set alight and burned like candles. (Too oily to be smoked or dried, they were allowed to putrefy before being boiled in boxes or old boats. Then the valuable oil was skimmed from the surface of the stew.) With lines and baited hooks of wood or shell, or harpoons, the Northwest people caught cod, 500-pound halibut and twenty-foot sturgeon—fish so large they had to be stunned with clubs before the fishermen could risk hauling them aboard, lest their thrashing capsize the boats.

As for the fabled salmon, they raced up the coastal rivers to spawn in such swarms they could be caught by hand, though an arsenal of tools proved more efficient. The Chinook Indians pieced nets together in 500-foot lengths, then walked them out into a river to surround the fish. Nootkas blocked rivers with complex weirs (fences made from saplings)

A finely carved, stylized owl head, opposite, adorns a wooden club discovered at the Ozette Village site on the northwest coast of the Olympic Peninsula in Washington. Archaeological excavations at Ozette, a whaling village that was inhabited for at least 2,000 years, have yielded over 50,000 artifacts. Above, a pictograph offers silent testimony to an ancient culture in a region of eastern Washington that is now the Colville Reservation, where a number of different tribes reside.

Northwest Coast

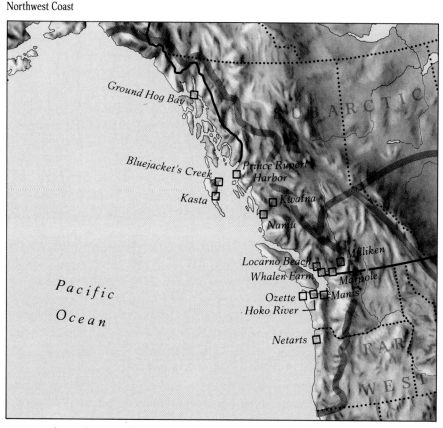

to trap the salmon, which they then speared with three-pronged leisters. These Indians shared a belief that salmon left the ocean for the express purpose of feeding the people, who observed the first catch of the year with special rites. The first fish caught was placed on an altar—facing upstream—while prayers were said, and then roasted. After every person tasted its flesh, its intact skeleton was returned to the river and thence to the submarine realm of the salmon people where, the Indians believed, the skeletons became new fish again. The reason for the ritual was self-evident to all who shared the fundamental belief that all living things possessed cogent spirits: prayer and ritual assured the quarry that their human captors would perform the acts necessary to enable the fish-spirits' safe transit back to the lower world of the sea where they could resume the form of living salmon.

The peoples of this rich environment spoke languages of four major groups: Athapaskan, Wakashan, Penutian and Salish. Despite wide linguistic differences, the life-styles of the Tlingit, Haida, Bella Coola, Kwakiutl, Chinook, Nootka, Eyak and Tsimshian and others, as they later were known by the Whites, were quite similar.

L ush rain forests such as that depicted in the nineteenth-century lithograph "A forest on Sitka Island," above left, offered both game and a wealth of vegetable foods, including abundant berries, to Northwest Coast Indians. A grizzly bear, above, feasts on salmon returning upriver to spawn. The protein-rich salmon was an important resource for many Northwest Coast peoples, and semipermanent riverside villages were often located at salmon harvesting sites.

Immigrants to this coast arrived relatively late. Several Northwest Coast peoples' appearance and inherited traits, including the Mongolian fold of the eyelids, suggest they come from stock that left Asia later than most. This was especially true for the Athapaskan speakers, whose languages show them to be members of possibly the next-to-last group of immigrants (the last being the Inuit of the far north).

At the end of the Pleistocene, peoples representing three cultural traditions, each characterized by different stone technologies, existed in the Northwest. Perhaps the first to inhabit the area were the coastally adapted peoples who followed the edges of the glaciers south. The two other traditions appear to have been brought by a proto-Arctic people arriving late from Beringia, bringing extensive Asian traits, and a proto-Plateau people who migrated from the east. These three combined into a maritime tradition along the Northwest Coast.

The immigrants settled at the mouths of rivers or in pockets of flat land between sea and coastal mountains; some lived inland by large rivers such as the Columbia and the Fraser. These settlement patterns tended to isolate these peoples from one another, accentuating differ-

This 2,000-year-old bowl in the shape of a seated human, right, exemplifies the extraordinary works in stone created by the people who lived at Marpole, a site in Vancouver on the north branch of the Fraser River. A Tlingit tobacco mortar bowl, below, is sculpted in marble in the shape of a bear. Opposite, an ancient stone mask from a coastal Tsimshian village in British Columbia portrays a human face.

Bills of two belted kingfishers form the handle of a mat creaser, above, used in making mats of tule — a wetland bulrush. The oldest wooden-carved work of art yet discovered in North America, the mat creaser is one of thousands of artifacts — particularly basketry, wooden fish hooks and cordage — that archaeologists have excavated from the site of a 2,800-year-old fishing station near the mouth of the Hoko River, right, in northwest Washington. Mudslides preserved wood and fiber artifacts that would have deteriorated in drier soil. Archaeologists used gentle spray from hoses to recover many fragile items, including a woven knob-top hat, opposite above, that was probably worn by an individual of high status. It resembles the hat worn by a Northwest Coast chief, opposite below, in an eighteenth-century drawing by John Webber, an artist with Captain James Cook's expedition of 1776 to 1779.

ences in languages and culture. Yet the environment they shared tended to make their ways of life similar.

The Indians of the Northwest Coast traded widely among themselves as well as with the Inuit and Subarctic peoples to the north and with inland dwellers of the Plateau. Some scholars believe that they may have traded directly with Siberians and other northeast Asians, and there can be little doubt that indirect links existed between Asia and North America via the Inuit or the Aleuts. Items of exchange included furs, walrus teeth, fish oil, roots or tubers, dried fish ground to powder, and basketry and the products of other crafts. Dentalia shells were sometimes used as a medium of exchange, and their collecting was regulated so that they would keep their value.

In addition to trade, the peoples of the region made war on each other and may have been especially hostile to their Inuit and Subarctic neigh-

bors. Captives taken in battle could be kept as slaves. Slaves, while of low status, were regarded as valuable possessions conferring prestige on their owners; they apparently could even change their own status if they proved skillful in acquiring wealth themselves by buying their freedom from their masters.

Ironically, the very environment that influenced these peoples' remarkably rich cultural evolution has also been responsible for tantalizing gaps in the archaeological record and, thus, in our knowledge of the region's prehistory. Heavy rainfall nurtured the area's forests, which in turn provided the abundance of wood that became a mainstay of the human inhabitants' material culture: red cedar, which splits easily into planks; soft yellow cedar and alder, which do not split and so are more readily carved into bowls and dishes; flexible yew for bows and harpoon shafts. Yet wood disintegrates, whether in the form of natural deadfalls or

Northwest Coast, A.D. 1400

A whaling canoe returns from the season's first successful whale hunt to a Makah village at Ozette, on Washington's Olympic Peninsula. In this artist's recreation, the tide has ebbed, stranding the dead whale and enabling the villagers to begin the hard but happy task of butchering the huge sea mammal. Months of preparation, including fasting and other ritual observances, preceded the expedition to intercept the humpback whales on their spring migration northward. The men killed the whale from their log canoes with harpoons and lances, and now the villagers salute the bravery and skill of the sea hunters with triumphant songs. The whalers themselves are distinguished members of the community — their woven hats denote high status, knob-topped hats the highest. Other bounty from the sea dries on racks above the red-cedar-planked houses.

The above is fiction, but it is based on fact. Life at the Ozette village came to an abrupt end about 500 years ago when a giant mudslide buried the community under ten feet of clay. A disaster for the inhabitants, the slide was a boon for archaeologists; the wet clay preserved artifacts of wood and other perishable materials. More than 50,000 objects were recovered, many of which are now preserved at the Makah Cultural and Research Center near the site.

Chalk-filled petroglyphs of faces and killer whales decorate rock near the ancient Northwest Coast whaling village of Ozette, where a devastating mudflow flattened, buried and ultimately preserved entire households nearly 500 years ago.

finely carved utensils—and rots all the faster because of damp conditions.

Thus, except at a few sites, relatively few prehistoric artifacts are to be found. Stone tools have survived, of course: projectile points of obsidian imported from the Oregon plateau; stone mauls and adzes; pile drivers (twenty-pound slabs with carved or "pecked" depressions to serve as handholds); sandstone abraders and even saws; basalt scrapers; slates ground with beveled edges for harpoon heads and crescent-shaped knives for slicing fish or blubber; soapstone effigy bowls and oil lamps. A great number of prehistoric garbage dumps or middens, full of shells, stone and bone trash, have helped archaeologists piece together types of utilitarian artifacts. It is largely through these objects from the middens that the descent of later forms and styles can be traced back in an apparently direct line for several thousand years.

One of the rare sites where perishable artifacts were preserved is Ozette, located on Washington's Olympic Peninsula. About five centuries ago a mudslide buried a thriving whaling village, encapsulating an entire way of life in a few moments. More than 50,000 artifacts have been recovered from Ozette, including nets, baskets, hats, beautifully carved wooden boxes, dishes and an extraordinary life-sized wooden effigy of the dorsal fin and back of a killer whale, studded with more than 700 sea otter teeth. Archaeological evidence showed that the village had existed for more than 2,000 years and had survived several previous mudslides before the catastrophic one. Excavators clearing mud from the floor of a house found still-green alder leaves and cedar bark, indicating that the slide took place in June. The Makah Indians who occupied the site until the late nineteenth century lived much as had their prehistoric forebears, fishing and whaling, making their living primarily from the sea.

As early as 7000 B.C., people were harvesting food offshore along the Northwest Coast. Early sites have yielded harpoons along with the remains of sea mammals, marine fish and albatrosses, which suggest the existence of boats. Whether the boats were of skins stretched over wooden frames or hollowed logs or took some other form is unknown. However, one of the undeniable technological achievements along these shores was the evolution of great log vessels.

To build seaworthy sixty-foot boats capable of weathering the sudden squalls that beset these waters required special raw materials and ingenious technology. The forests supplied the wherewithal in redwood, red cedar and fir trees growing up arrow-straight for 200 feet and eight feet thick at the base; the Indians supplied the know-how. The Haida and Nootka learned to fell these arboreal behemoths with controlled burning,

onservator Gerald Grosso resets some of the 700 sea otter teeth originally placed in a killer whale fin effigy carved of red cedar, above left, a unique find at Ozette. Also from Ozette, a sea monster with a bear's head is carved into a wooden double comb. The design continues to the reverse side.

subsequently splitting a section of log lengthwise with stone wedges hammered by stone mauls. Then they removed most of the inner wood —by burning and with stone adzes hafted to wooden, bone or antler handles. To assure a hull's even thickness—lest the finished boat list or lie end-down in the water—they developed the technique of drilling holes of chosen depths from the outside, then cutting away inside wood until they reached the holes. (The holes were later plugged.) In this manner they could shape a hull so that it was thickest (and heaviest) below the waterline, the better to stay upright in a stormy sea. To enlarge a boat's capacity—and broaden its beam, which gave it greater stability—called for an even more sophisticated technique. The boatwright would fill the unfinished craft with water and then heat the water with hot stones. This procedure made the wood temporarily flexible, so that the builder could force out the gunwales with thwarts that later served as rowers' seats. (Officers sailing the coast with James Cook and Vitus Bering during their eighteenth-century voyages remarked on the seaworthiness of the log canoes and the skill of the Indian mariners.)

The Haida and other coastal peoples who made canoe building a high art also wrought boxes of wonderful design and utility. Typically the sides were formed from a single plank, which was scored across the grain in three places and then bent along the grooves at right angles. The only open joint, where the two ends met, was sealed with a clamshell paste and reinforced with a sewn binding of plant-fiber thread. Then another plank, grooved to accept the sides, served as a bottom. These boxes were

U sing hafted mauls as sledgehammers to pound in wedges, northern Pacific Coast Indians split planks from a tree without felling it, above. Stone hammer heads were often carved with zoomorphic designs, such as the masterful Haida "Thunderbird" with a whale in the curve of its beak, right. Opposite, finely engraved bone artifacts include what may have been a decorative comb; they were excavated at the Minard site in the region of sheltered bays at Grays Harbor, Washington.

fitted so tightly they could hold liquids such as water or fish oil. The Haida in particular were also accomplished weavers who created striking textiles that combined wool (from mountain goats or dogs) and bark-fiber thread. Women wove ceremonial garments, using symmetrical designs that shamans drew on wood panels.

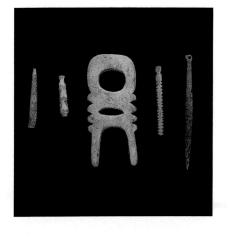

The same skills and stone gouges required for their boats and boxes also enabled the Northwest peoples to construct wooden buildings that were large by any standard. Built of logs notched and fitted together without pegs, these dwellings accommodated several families who shared the area around a central hearth and retired at night to private spaces. Roofed with bark slabs and walled with planks split from standing trees, the houses were graced with carved log pillars that supported the roof beams. These pillars originally provided stately entrances. Later, in certain tribes, these carved pillars would evolve into one of the several kinds of heraldic or story-telling "totem" poles.

Dwellings like these, along with houses for women coming of age, for birthing mothers, and charnel houses for the dead, were raised on well-chosen seaside sites. These permanent villages were occupied in winter by as many as 1,000 people. With the coming of spring—and the return of the salmon—many moved to locations along the rivers. Often they removed planks from their winter homes' walls to use as temporary shelters, freighting the good lumber back in the fall. One common method of transport was to lash planks across two canoes, making a sort of catamaran. The planking then served as a platform for goods.

Winter, spent in the permanent villages, was the rainiest season and a time for the most elaborate social activity. This was the time for the pot-latch, a term that some authorities attribute to Kwakiutl and others to Chinook, the language that became the basis for a widely understood pidgin. Whatever the word's native source, the potlatch meant "to give away" in a tradition practiced by most tribes in the region.

A potlatch was held when a tribal chief chose—or was obligated—to celebrate an event of importance, such as the death of his predecessor, a marriage or a child's coming of age and admission to a secret society. The occasion's underlying purpose was to validate the chief's (and thus his village's or tribe's) social status by giving away valuable goods. Material wealth—in food, baskets, cloaks woven from mountain goat wool and bark fibers, ingots beaten from native copper, shell ornaments, canoes and other goods—thus provided the symbols of status and social ties within societies of the Northwest Coast.

Social rank was inherited among these largely matrilineal tribes, but within each social stratum individuals could either gain or lose standing.

This early twentieth-century Edward Curtis photograph of masked Kwakiutl dancers depicts gigantic masks that were worn at winter ceremonials. Masks often represented family totems, including the sea eagle, mountain goat, wild man, grizzly bear, killer whale, wasp, bee and raven seen here.

This was especially true among rival chiefs whose competitive arena, the potlatch, was governed by protocol so strict it would test a diplomat's observances of formal rules.

Because the archaeological evidence is relatively scant, it is not known how far back the potlatch pattern goes. Large-scale, elaborate potlatches are clearly historical phenomena. (Many Northwest Indians died from diseases brought by the Whites and the rise of commercial fishing made those remaining much wealthier.) In historic times, a major potlatch, which might last for several days after years of planning, began when invited guests appeared at the host's village in their finest canoes. Coming ashore in rigidly formal order, each guest was greeted aloud and at length by the host's herald, who declared the visitor's pedigree and acquired honors—most of them inherited. In so doing the herald did not fail to announce his own chief's credentials, which, after all, qualified him to play host in the first place. The feasting that ensued provided

A historic-era grizzly bear helmet not only provided a Tlingit warrior protection but also made him a more fearsome foe. The skin of a grizzly's head was pegged to a carved hardwood form, with iron domes serving as eyes and small wooden carvings of humanlike bears—only one of which remains—filling the ears.

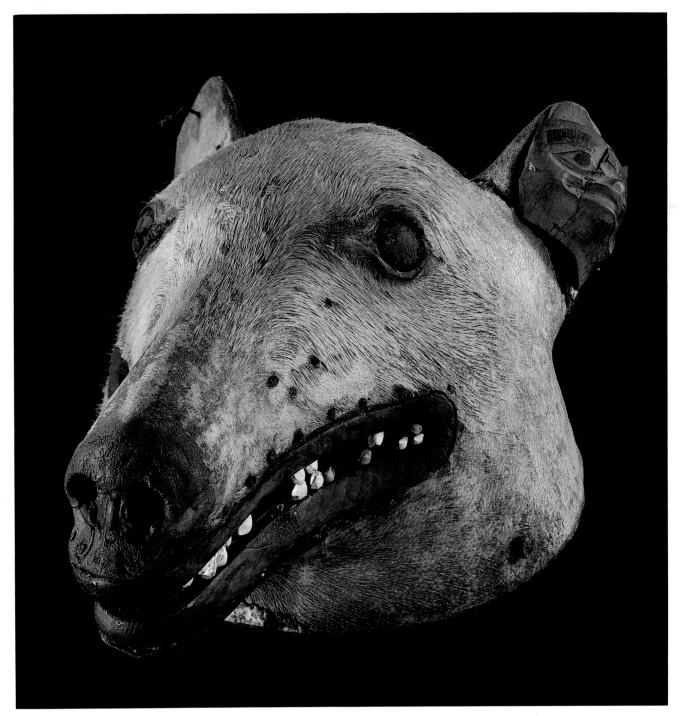

The "tail-bird" was long ago broken off the raven rattle, above, whose particular carvings and detail represent early Tlingit style. With its upraised tail forming another bird's head and a reclining man on its back, such raven rattles were commonly carried by Northwest Coast chiefs at potlatches and on other public occasions. Depictions of whales embellish the front of a wooden box recovered at the Ozette site, right.

new opportunities for the host's stature to be revealed through spectacular acts of largesse, as his measure was taken by the grandness of his hospitality. Not only did he provide vast amounts of food, but he tested his guests' worthiness by their ability to consume. Indeed, consumption became a kind of competition. Huge ceremonial bowls—sometimes boats—were filled with delicacies such as salmon roe or berries preserved in fish oil. Then a guest's party would be challenged to eat it all or lose stature before the other guests and be humiliated by the hosts.

The bowls were named and had their own lineages, which were rehearsed as ceremonially as a chief's genealogy. They would be among the many gifts presented to the guests in displays of prodigality; thus, when a bowl was given away its lineage would gain a new degree and its value would be enhanced. Among even more valued objects given away at the potlatch were embossed tablets hammered out of native copper brought from the Coppermine River of Canada's Northwest Territories. Like the ceremonial bowls, these objects had names and histories of their own.

The Northwest Coast peoples defined themselves by property. A chief was what he owned—namely what he had inherited and created or acquired through other potlatches. Possessions included the hunting, fishing and gathering territories he controlled, the goods his village produced, the objects he previously acquired from rival hosts and—most important in some respects—his intangible possessions. The right to display a bear totem or orca (killer whale) crest resembled a Scot's privilege to wear his clan's tartan or an American merchant's exclusive license to use a trademark. The Indians took this form of owner's privilege several steps further. Myths and dances were owned as certainly as objects; they were considered exclusive property and could only be performed (or declared) by their acknowledged owners. So were lineages, the chiefs' treasured pedigrees, which typically harkened back generation by generation to the founder of a clan or tribe who had been given a legacy by a god or spirit. Curiously, these intangible assets could be bought or more often stolen. An interloper at a public ceremony could declaim a heritage, which then became his own unless he was challenged on the spot and disposed of through ridicule.

The peoples of the Northwest Coast, bearers of these rich and complex cultures, were among the last of the continent's Indians to be touched by the Whites. The results of contact were much the same as elsewhere: disruption, displacement and decimation by disease. Nonetheless, they have managed better than many others to carry their traditional ways over into the modern world. ✸

A boldly executed design of an oyster catcher and two skates decorates this blanket, possibly Nootka, woven from a mixture of cedar bark and mountain goat wool. As this wool was highly valued, only chiefs could afford to own such elaborate blankets, which they wore on ceremonial occasions.

THE SOUTHWEST

 The Mogollon potters of New Mexico's Mimbres River Valley made pots still regarded as among the finest of North America. As Chicago's Field Museum archaeologist Paul S. Martin once exclaimed, "Mimbres Classic pottery demonstrates such originality and such care in craftsmanship that it is in a class all by itself; no prehistoric Southwestern pottery can compare with it as an expression of the sheer ecstasy of living." In fact, had this group of people not produced such splendid ceramics, we might know more about them; unfortunately, pot hunters found such a ready market for Mimbres vessels that their sites have been systematically looted and destroyed for most of this century.

Ancestors of the Mogollon and most of the other early Southwestern peoples seem to have entered the region sometime between 10,000 and 9000 B.C. Clovis-style projectile points mixed with butchered bones of mammoths and other long-extinct mammals at sites such as Naco in southern Arizona attest to the skill and bravery of the Southwest's Paleo-Indian hunters. Finds made by the University of Arizona's Emil Haury in Ventana Cave, on the present-day Papago Indian reservation in southern Arizona, have revealed continuous human habitation in the region from the end of the ice ages to the present.

Ventana Cave's many layers have preserved an extraordinary record of an evolving hunting-gathering life-style lasting hundreds of generations. Finds at Ventana Cave and other sites in the Southwest indicate that several subregional toolmaking traditions arose after the end of the Paleo-Indian period about 5000 B.C.: the San Dieguito-Lake Mohave in the west, the Oshara in the north and the Cochise in the south. During the early Archaic period the hunting-gathering way of life was common to all of the peoples of the Southwest. Cynthia Irwin-Williams of Reno's Desert Research Institute suggests that by 3000 B.C. the Southwest was "occupied by a broad continuum of interacting culture systems that have been termed the Picosa or Elementary Southwestern culture."

In the late Archaic, sometime around 1500 B.C., agriculture seems to have reached the Southwest, probably from Mexico. While hunting and gathering continued throughout the rest of the prehistoric era, agriculture played an increasingly important role in subsistence, particularly after the first century A.D. Ceramics, too, seem to have come from Mexico. Together, agriculture and ceramics would contribute greatly to the industry and art of the Southwest, and particularly of the three major cultures to develop in the region in late prehistoric times: the Mogollon, the Hohokam and the Anasazi.

Although geographically and culturally distinct, these three cultures

People of the Anasazi culture of Chaco Canyon built the great *kiva*, far left, in the 500-room pueblo today preserved as Aztec Ruins National Monument in New Mexico. Restored by the National Park Service, this kiva once served as a meeting place for ceremonies involving members of many clans. Chacoans began the construction of Aztec pueblo about A.D. 1100. It was abandoned late in the thirteenth century, perhaps because a great drought forced its dwellers to disperse. Above, gray and red Anasazi pots from A.D. 700 to 1100 demonstrate potters' command of various techniques even in this early period. The pot on the left is eight and one-half inches tall.

Southwest

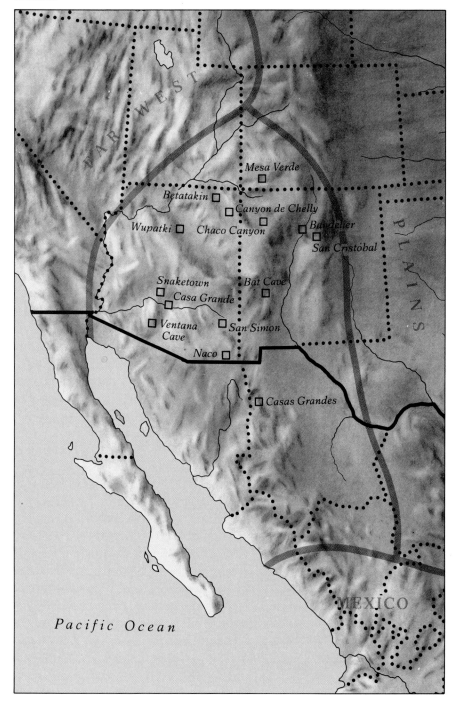

Paleo-Indians dispatched mammoths and other large prey with these projectile points at two sites in southern Arizona more than 10,000 years ago. Called Clovis points after the New Mexico site where they were first found in association with the bones of long-extinct bison, spear points of this style have been discovered in almost every region of North America. Above, Paleo-Indians of Arizona may have straightened spear shafts with this wrenchlike tool, probably of mammoth bone, more than 11,000 years ago.

were by no means self-contained and aloof. Their peoples traded raw materials, finished goods and technologies among themselves and their neighbors. Nor were they the only inhabitants of the region. There were the peoples of the Sinagua culture, from the Spanish words for "without water," who dry-farmed crops in the volcanic soil around present-day Flagstaff, Arizona.

The people of another culture, the Salado ("salty"), farmed the upper Salt River Valley for generations and built complex houses in cliffside caves a thousand feet above and as much as five miles from their valley fields. In addition to corn, beans and squash, they raised amaranth (pigweed) for its nutritious seeds, and cotton, which they wove into patterned fabrics. They also made use of the region's varied wild plants, among them saguaro cactus, yucca and mesquite.

In Arizona's western central desert and along the Colorado River lived the predecessors of today's speakers of the Yuman family of

Master potters of North America, people of the Mogollon culture who lived in New Mexico's Mimbres Valley built pots of smoothed coils of clay and then painted them with long brushes made from fibers of the yucca plant. The pots were often placed in graves to accompany the dead. Mimbres Valley people punched holes in the bottoms of the pots before burial, perhaps to "kill" the pots or to release the spirits of the painted figures or symbols. Below left, the two figures on this bowl from about A.D. 950 may represent male and female or perhaps life and death. Above left, a bird decorates this bowl from the Mimbres Classic

black-on-white tradition of the tenth to thirteenth centuries. Bats often appear on Mimbres bowls; the extraordinarily well-preserved example above comes also from the Mimbres Classic black-on-white style. Above right, figures of what appear to be a bighorn sheep ewe and a more mysterious creature grace the lower two Classic black-on-white bowls, while the upper bowl is from the earlier Mimbres Boldface black-on-white tradition of A.D. 750 to 1000. Below right, insects were another common motif of Mimbres Valley bowls; this example of the Mimbres polychrome tradition is dated between 1050 and 1200.

languages: the Yavapai, the Havasupai and Walapai, and the Mohave. These peoples farmed, hunted and foraged along the Colorado or on the desert plateau to the east. To the south were such cultures as the Chametla-Aztatlán and the Chalchihuites of northern Mexico, whence came much of the Mesoamerican influences on the Southwestern peoples.

Very late arrivals in the Southwest were the Apacheans, Athapaskan-language-group speakers who had migrated over the course of many generations from northern and western Canada down into the Plains and Southwest. The peoples who would be called Navajo and the various Apaches arrived in the Southwest sometime in the fifteenth century A.D. There most lived in small groups of a few families and followed a lifeway that included some farming but much more hunting and gathering than had been typical of the Pueblo peoples. The Apacheans often coexisted uneasily with their more settled Pueblo neighbors, alternately raiding or trading with them.

Each of these peoples developed in a different way to find a niche. For varying periods (and with varying degrees of success), Anasazi, Hohokam, Mogollon, Salado, Sinagua and the other non-Apacheans found ways to manage scarce water and thus sustain agriculture. If they appear to have shared many common denominators, it is because they lived close enough to each other in time and space to address similar challenges and to exchange innovations such as corn and pottery.

As Paul S. Martin wrote, "For the most part, the recognizable differ-

A bove, a bone hair ornament, an awl of grizzly bear bone and a carved wand, also of grizzly bear bone, were crafted by people of the Late Mogollon culture between the thirteenth and fifteenth centuries A.D. The objects were found at the Grasshopper site in north central Arizona. The Salado people of central Arizona made human effigy pots such as the one opposite between A.D. 1100 and 1300. The pot is seven and three-quarters inches tall.

ences between the Hohokam, Anasazi and Mogollon seem to reflect the existence of functionally different ecological niches.... An expert can readily distinguish among the material facets of the three great subcultures of the Southwest, but actually there is a majestic parallelism of likeness among them."

Let us now consider them individually.

The mountains of eastern Arizona and southwest New Mexico are semiarid or arid, although at higher elevations some are graced with rushing streams, vast expanses of forest and lovely meadows. They were inhabited by people of the Mogollon culture, whose name derives from the Mogollon Mountains, in turn named for a Spanish colonial governor. The territory of the Mogollon culture also extended down into the dry deserts of Chihuahua.

The Mogollon peoples may have descended from the hunter-gatherers of the Archaic period's Cochise culture. Mogollon influence extended from central Arizona and New Mexico into Chihuahua, bounded by the Sonoran Desert to the west, the grasslands to the east and the Colorado Plateau to the north. As finds in Bat Cave, New Mexico, have shown, by around 1000 B.C. these peoples not only grew corn but had implements to grind it into flour—mortars, pestles and metates, the ubiquitous stone slabs that acquired deep grooves from hours of grinding with handstones, or manos. By A.D. 700 there were locally adapted strains of maize, from pod corn through sixteen-, fourteen- and twelve-row varieties to the larger-kerneled eight-row variety. Mogollon village sites also contain the remains of wild foods: pine nuts, Indian rice grass, lily bulbs, walnuts, acorns, prickly pears, wild tomatoes (wolfberries) and sunflower seeds. The people hunted deer in particular, as well as bison, turkeys, muskrats and other animals and birds.

Early Mogollon villages consisted of a few pit houses placed in no particular pattern except that the entrances usually faced east or southeast. The houses were built on well-drained, breezy hills, mesas and ridges, which enabled the inhabitants to keep a watchful eye on their fields. To build these dwellings, the Mogollon dug round, knee-deep depressions. Inside, they placed an upright post in the center as the hub for a circle of sloping poles resembling wheel spokes. The poles were covered with reeds, grass and sticks and then covered with mud to enclose a cone-shaped hut. As time passed, construction materials changed little, although the circle became D-shaped and then rectangular when corner posts replaced the center post.

When Mogollon architecture changed during the ninth century A.D., dwellings featured smaller rooms but more of them. While large, separate

Typical cacti of the Sonoran Desert, giant saguaros bear fruits, above, harvested by historic Papago Indians of the region as well as prehistoric peoples of Arizona's Hohokam culture. Also from the Tucson area, these Rincon red-on-brown human effigy jars, opposite, represent a face and baby (left) and a dotted face with the lip of the jar at the top (right). Hohokam potters sculpted the vessels sometime between A.D. 900 and 1200.

pit houses had characterized earlier villages, surface pueblos now began to appear. These above-ground complexes were built of cobbles, piled in rough walls and mortared with quantities of mud. Nonetheless, underground rooms were not abandoned; they continued to be used for storage and as round *kivas*, centers for ceremonial and other group activities.

The Mogollon peoples crafted many kinds of ritual and decorative artifacts, among them painted stone animals and tobacco pipes, sun disks for unknown purposes, masks, pottery showing masked dancers, copper bells probably imported from Mexico, turquoise, stone and shell beads, bone and shell bracelets and effigy figurines. They are best known, however, for their spectacular pottery.

The tradition of plain brown and red pottery-making had come at least a millennium earlier, possibly from Mexico. The Mogollon manufactured their pots by building up coils of clay, then scraping them and finishing them to leave a smooth surface. Red-on-white painted styles appeared, to be followed by the striking black-on-white Mimbres tradition and other black-on-white styles. Mimbres bowls were decorated with complex geometric designs, and crisply stylized realistic images: human figures in all sorts of postures and activities (including coitus), and animals such as bats, turtles, lizards, rabbits, insects, frogs, bears, mountain sheep and deer. When these vessels were buried with the dead, each vessel was ritually broken by punching a hole in the bottom. Although the pot-breaking must have had a religious significance, archaeologists can only guess at its meaning.

Starting around A.D. 500, the peoples of the Mogollon may have gone into a temporary decline. During that time their diet seems to have included more wild foods and fewer domesticated foods. Two centuries later, however, corn and squash returned to the larder in greater quantities, judging by the contents of middens. Before A.D. 1000, agricultural activity increased and many other changes became evident. Villages were located in valleys instead of on high ground, and many-roomed, above-ground pueblos of masonry featured rectangular kivas.

Around 1100, the Mogollon culture entered another decline that lasted for more than a century. Then a brief resurgence was followed by what amounted to complete eclipse about 1250. Contributing factors may have included a changing climate and the still-rising dominance of the Anasazi to the north and the Hohokam to the west. In any event, the Mogollon culture virtually disappeared save in the northern Mexican pueblo of Casas Grandes and related sites, which survived into the fifteenth century.

Casas Grandes was a city of multistoried apartments and colonnades, where warehouses held tons of marine mollusk shells as well as iron

crystals, paint pigments, copper and turquoise. Possibly a political center, it certainly served as a center of commerce, since the ruins reveal a large, central marketplace. Here turkeys and macaws were bred, probably for their plumes, which were used in religious ceremonies. By the time Casas Grandes reached its peak, it was allied with more distinctly Mexican cultures, although Mogollon influences would linger. The people themselves left no clearly defined descendants.

The Sonoran Desert, below and generally to the west of the Mogollon region, was the territory of the Hohokam. The Hohokam name derives from a term in Piman, the tongue of today's Pima Indians, who occupy some of the Hohokam's ancient range. The Piman language forms plurals by doubling a noun's first syllable. *Hokam* refers to a thing "used up," such as a punctured tire, as their preeminent student, University of Arizona archaeologist Emil Haury, explains. Thus the *Hohokam* are "many things used up," or in more delicate translation, "the vanished ones."

The Hohokam were a desert people, but the Sonoran Desert is generally not an environment of dunes and drifting sands. Vegetated with more species of plants than are typically found in an Eastern hardwood forest, the Sonoran Desert today receives enough rain to place it on the borderline between arid and semiarid, and there are many indications

Mid-nineteenth-century watercolorist Seth Eastman captured a moment in the lives of a group of Pima Indians living near the Gila River of central Arizona, territory occupied centuries before by peoples of the Hohokam culture. In the 1930s and 1960s, University of Arizona archaeologist Emil W. Haury excavated Snaketown, a principal town of the Hohokam. Around A.D. 850, he concluded, Snaketown would have looked much like the later Pima village.

that the area was somewhat wetter at times during the past. It is fertile and quite productive cropland when adequately watered.

Speculation on the origins of the Hohokam culture has provoked lively debate for decades among scholars of Southwestern prehistory. Some, notably Haury, argue that a people migrated from Mexico into Arizona's Gila River Basin about 300 B.C. and evolved the Hohokam way of life. Some agree with the migration hypothesis but place it later, at about A.D. 300. Others reject altogether the idea that a people migrated north and suggest a local origin for the Hohokam, perhaps an Archaic culture such as the San Pedro Cochise, which also gave rise to the Mogollon.

In any event, a village of permanent square houses arose where previously only hunter-gatherers of the Archaic Cochise people had made their temporary camps. Snaketown, the landmark Hohokam site in central Arizona, has been excavated twice and covered over; it now lies again beneath desert ground, its location betrayed only by undulating rises in the nearly level land beside the Gila River in country that looks parched—and probably has been dry since humans first came this way. Yet the Hohokam became "desert farmers and craftsmen," to borrow the subtitle of Haury's monumental study of the long-lived settlement. They contrived ways to divert the Gila into a complex system of canals that at one point may have stretched fifteen miles. (Eventually the Hohokam built hundreds of miles of canals throughout their region.)

Snaketown's name, taken from the Piman word for "place of snakes," was apt. Rodents found the prehistoric trash heaps better places to burrow than the surrounding natural soil, and the large, permanent rodent population attracted multitudes of snakes. (The rattlers did not deter the archaeologists, who encountered only a dozen snakes in the course of digging. "If anything, they sharpened our powers of observation," Haury writes.) In prehistoric times, as now, the environment was harsh, with annual temperatures ranging between 7 and 119 degrees Fahrenheit. Although rainfall averaged a marginal ten inches a year and snow was rare, there were flash floods and sand storms to contend with.

"The Hohokam habitat had an ethos peculiar unto itself,..." Haury mused, "[in] the contrasts between the searing heat of the day and the bone-rattling chill of the night; the powder-dry land one minute, a quagmire the next; the unbelievable mirages in the morning and the crystal-clear night sky; the dust devils, the dimensionless vistas ending in a ragged mountain backdrop that reminds one of pasteboard cutouts, and the smell of the desert after a rain."

It was ever thus. He continued, "The enduring character of Hohokam society was, in large measure, a product of their nearly perfect adaptation to a desert homeland....a mode of living that stretched back in time more than 2,000 years."

At Snaketown the early Hohokam solved the irrigation problem by digging a three-mile canal to draw Gila River water onto the plain. (This

A raised irrigation canal near the Gila River, the Santan Ditch, above, probably follows the course of an ancient Hohokam canal. The site of the Hohokam town, Snaketown, lies just beyond the mountains in the background. Hohokam irrigators built hundreds of miles of ditches in central Arizona. Left, one of two "ball courts" excavated at Snaketown suggests Mesoamerican influences on the Hohokam. Archaeologists believe that inhabitants played some form of ball game on such courts, many of which have been found in the Southwest and in Mesoamerica, where the game originated. This court measures about 130 feet long and 100 feet wide and was constructed sometime between A.D. 600 and 900. Almost nothing is known about the game itself, except that it probably had religious as well as competitive significance.

canal was maintained, improved and used until 1450. And it is a credit to Hohokam engineering that modern Phoenix depends on a canal system nearly superimposed on the early Indians' plan for diverting the Salt River.) In prehistoric times, natural river flow was plentiful in spring when the mountain snowpack melted and again in August with the onset of late summer rainstorms. These farmer-engineers may have learned to marshal the seasonal flow ably enough to raise two crops a year. They supplemented maize, beans and squash with wild foods, including the seedpods of mesquite trees and a variety of cacti such as prickly pear, cholla and saguaro (the giant cactus that also provided woodlike ribs for building material). For meat they hunted deer, rabbits and smaller animals of every description, although today game is scarce in most of the region formerly occupied by the Hohokam and may have been so in the past.

Snaketown was the hub of an extensive trade network between the Southwest and California. Its inhabitants imported marine shells from the Gulf of California to make carved ornaments. Trading turquoise from New Mexico and eastern California for Mexican copper bells, they apparently served as active middlemen between the south and the northern hinterlands. Soon Hohokam villages featured scattered shallow pit houses, with wattle-and-daub roofs supported by four interior posts and with a fire pit near the door. Snaketown, which eventually covered more than a third of a square mile, boasted raised platform mounds for public ceremonies and ball courts, probably for a ball game imported from Mexico. Later, historical observers of the game as it was played in Mexico would liken it to a violent scrimmage between teams engaged in a contest with apparently sacred functions.

Maintaining strong ties with Mexican peoples, the Hohokam followed the cultural lead of their southern neighbors as they began weaving cotton cloth and painting their pottery with red designs. As artisans the Hohokam were both skilled and innovative. Hohokam potters shaped their vessels with paddle and anvil and achieved novel effects with mica-flecked clay. Their later pottery featured an almost infinite variety of red geometric designs on a buff ground. Nor was decorated pottery their only medium of artistic expression. Incense burners and other vessels were sculpted in the forms of stylized animals. Seashells were adorned with turquoise mosaics. Not content with carving the shells, the Hohokam turned to etching. They first covered a shell with pitch or wax and scratched a design through the protective layer to the shell beneath. The exposed parts of the shell were then daubed with acidic fermented cactus juice to eat away the shell's surface at the selected

A Hohokam potter made this animal effigy censer in the form of a bighorn sheep sometime between A.D. 900 and 1150. Used to burn incense, the censer represents the style called Sacaton red-on-buff. Archaeologists consider the Sacaton phase of Hohokam pottery to be the beginning of a decline from earlier styles to a period when production quantity became more important than quality.

ost holes outline house floors at Snake-town, site of a large Hohokam town on the Gila River. Snaketown was inhabited from about 300 B.C. to A.D. 1450. During that time house styles changed; newer houses were built over old floors — thus the mosaic of overlapping dwellings seen here. Though the entire site covers about one-third of a square mile, no more than about 125 houses existed at any one time.

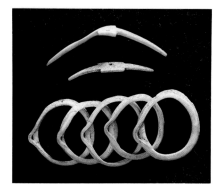

The manufacture of shell bracelets and ornaments such as those above was an important Hohokam industry. Nearly every area of Snaketown contains debris from shell work. Considerable archaeological evidence suggests that Hohokam shell crafters made periodic treks to the east coast of the Gulf of California to collect various kinds of shells, including giant bittersweet clamshells from which bracelets and other objects were made.

places. This method of decoration would not be invented in Europe for several centuries.

As time passed, Hohokam culture changed, taking on so many characteristics of surrounding societies that some authorities, Emil Haury among them, have suggested that perhaps the Hohokam were not Hohokam any more. Particularly noteworthy was a shift during the twelfth century from the pit houses favored for many generations to large, above-ground complexes. One of these is Casa Grande, near the Gila River south of present-day Phoenix. Today the ruin rises like a castle on a level plain, surrounded by mesquite trees and protected from the elements by a huge steel roof. But when it was occupied, the three-story structure stood at the center of a walled town of *caliche*, concrete-like soil that the builders mixed with precious water to make walls. Such towns became hubs for widely scattered villages, indicating the evolution of a more complex society.

By about 1450, however, classic Hohokam culture had declined. A number of hypotheses have been offered to explain the phenomenon. Scholars have suggested that perhaps the intensive irrigation projects of the Hohokam increased the salinity of the soil, a common problem in irrigated desert lands in our own time. Others have pointed to a great drought that afflicted all Southwestern cultures during the thirteenth century. In any case, when the Spanish arrived in the late sixteenth century, probably preceded by epidemic disease, they found the eastern part of the area occupied by Pima Indians and the west inhabited by Papagos. Although some circumstantial and cultural evidence suggests connections between these modern tribes and the Hohokam, direct genetic links between the newer and older peoples have never been proven. But along the Gila River where the Hohokam once lived, farmers—Indian and White—still divert water into canals to irrigate their fields.

The high desert of the Colorado Plateau of northern Arizona and New Mexico and southern Utah and Colorado, a land of majestic mesas, canyons and open sagebrush country, was the domain of the Anasazi. At first these people used natural rock shelters as burial sites and places to cache stores of food and utensils. Bags of hand-twisted cord, coiled baskets, flat winnowing trays, curved throwing sticks to bring down small game, large rabbit nets and milling slabs and cobble manos for grinding corn have all been found preserved in dry caves. Early middens also contain the remains of turkeys, though it cannot be said whether these are the bones of hunted or domestic birds. The early Anasazi hunters used atlatls to hurl hardwood-shafted darts with big, notched

Toad or frog effigies, left, were made of tiles of blue turquoise and red *Spondylus* shell or the red mineral argillite, glued to bittersweet clamshells combed from beaches of the Gulf of California. Worn on necklaces by men of high status in a number of Southwestern cultures, the amphibian effigies may have signified participation in a religious society. The effigy at upper left was found at Limestone Ruin in Arizona's Verde Valley and is dated at about A.D. 1300 to 1400; that at lower left is from the Keystone Ruin of Arizona's Tonto Basin, A.D. 1300 to 1400; and the largest effigy is from Kinisba Ruins, a pueblo on the Fort Apache Reservation in Arizona, and is dated at about A.D. 1200 to 1400. Above, a craftsman of the Hohokam culture etched an effigy of a horned lizard in a cockleshell, using dilute acid made from fermented cactus juice to dissolve the shell. The etching was made sometime between A.D. 900 and 1100.

stone points. Archaeologists have long referred to these early people as the Basketmakers because of their distinctive wicker containers; ceramics were so rare at this stage that none had been found when archaeologists named the culture.

By about A.D. 700, most Anasazi communities used ingenious dryland farming techniques to support their maize-and-squash agriculture. The villagers lived in pit houses. The larger ones, about twenty-five feet in diameter, were substantial dwellings with walls of earth and wattle and daub and domed roofs made of wattle and daub with logs framing smoke holes and entryways. As these houses became deeper, what had been the smoke hole gained a ladder and became the entrance, while the old entrance became a ventilator shaft with a deflector in front to control the draft. The pit house also featured a *sipapu*, a small hole in the floor to provide symbolic access to the lower world whence humans had originally come, according to the lore common among many later Southwest Pueblo Indians.

By the late Basketmaker period, the Anasazi planted beans in addition to maize and squash. They raised or kept turkeys. Bows and arrows joined atlatls and spears in the hunters' arsenal. Wicker workers continued to make baskets and twine bags, but coiled pottery appeared

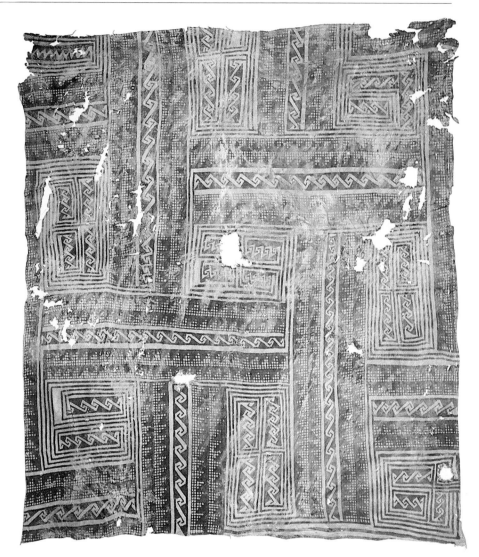

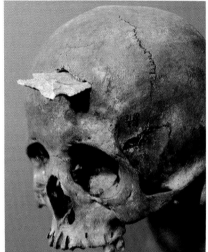

G em of the Anasazi cliff dwellings, Cliff Palace, opposite, boasted twenty-three kivas and 200 rooms. Here it looks much as it did when discovered by cowboys Richard Wetherill and Charlie Mason on a snowy December day in 1888 at Mesa Verde, Colorado. Built about A.D. 1100, Cliff Palace was abandoned sometime around 1275. Although evidence is scanty and contradictory, warfare and drought may have forced the abandonment of Anasazi cliff dwellings: above, an Anasazi woman of Mesa Verde died about A.D. 1300 when a spear point pierced her forehead. Above right, influenced by Anasazi, Mogollon and Hohokam cultures, people of the Sinagua culture, centered south of today's Flagstaff, Arizona, painted intricate designs on this woven cotton blanket sometime between A.D. 1200 and 1300.

in the form of black, gray and white vessels. In southeastern Utah, Anasazi potters made red-on-orange ware. The addition of these colored vessels to the Anasazi potters' black, gray and white ware demonstrated a new technology. Gray pottery was fired in oxygen-poor (reducing) conditions, probably beneath a bed of mulch, while the brighter-colored wares marked the new technique of well-ventilated firing. These techniques for firing colored wares were used also by the Mogollon peoples.

During the next phase of Anasazi culture, called the Pueblo period by archaeologists, the Anasazi began to congregate in larger settlements both at high elevations and in the canyons. Most villages remained small, but some soon expanded to 200 structures. Also during this period, the Anasazi built greater numbers of surface structures—initially for storage. At the same time they constructed partially subterranean kivas. Their pottery became more diverse and carefully finished. They polished many vessels and covered them with a wash or slip before adding painted designs. Weavers still twisted fibers into rough twines, but they also learned to use vertical looms and to weave fine cotton. Instead of swaddling their babies on flexible wicker cradleboards, the Anasazi now began to make these carriers of wood, which permanently flattened the children's skulls. Ten centuries later archaeologists would suspect that the flat-skulled people they found in early Pueblo graves had belonged to a race

The Anasazi of Chaco Canyon

The most remarkable example of Anasazi culture is located within the thirty-two square miles of present-day Chaco Canyon National Historical Park in northern New Mexico. From about A.D. 900 to 1200, Anasazi culture flowered, giving rise to what has been called the "Chaco Phenomenon," a sustained burst of activity in engineering, architecture, trade and social organization. The ten-mile-long canyon boasted eight major pueblos, such as Pueblo Bonito, some containing several hundred rooms.

The Anasazi understood the intricacies of building walls that could support structures up to five stories high. Archaeologists estimate that 200,000 logs — brought from twenty-five miles away — were used in the construction of the canyon's buildings.

The Anasazi of Chaco Canyon also turned their considerable engineering talents to agriculture and the problems of limited water and poor soil. They built diversion dams and canals to capture and divert rare but torrential downpours into bordered gardens of corn, beans and squash.

Clearly, Chaco Canyon was a hub of the Colorado Plateau — 400 miles of roads linked at least seventy-five settlements within a 33,000-square-mile basin. Beads were made in Chaco from imported turquoise, and many goods were brought from as far south as Mexico.

As many as 5,000 people may have inhabited the canyon's pueblos during the height of its civilization. In the twelfth century drought overtaxed the water resources of a culture that had already strained them to the maximum, and the canyon was gradually abandoned.

Greatest of all of the "Great Houses," Pueblo Bonito sprawls over more than three acres of northern New Mexico's Chaco Canyon. Perhaps as many as 1,000 people lived here. Shaped like a capital D, the structure was begun in about A.D. 920. During the 150 years that construction of the five-story pueblo continued, the plans of the original builders appear to have been followed closely. Inner and outer walls, left, were built of carefully dressed courses of sandstone mortared and plastered with wet clay; the space between the walls was filled with rubble.

Roofs long gone, some of Pueblo Bonito's many clan kivas, most about twenty-five feet in diameter or less, gape at the sky. Not visible are the huge pueblo's two great kivas, forty and sixty feet in diameter, capable of holding hundreds of people for important ceremonies and meetings involving the whole population of the pueblo. Religion and ceremony were inextricably woven into the life fabric of the inhabitants of Pueblo Bonito, as they are among today's Pueblo peoples.

Cliff dwellers carved footholds in cliffs to reach the canyon floor or mesa-top garden plots. Those at right are at northeastern Arizona's Canyon de Chelly. Pueblo and cliff dwellers reached upper stories with ladders such as the one below, photographed recently at Acoma Pueblo in New Mexico. Rectangular doorways, bottom, pierce some of the finest prehistoric masonry in North America at 800-room Pueblo Bonito in Chaco Canyon, New Mexico.

of interlopers or invaders. Research would show, however, that these were the same people as before, but with the shapes of their heads changed by the custom of strapping babies to hard cradleboards.

Evidently, the Colorado Plateau experienced especially favorable weather for almost three centuries after about 850, as rainfall—especially in summer—increased slightly over the norm of eight to twelve inches a year. The Anasazi thrived as they expanded their territory. They built check dams and efficient catchment basins to trap the runoff from mesas during summer squalls. Their irrigation and dry-farming techniques enabled them to farm areas that had not been arable before (or since, for that matter), while they continued to make wide use of wild animal and plant foods. These clever and adaptive people took maximum advantage of the benign climate for the dozen generations it lasted.

The Anasazi of Chaco Canyon in northern New Mexico built pueblos with masonry walls of stone rubble faced with dressed stones or with one or more courses of dressed stone. These walls, some of them surviving 800 years or more, rise almost perfectly flat and vertical, some to four stories. Many pueblos were planned structures of several hundred rooms. Throughout the area of Anasazi influence, kivas took on their fully developed form: each ceremonial space was a partially underground round room lined with masonry walls, sometimes including a built-in bench around the perimeter. Each featured a central fire pit, a ventilator shaft and deflector, a southern recess, and the sipapu, "Earth Navel or Hole of Emergence from the Underworld."

Pottery continued to flourish with painted designs on serving bowls and ceremonial vessels. For cooking vessels, a new sort of ware became popular: the clay coils were not smoothed on the outside but instead pinched around the surface to produce a "corrugated" texture. Artisans crafted many sorts of goods: sandals of yucca fibers, bone scrapers, wooden combs, stone pipes, spindles and distaffs for yarn, black-on-white bowls and ladles, black glazes, jewelry of shell, stone and turquoise, and digging sticks with blades made from the horns of mountain sheep. After 1300, ceramics continued to flourish and kiva walls were decorated with murals.

The Anasazi's strategies worked so long as the climate favored them. However, Southwestern rains are often quite localized; if a particular canyon received no rain for a year or more, the inhabitants of its small, scattered pueblos might have to abandon them. That this happened many times seems evident. Many small pueblos were occupied for no more than 100 years, or even less.

But perhaps severe, long-term drought, extending over the whole region,

A ladder in the foreground protrudes from the ceiling entrance to a kiva at a Mesa Verde cliff dwelling. Clans and other groups used kivas for ceremonies and meetings of various kinds. Keyhole-shaped "windows" in the structure beyond are actually doors reached by ladders. Such doors may have afforded easier access for inhabitants bearing loads on their shoulders or may have been easier to defend against attackers.

Southwest, A.D. 1100

Great Basin hunters gaze from hiding at huge, multistoried Chetro Ketl pueblo at Chaco Canyon, New Mexico, in this artist's rendering. Ceremonies held in the circular kivas may have been critical in maintaining the high degree of social cohesiveness that not only enabled the Chacoans to survive the arid conditions but also to accomplish extraordinary feats of architecture, road building and irrigation. Corn grows in bordered gardens supplied with carefully channeled run-off water from the mesa tops. Laborers bring wooden beams from forests more than twenty-five miles away to reinforce the sophisticated masonry walls, ruins of which still exist. One archaeologist estimates that fifty million pieces of stone were quarried, transported, cut and used to build Chetro Ketl's walls. Scholars believe that the 500-room, three-acre complex, together with other great pueblos in Chaco Canyon, such as Pueblo Bonito one-half mile to the north, served as centers of civilization to many peoples in the Southwest.

H opis and other Pueblo peoples have
clung to their ancestral religions and lifeways with greater tenacity than many
other Indian peoples. *The Delight
Makers*, painted by Hopi artist Fred Kabotie
in 1940, portrays the clowns called *koshares* as
they poke fun at human folly and weaknesses. Their
stylized antics, use of obscenity and heckling of
onlookers provoke great hilarity — and reinforce
traditional ways and mores.

was the factor that forced these people to abandon many of their spectacular architectural accomplishments and retreat to larger population centers. For from about 1150, when we know that such a prolonged dry period set in, the Anasazi inhabited fewer but larger pueblos. Many of them, such as those at Mesa Verde in southwestern Colorado, were built in natural rock shelters beneath precipitous cliffs. These were virtually impregnable to attackers and might have been designed with defense in mind. During the later Pueblo period, the Anasazi were moving south and east, abandoning their more northern range, possibly, and searching for areas of greater environmental stability where they could continue their pueblo life-style. Much later, the Spanish found Apacheans farming in northern New Mexico on lands abandoned by the Anasazi. Presumably they were able to live on those lands because their population density was much lower than that of the Pueblo peoples and they could supplement the produce of tiny plots with game and wild plants.

Today a group of Pueblo Indians who speak Keresan dialects inhabits seven pueblos along and near central New Mexico's Rio Grande River Valley, one of which, Acoma, has been occupied continuously for 1,000 years. The origin of the Keresan language is unknown, but its speakers believe that their first homes were in the west and north. Archaeological evidence substantiates their tales; many scholars consider the Chaco Canyon region, once part of the territory of the Anasazi, to have been the former homelands of these Keresan speakers. The people of Taos Pueblo, speakers of Tanoan, probably had a Plains origin and were influenced by the Chacoans after their arrival in the Southwest. Also Tanoan speakers, the Tewa live with the Uto-Aztecan-speaking Hopis and in several Rio Grande pueblos, while the Towa are concentrated in the Rio Grande pueblo of Jemez.

Farther to the west, the best-known inheritors of the Anasazi culture are the peoples of the Hopi and Zuni pueblos. Their pottery traditions can be traced archaeologically to the Anasazi Basketmaker period of 1,500 years ago.

The Hopi and Zuni may be able to trace their roots to the Mogollon as well. Because of past population movements, the Hopi, the Zuni and the people of the Rio Grande pueblos are heirs to a rich cultural commingling. Fred Plog of New Mexico State University has observed that "People, not cultures, moved...and arranged their organizational practices in response to the changed circumstances in which they found themselves." Whether of Puebloan, Apachean or other origin, the Indians of the Southwest today maintain a proud link to their past and their environment that few recent cultures can boast. ✴

Pueblo peoples represent the supernatural beings called *kachinas* with small painted dolls. The thirteenth-century A.D. figurine above, from a cave in southwestern New Mexico, may be an early form of such a doll. The clowns in the painting, opposite, are regarded by the Hopi as the fathers of the powerful kachinas, who number in the hundreds.

MEXICO

We all know of the glory of ancient Mexico and of its source of power—the cultivation of maize and other plants. But did New World agriculture begin in Mexico and, if so, how and where? How did the rise of the great civilizations of Mesoamerica affect other North American cultures? These two fundamental but persistently perplexing questions have challenged archaeologists for the past half century.

The development of *Zea mays*—corn or maize, as it is known to most of the world—is especially significant. In ancient times, "Indian corn" became the staple of almost all sedentary native groups both in Mesoamerica and in temperate North America and eventually became the world's third most important crop. But before we can consider the origin of New World agriculture and its spread, we must go back to the beginnings.

First, let us review the geographic arena where such greatness arose. Mesoamerica—archaeologically defined as the central Valley of Mexico; southern Mexico, including the Yucatán Peninsula; and the lowland region called the Petén that straddles the modern borders of Mexico, Guatemala and Belize—was the cradle of the most splendid civilizations of the continent: the Olmec, Teotihuacáno, Zapotec, Mayan, Toltec and Aztec.

In the earliest days, small bands of hunters following Pleistocene animals across the continent's breadth pursued them into Mexico, then to the Isthmus of Panama and beyond. The stone tools of Paleo-Indians discovered in Mesoamerica resemble those found scattered throughout the continent. Even the lifeways of later Archaic era natives in Mexico resembled those of northern peoples as cultures everywhere adapted to the changing climates and resources that accompanied the waning of the ice ages. Yet as Archaic traditions developed in Mexico, a new element appeared on the scene, one that would accelerate the region's pace of social evolution and radically alter the course of events throughout much of the New World. That element was agriculture.

To call the adoption of agriculture a revolution is to misname it, for its impact seems sudden only when viewed through the foreshortened lens of historical hindsight. As Robert McCormick Adams has written: "In short, the Food-Producing Revolution was a 'process' and not an 'event' in that it developed gradually"—indeed, over a long enough span for potential crop plants to be altered genetically. Adams, now Secretary of the Smithsonian, wrote in his classic study of Mesoamerican and Mesopotamian cities, *The Evolution of Urban Society*: "It is a truism that complex, civilized societies depend upon a subsistence base that is sufficiently intensive and reliable to permit sedentary, nucleated settle-

The jade and serpentine figurines, above, came to light at La Venta, a once spectacular island center of the Olmec culture—Mesoamerica's first great civilization. From six to ten inches high, the effigies appear as they were found, grouped around a leader to whom they seem to be listening intently. Consummate Olmec sculptors carved figurines by the thousands, often portraying infants and dwarfs. Opposite, a jade mask from about nine centuries before Christ offers further testimony to the magnificent artistry of the Olmec. Highly prized jade was sought far and wide, and provided impetus for this civilization's expansion.

247

Mexico

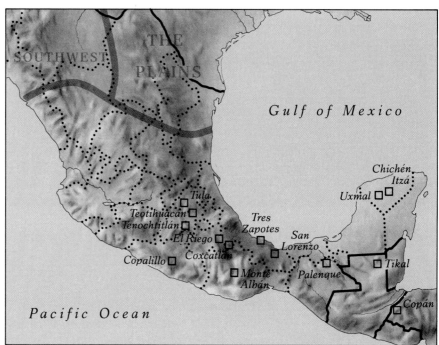

ments, a circumstance that...certainly in the long run has implied agriculture."

As some hunter-gatherer societies, propelled by local circumstances, evolved into village communities, the harvesting of domesticated plants fostered increasingly complex social organization. The final results of this cultural process were the great Mesoamerican civilizations.

Eighty years ago scholars began to realize that the first agriculturalists probably lived in regions where a good deal of energy was necessary to gather sufficient plant and animal foods. To find the original setting of agricultural beginnings— a place where people started controlling the source of their food supply—archaeologists began looking in semiarid areas, marginal environments in which Archaic peoples might have been pressed to nurture useful plants to augment naturally occurring forage. By the 1960s, the search for the homeland of corn cultivation had been narrowed to the highlands south of Mexico City, and Richard S. MacNeish, then with the R. S. Peabody Foundation, brought his practice of systematic theoretical and practical investigation to bear upon the central regions of Mexico.

Starting in the lower reaches of the region where farming might have begun, MacNeish meticulously surveyed dry caves and rock shelters— sites where organic materials had the best chance of being preserved for thousands of years. His search finally led to the Tehuacán Valley in Mexico's south central highlands.

After investigating thirty-eight caves with no success, MacNeish was rewarded by the thirty-ninth. He and his local guides found six preserved cobs of early domestic corn, three of them smaller and more primitive than anything ever seen by modern eyes, including 3,000-year-old corn found earlier in New Mexico's Bat Cave. These southern Mexican specimens proved to be 5,600 years old.

MacNeish has written: "The people of the valley of Tehuacán lived for thousands of years as collectors of wild vegetable and animal foods before they made their first timid efforts as agriculturalists. It would be foolhardy to suggest that the inhabitants of this arid highland pocket of Mexico were the first or the only people in the Western Hemisphere to bring wild corn under cultivation. On the contrary, the New World's invention of agriculture will probably prove to be geographically fragmented."

Indeed, other plants were grown first in different parts of Mesoamerica. As Muriel Porter Weaver has written in *The Aztecs, Maya, and Their Predecessors*, "squash, avocado, chili peppers, and amaranth, followed by corn, were the first domesticates in the Tehuacán sequence, while pumpkins, bottle gourds, beans, and chili peppers preceded corn in the north." Despite geographical variations in the sequence of plant domestication, the general development of agricultural practices can be discussed for the entire culture area.

In the Tehuacán Valley, corn was fully domesticated by 5000 B.C. It is also possible that cotton was being planted by this time. Avocados and chili peppers had been domesticated as early as 8,500 years ago. But the presence of these domesticated plants in the archaeological record does not mean that the older hunting-and-gathering way of life was quickly and simply abandoned.

In the Valley of Oaxaca, the University of Michigan's Kent V. Flannery and his colleagues excavated a small cave site called Guilá Naquitz. They unearthed remains of bottle gourds and a single domesticated squash seed in a layer later radiocarbon dated at between 8750 and 7840 B.C. These are the earliest dates yet established for any domesticated plant in North America. It is possible, postulates Flannery, that the use of dried bottle gourds to transport water represented a technological breakthrough enabling people to range farther afield in their search for food. Also at Guilá Naquitz, Flannery found other squash remains dated at 7000 B.C. and wild runner beans dated at 8750 to 6700 B.C.

There was a 6,500-year period between the initial domestication of the

From the great Olmec center of La Venta came this colossal head, above, and three others. Huge blocks of basalt, a hard volcanic stone, were dragged from the quarry through twenty-five miles of jungle by hundreds of laborers and then floated on rivers to sites in the states of Tabasco and Veracruz. There, artisans produced images weighing up to twenty tons.

On an artificially flattened mountaintop called Monte Albán in southern Mexico, Zapotec culture reached its zenith between A.D. 400 and 600. Surrounding the Grand Plaza are twenty-two tombs, twelve graves, fifty-one burial offering sites and a multitude of dwellings.

avocado and the chili pepper and the appearance of sedentary farming villages about 2000 B.C. During this long period the Archaic peoples of central Mexico gradually began to gather in groups during the wet season and cultivate the crops they had purposely planted earlier in the year. In the drier seasons the groups would split into smaller bands and proceed into their traditional territories to hunt and gather until the rains came again. These seasonal shifts began about 4800 B.C.

By 3500 B.C. some peoples were probably living in pit houses year-round. Corn was certainly being planted by this time, and the *sapote*, the sapodilla or marmalade tree, which produces an edible fruit, had also been domesticated. The sapote and other plants were not only domesticated but exported from region to region, where new genetic varieties established themselves.

Other innovations arose, some not of a biological nature. Pottery first appeared in Mesoamerica about 2300 B.C., when truly settled villages began to emerge. Crude vessels of gravelly clay have been recovered from cave sites in Tehuacán and at Puerto Marques near Acapulco. During the same time, older types of hunting artifacts such as dart or spear points and atlatls began to give way to the characteristic Mesoamerican obsidian blades—long, prismatic, knifelike blades more suited to cutting tasks such as leather work and food preparation. In the centuries before 2000 B.C., the dog, which had accompanied humans from Asia to the New World, appeared in the region. Dogs apparently became a source of food, for numerous canine bones have been found in middens. All this archaeological evidence reveals that while hunting and gathering still played a role in food production, by about 2000 B.C. most Meso-americans lived in villages and farmed.

Mesoamerica's Pre-Classic period (2000 B.C. to A.D. 300) marks the beginning of the increasing evolution and spread of civilization. The Classic (A.D. 300 to 900) and Post-Classic (900 to 1520) periods span the magnificent era of pyramids, temples, huge administrative "palaces," sculptures and paintings, all testimonials to the cultural transformation that had had its origins in small plots of primitive corn, beans and squash.

Villages dotted the Mesoamerican landscape at the beginning of the Pre-Classic period. Most of these sites are less than five acres and contain about ten or twelve houses. The houses were rectangular, about ten by eighteen feet, and the floors were sunk slightly below ground level. Sand from nearby streams was poured on floors to keep the houses clean and dry. Wattle-and-daub construction techniques were used, and in the highland Valley of Oaxaca a whitewash similar to a pottery slip covered the walls.

In a typical pre-Classic village in the Valley of Oaxaca, described by Flannery and Marcus C. Winter, graves and bell-shaped storage pits usually were dug beside each house. Specialized crafts such as leather working, shell and macaw feather ornament production and obsidian blade making took place in specific houses in the village. Trade was already extensive; obsidian blades have been found along trade routes that traversed hundreds of miles.

From this socioeconomic foundation grew the first great Mesoamerican civilization, the Olmec. The earliest Olmec remains have been found at San Lorenzo, near the Mexican Gulf Coast, and are dated at 1250 to 1150 B.C. La Venta is the largest Olmec site, occupied from 1100 to 400 B.C. Tres Zapotes, the other major center, was occupied for only 400 years by the Olmec, from 500 to 100 B.C. Recently, a fourth Olmec site has been located at the town of Copalillo, near Acapulco, a find that pushes the first appearance of stone architecture back to 1200 B.C.

Rich funereal art, right, perhaps the most characteristic Zapotec cultural trait, appears in mural form at Mexico's National Museum of Anthropology and History. Recovered from a tomb at Monte Albán, the designs include representations of temples, the Plumed Serpent and other deities.

La Venta is famous for its 100,000-cubic-foot, heavily eroded earthen mound. The site's central plaza and surrounding earthen mounds display the distinctive form of what would become the typical Mesoamerican religious center.

In 1939, the Tres Zapotes site yielded convincing evidence that the Mesoamerican calendar had originated in the Pre-Classic period and not with the later Maya. The Smithsonian's Matthew W. Stirling discovered a stela or stone pillar inscribed with both an Olmec-style jaguar head and a date in the distinctive bar-and-dot numerical notation previously thought to be a Mayan invention of the first century A.D. Since the 1940s, many numerical symbols in the Olmec style have been found at the great sixth-century-B.C. Zapotec center of Monte Albán, in south central Mexico.

The Olmec are known for their monumental stone heads as well as for bas-relief sculpture, massive ceremonial centers and sophisticated drainage systems. Their extensive drainage systems were built to maintain reservoirs and perhaps ceremonial pools. The colossal stone heads — weighing as much as twenty tons — are either the individual portraits of Olmec rulers or the stylized portrait of an Olmec deity. The basaltic stone from which some were made was transported forty-five miles from the quarry to San Lorenzo.

Today many archaeologists regard the Olmec as an "interaction sphere," analogous to the Hopewell of the Northeast, rather than as a unitary culture. In an interaction sphere, a number of distinct regional cultures share symbols, rituals, religious concepts and perhaps other

Zapotec astronomers may have used Monte Albán's central structure, above left, as an astronomical observatory. Rulers and ritualists of the highest rank inhabited some of the buildings around the Grand Plaza, while the majority of the people lived in structures that clung to mountainside terraces. Above, modern Zapotec Indians recreate an ancient dance. In ancient times, their headdresses would have indicated status.

cultural traits. Nevertheless, the Olmec are considered Mexico's "mother culture." Their economic and perhaps even military influence stretched from central Mexico to El Salvador, and highly prized jade, serpentine and obsidian were traded throughout the area. The Olmec religion, which included the frequently found symbol of the half-human, half-jaguar figure, became the basis for the religious practices of the later civilizations.

The Classic period began about A.D. 300 with the rise of the astonishing city of Teotihuacán in the central Valley of Mexico. With a population of 200,000 during its height between the fourth and sixth centuries A.D., Teotihuacán rivaled the glory of ancient Greece and Rome. The city's ceremonial center, nearly two miles long, was dominated by the Pyramid of the Sun. This awe-inspiring structure measures 200 feet high and 700 feet on a side. Religion was a vital part of the people's daily lives; from the many large apartment complexes that made up this crowded city, thousands of figurines, censers and ritual vessels have been recovered. A large elite class of priests and scholars must have been necessary to maintain the temple complex. Teotihuacán was sectioned into different neighborhoods or *barrios* for the specialized production of obsidian blades, pottery and cloth. Even farmers lived within the city and walked out to the irrigated fields to work.

Teotihuacán dominated central Mexico for the first six centuries A.D.

A serpent's head, above, juts from the elaborate Temple of Quetzalcoatl, built at the same time as the famed Sun Pyramid, right, both from the site of Teotihuacán, a powerful city-state predating the Toltec and Aztec cultures. Such was this city's architectural and mythic magnitude that its ruins became a place of pilgrimage and adulation for later cultures — the Aztecs may have held religious services at the base of the pyramid 700 years after the city was abandoned.

and was even able to influence the Mayan civilization to the south for a time when a king with northern Mexican ties ruled the city of Tikal in what is today Guatemala. The power of Teotihuacán resulted from its extensive irrigation system, which made possible the production of crops sufficient to feed its enormous urban population, and from its control of the highly valued, green-gold obsidian of the Cerro de las Navajas near Pachuca, Mexico.

Sudden and mysterious, the collapse of Teotihuacán began about A.D. 650 after a large part of the city's population moved away to the east. Although no direct evidence exists for warfare or invasion, the city was burned fifty years later, and by 750 only a few lived in what had been one of the world's great urban centers.

As mighty Teotihuacán approached its decline, the Mayan civilization to the south began its most explosive period of creative energy and cultural dynamism. The Classic period receives its name from this efflorescence. Located in the Yucatán Peninsula and in the tropical lowland region of Guatemala, Belize and southernmost Mexico called the Petén, such Mayan cities as Uxmal, Copán, Tikal and Chichén Itzá became great centers of art and commerce between A.D. 300 and 900.

The first clearly Mayan artifacts date from about 500 B.C. With the passage of time, hundreds of ceremonial centers arose with surrounding populations comprising a society of competing, warlike city-states. At

L eft, Mexican artist Diego Rivera's conception of a market at the great Aztec city of Tenochtitlán centers on the bounty of the earth and, above all, the importance of maize in Aztec life. While cobs rarely exceeded an inch in length 7,000 years ago, they eventually enlarged through hybridization, perhaps with such species as the wild grass *Tripsacum,* above.

their zenith, the Maya created a dramatic architectural style based on the corbeled arch, a stepped rather than curved form, and introduced the mathematical concept of zero. Their astronomers made long-term, highly accurate observations of celestial movements from which they constructed a calendrical system called the Sacred Round. They based it on a 260-day year and a 52-year cycle. With their superb calendar and the only known form of writing in the New World, a phonetic system using glyphs carved on stone or written on processed bark paper, the princes of the Mayan city-states recorded their accomplishments in detail. Some glyphs have survived to be deciphered.

Mayan society consisted of four classes: the semidivine elite; the scribes, accountants and sculptors; the artisans, including toolmakers and weavers; and the peasant farmers. The civilization rested on intensive agricultural methods. Forest and brush were cleared with fire, and sophisticated terracing and drainage systems created arable land. Two crops per year were probably harvested in the most fertile areas.

Yet, despite their ingenuity, originality and energy, many of the Mayan cities suffered a swift collapse when in the ninth century A.D. the Maya abandoned their cities. Temple and administrative construction ceased, and defensive works became more common. Some scholars have attributed the decline to increased competition and warfare among the city-states, while others argue that Mayan populations overtaxed the productivity of the available agricultural lands, soil infertility leading inevitably and quickly to the dispersal of the urban populations. In any case, by about 950 the Maya were no longer so competitive a force in Mesoamerica. Their descendants, however, still live in the region and speak Mayan languages.

Other Mesoamerican urban centers existed outside the Mayan and Teotihuacáno spheres of influence. The Zapotecs of southwestern Mexico built chains of hilltop fortresses all around the Valley of Oaxaca and a great mountaintop temple complex at Monte Albán. There they entombed the bodies of deceased nobles with some of the most astounding treasures ever found in North America. The Toltecs of the city of Tula, north of Teotihuacán, extended their influence as the Maya declined. In the tenth century A.D. the Toltecs conquered the Mayan city of Chichén Itzá and succeeded the Maya as the dominant culture in Mesoamerica.

But it was the Aztecs who built the last and in some ways most spectacular of all the pre-European civilizations of Mesoamerica. Migrating from the north to the Valley of Mexico in the 1200s, by 1345 the Aztecs founded the fabulous city of Tenochtitlán on the swampy shore of Lake Texcoco and began to expand their own power. Tenochtitlán

Time has deeply eroded a wooden sculpture of a Mayan dignitary, opposite, of the sixth to ninth centuries A.D. Carved ornaments, a stole and a heavy belt clothe the figure—the only surviving piece of its kind. Above, sun god embraces moon goddess in a Late Classic (A.D. 600-900) figurine from the Mayan necropolis island of Jaina. Mayan myth explains that the sun god eternally pursues the moon goddess across the sky.

Wind-driven waves crash against cliffs at Tulum, a Mayan city of the thirteenth century. Some anthropologists suggest that Tulum may have been a point of departure for Mayan voyages to Mexico's Gulf Coast or to the Caribbean shore of Central America.

grew to be one of the largest cities anywhere on earth. When the Spanish under Hernán Cortés entered Tenochtitlán in 1519 they found a city more populous than any in Spain, perhaps larger than any in Europe save London. The marketplace of Tenochtitlán could accommodate 60,000 people. The recently excavated *Templo Mayor*, or Great Temple, buried for more than four centuries beneath post-conquest Mexico City, rivaled in splendor and magnificence any temple complex ever built anywhere. The Aztecs created a city surrounded by the water of Lake Texcoco and crisscrossed by canals. Even their agricultural lands were raised from the lake bottom into low mounds of fertile soil called *chinampas*. Some suggestion of the *chinampas* can still be seen in the "floating gardens" of Lake Xochimilco, the surviving remnant of Lake Texcoco.

Much has been written of the splendor and the cruelty of the Aztecs, of their ruthless subjugation of the peoples around them, of their human sacrifices and stern deities. For all of their monuments and display, the empire of the Aztecs rested on the tribute of often reluctant and resentful vassals. When Hernán Cortés and his small band of Spanish adventurers landed on Mexico's east coast in 1519, they quickly defeated the allies of the Aztecs, who then joined the Spanish. With their assistance and because of weakness and uncertainty among the leaders of the Aztecs, Cortés and his men were able to overthrow the Aztecs, thus ending Mesoamerica's Post-Classic period.

Ever wakeful Chacmool, sacred sentinel of the Toltec empire, guards the threshold to the temple of the rain god in the Mayan city of Chichén Itzá, top left. Top, archaeologists use a satellite-linked positional locator to pinpoint the exact longitude, latitude and altitude of the Mayan temple at Chunhuhuv. Above, a death's-head frieze graced a ball court at Chichén Itzá. Losers in a sacred game often forfeited their lives.

259

Uxmal, an astonishing city-state of the Maya, rises in the Yucatán Peninsula and bears witness to the architectural genius of its builders. An elaborate door lintel, bottom, reveals the skill of Mayan sculptors. The city itself contains a rounded pyramid on an oval base and a palace frieze created from 20,000 dressed stones.

The archaeologists who first began to explore the ruins of Mesoamerica were easily convinced by these great civilizations' lost splendors that Mesoamerica must have been the creative font for all the important cultural traits and technical achievements of North America. It seemed to them that everything from moundbuilding to cosmology and human sacrifice in the Southeast and pottery design and rubble-wall masonry in the Southwest must have derived from Mexican influences. The burial mounds and earthworks of the Adena and Hopewell peoples seemingly had their origins in the pyramids of Mesoamerica.

These all-embracing cultural "diffusion theories" held great weight for a long period because of the general similarities between the material culture of Mesoamerica and that of some North American societies. For example, the Mississippian practice of arranging flat-topped mounds around a central plaza and intriguing parallels among art motifs and styles of the Southeast and Mexico tended to award the diffusion theories precedence over other possibilities.

Continuing research, however, has brought many authorities to the belief that these cultural traits did not derive directly from Mesoamerica. This opinion, says State University of New York archaeologist Vincas Steponaitis, is based in part on the compelling fact that not one clearly

ifteen-foot-tall warrior effigies watch over the site of Tula, capital of the Toltecs. These basalt columns may once have supported the wooden roof of the great temple at Tula. Each figure holds an atlatl and a bag of incense.

Mosaics of shell and turquoise on a double-headed serpent and the handle of a sacrificial blade of flaked chert still gleam after half a millennium. Seventeen inches long, the snake served as a pectoral, a dramatic chest ornament. Aztec emperor Moctezuma II may have presented both pieces to Spanish explorer and conqueror Hernán Cortés in the early 1500s.

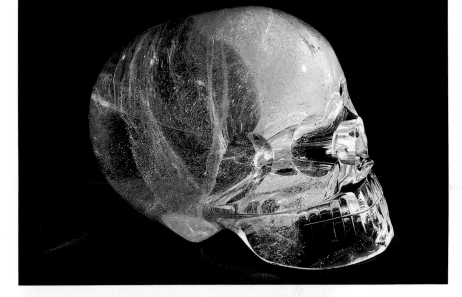

A transparent skull, top right, exquisitely wrought from rock crystal, reflects the Aztec preoccupation with death. Right, a gentle reminder of domestic life, the Lord of Fire, Xiuhtecuhtli, reposes. Such a figure occupied every Aztec hearth — new fires were kindled in a hollow of the idol's head.

Mesoamerican artifact has been found in the Southeast—nor have Southeastern artifacts been found in Mexico. James B. Griffin, the University of Michigan's senior authority, states the case even more emphatically:

"There are no proven indications of either large or small group movements from Mexico into the Southeast at any time period.... It is accepted that on a hunting-gathering level, populations in south Texas did have some amount of interaction with similar groups in adjacent northern Mexico. The early cucurbits (gourd and squash) of the Southeast are evidence of this. The southeastern use of earspools may indicate transmission. The platform mound and plaza has always been a prime candidate for derivation from Mexico, but... this is not the only possible interpretation. Maize and beans arrived at different times from the Southwest, and direct introduction from Mexico of either cultigen at any time is not likely. The known religious practices and beliefs of Southeastern Indians are viewed as essentially a product of regional development over millennia."

Yet even if many archaeologists agree that it is unlikely that Mesoamerican "missionaries" came to the Southeast to teach its inhabitants how to build mounds, still some diffusion in both directions took place. It is inconceivable that ideas did not diffuse from culture to culture. Ideas have crossed cultural boundaries in every other part of the world and must have done so in the New World. And some seeming diffusion may not have been diffusion at all. Recent evidence suggests that peoples of the Southeast may have independently domesticated squash.

Some scholars have suggested the existence of an Indian core culture, a set of shared beliefs or concepts that came with the peoples from Beringia. Such a core culture would be somewhat analogous to the Graeco-Roman, Judeo-Christian heritage shared by most European peoples.

And the fact remains that perhaps the most influential achievement of all occurred in Mexico—the development of corn, which then spread to the Southwest and elsewhere in North America. Surely no other American invention had so profound an effect on the lives of many of the continent's peoples.

Thus ends our story of North America before the Europeans. Who can help but wonder what might have happened if for some reason the Europeans had not come? What might the continent have brought forth? Of course, we will never know. The Europeans did come, beginning with the Norse, and in the ensuing centuries wrenched the continent and its peoples out of their old ways and into new patterns of change, conflict and accommodation. ✺

Aztec priests ripped human hearts from the chests of sacrificial victims and deposited them in this imposing font, opposite. The altarpiece, a massive jaguar, measures seven feet in length and weighs six tons. Above, image of a dismembered goddess came to light during commercial excavations at Mexico City in 1978. The eleven-foot-high sculpture represents Coyolxauhqui, slaughtered by her brother Huitzilopochtli, the war god and patron of the Aztec capital. The abasement of the goddess, shown naked and cut asunder, reminded conquered peoples of the power of their Aztec overlords.

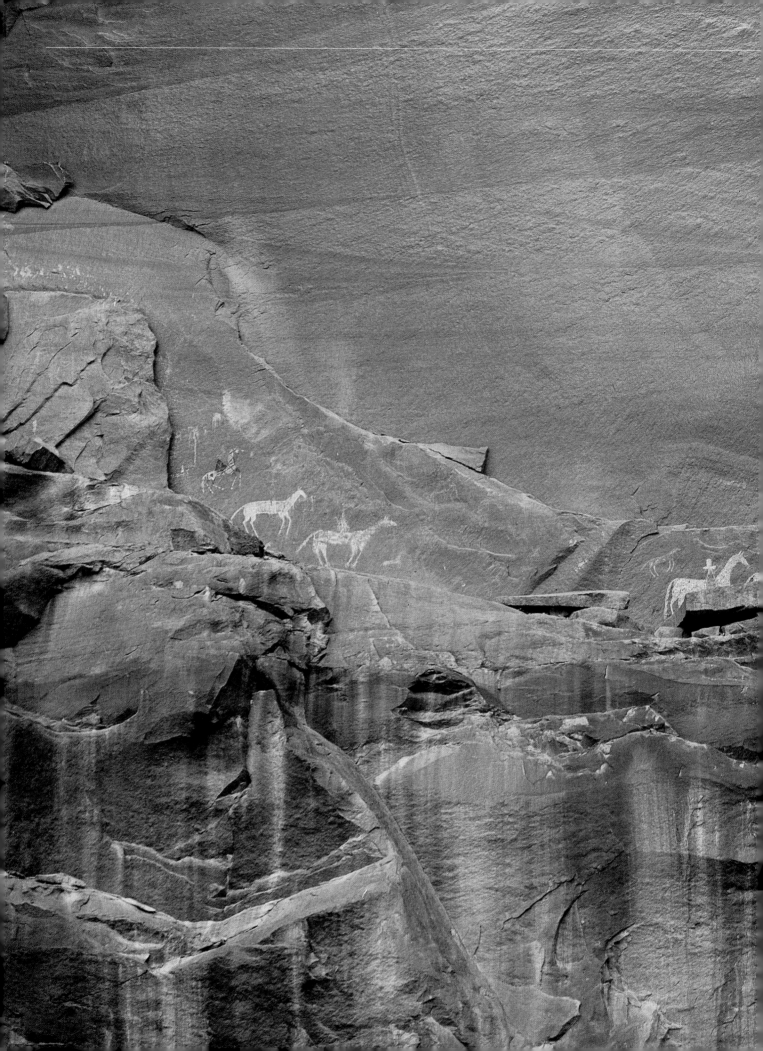

THE COMING OF THE EUROPEANS

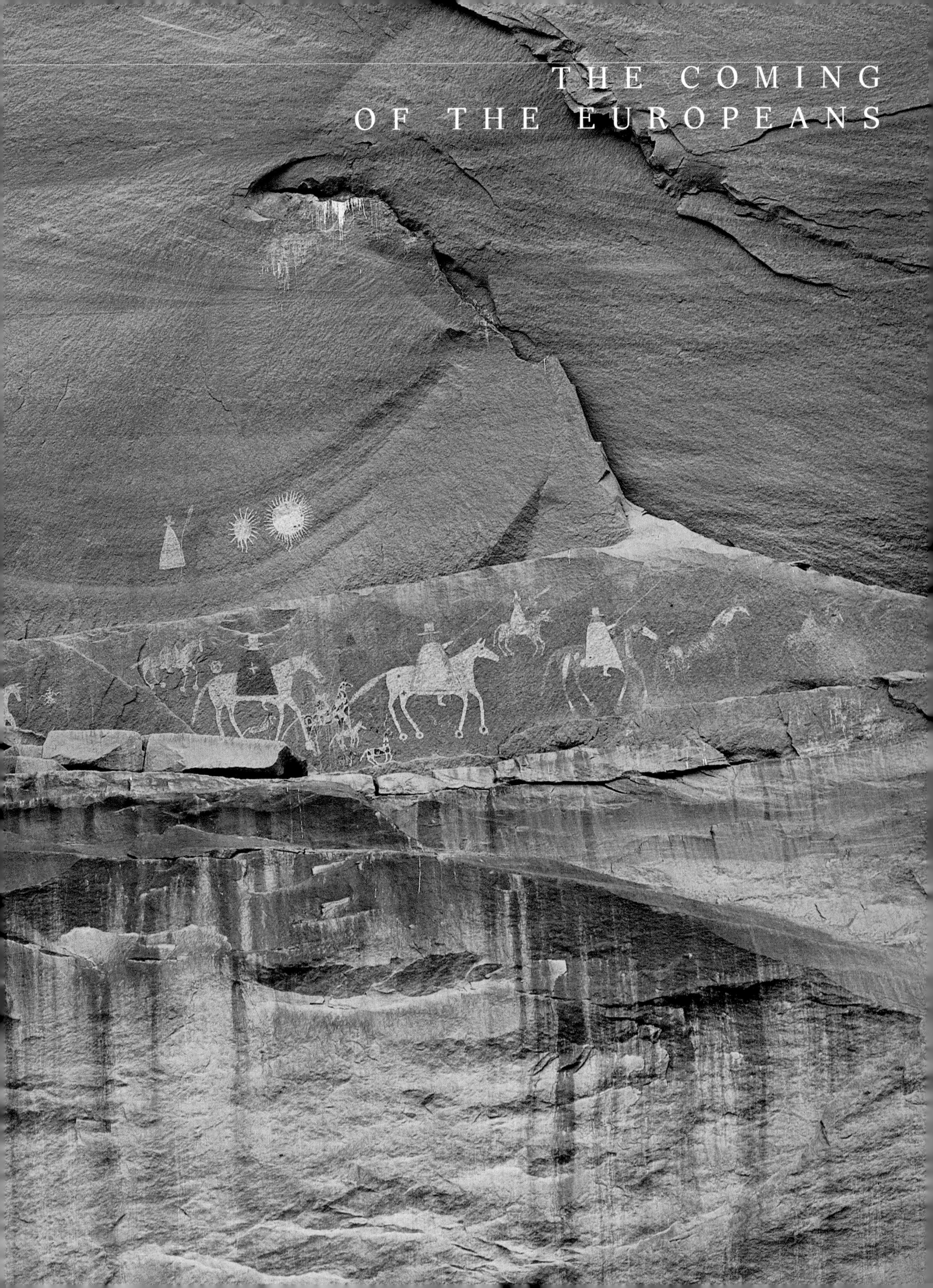

EPILOGUE

by Wilcomb E. Washburn
Director, Office of American Studies,
Smithsonian Institution

The first Europeans came to the New World much in the manner of the first Indians: moving out from the farthest northern reaches of the Eurasian landmass across the sometimes frozen waters that separated it from the unknown world. The ancestors of the native Americans approached from the west on foot; the Europeans from the east in ships. We know now that what differentiated the two movements was not only the times they occurred but also their levels of technical sophistication and degrees of immunity from disease.

In fact, when the earliest immigrants from Europe met the descendants of the earlier arrivals from Asia, the technological levels of the two peoples were not far apart. Indeed, the Norse explorers from Scandinavia, who late in the tenth century reached Vinland (the North American mainland) after colonizing successively Iceland and Greenland, were repulsed by the natives. The Norse sagas provide us with the dramatic story of the conflicts between the Norse and the "Skraellings," the native peoples whom they encountered. One such account describes how the Norse women had to rally their men to protect their settlement against a Skraelling attack.

Because the power differential between the Skraellings and the Norse was minor if not nonexistent, and because the Norse were operating in an inhospitable environment far from their home bases in Greenland, Iceland and the Scandinavian peninsula, the settlements they established on the mainland (and indeed those in Greenland) were eventually abandoned or overrun.

By that time, explorers and adventurers from southern Europe were about to make the breakthrough that is usually associated with European settlement in the New World. But even Columbus and his followers did not arrive with overwhelming technological superiority. The native inhabitants of the New World had the same bow-and-arrow technology from which Europeans had only recently graduated to crude firearms. Both sides had shields and protective clothing, but Europeans had iron, which gave their sharp weapons and durable household utensils (such as cooking pots) a decisive advantage over stone tools and clay utensils. Nevertheless, the disparity in power could have been overcome by effective leadership and by the weight of numbers. But it was not. In part, this outcome was the result of superior European organization; in part, from the use of terror weapons such as horses and dogs of war. Even more devastating were the epidemic diseases brought by Europeans, against which the natives lacked immunity.

The tale of the Spanish conquest of much of what is now Central and

Karl Bodmer painted the Sioux woman Chan-Chä-Uiá-Teüin, opposite, while on an early nineteenth-century trip to the Great Plains as artist for a German prince whose interest was natural history. Although the woman pictured was a member of the Teton Sioux, the translation of her name — "Woman of the Crow Nation" — implies a connection with the Sioux's bitterest enemy, the Crow, suggesting that she may have been taken captive in a raid. Above, the hooded figure carved in bone by a Thule artisan may be a Norseman. The Norse inhabited settlements on southwest Greenland between A.D. 1000 and 1500. Inuit contact with the Norse was sporadic; most scholars agree that it did not dramatically affect Inuit lifeways.

Early seventeenth-century French explorer and fur trader Samuel de Champlain led the Hurons against the Mohawks in a battle on the shore of the lake bearing his name. The French believed that by helping their Indian allies secure the St. Lawrence valley, they could increase their profits from the volume of highly prized furs. The palm trees and hammocks support the notion that the artist was unfamiliar with upper New York State and certainly did not witness the battle.

South America has been dramatically told many times. Nothing can add to its grim pathos. The Spanish conquered, as the Aztecs and the Incas had conquered before them. But in the process they stamped out—deliberately and ruthlessly—the rich culture of those they defeated. They burned the codices containing Indian writings; they melted down the exquisitely wrought gold ornaments that now serve (in the few examples coming down to us) as expressions of an elevated native aesthetic tradition.

Historians fiercely continue the debate over the "black legend of Spanish cruelty." The issue turns on the veracity of Bartolomé de Las Casas, the Spanish priest who spent his life decrying Spain's crimes in the Indies and attempting to ameliorate the lot of the natives who were its victims. Since Spain was, throughout the centuries of conquest and settlement of the Americas, in constant rivalry with other European powers, particularly the English and the Dutch, Las Casas's books were grist for the mills of Spain's enemies, and they gleefully translated and reprinted his accounts of terror and cruelty in the Indies as justifications for their own ambitions to share the spoils of the New World. The argument over the "black legend" should by now be a technical investigation among historians of all nations, and should center on how many natives were killed in fact and on how accurately Las Casas reported the cruelty of the Spaniards. Instead, because history is not entirely detached from national passions, historians have tended to line up on national grounds and to argue in generalities about Las Casas's probably exaggerated figures, his emotional commitment to the Indians and his medieval religious outlook. Yet the fact remains that the Spanish conquest *was* extraordinary in its destructiveness and cruelty: the only question is the extent of these elements.

The French, in contrast to the Spanish, are usually credited with a special understanding of the Indians and an ability to adapt to native ways even while encouraging an appreciation of French culture. This picture is only partly accurate. The French, who colonized the vast reaches of Canada and whose *coureurs de bois* and *voyageurs* traversed the enormous lengths of North America's great rivers, learned by necessity to coexist with the Indians. Outnumbered and distant from their sources of power, the French explorers and traders in the interior of New France ingratiated themselves with the locally powerful natives, marrying their daughters according to the custom of the land (that is, informally and not according to the rites of the Roman Catholic Church) and sharing in the profitable fur trade of the interior. The plenitude of present-day Indians bearing French names in the areas of French penetration, such as the Mississippi Valley and St. Lawrence Valley, bear witness to this process of physical integration.

Yet the French could, on occasion, rival the Spanish in severity. Their virtually total destruction of the Natchez Indians in the lower Mississippi Valley as a penalty for allegedly treacherous behavior in the early eighteenth century provides one example, as does their attempt to cut off the Chickasaws—allies of the English—during the international and intertribal rivalries in the Southeast in this period.

The ultimate prize of dominance, not only in the temperate north, but throughout the Western Hemisphere, went to the English and their rebellious offspring, the Americans. The Colossus of the North, as the United States is often termed by its neighbors to the south, springs from the heritage bequeathed by the last of the active European powers to explore and settle the New World.

The English were not the most lovable of the European settlers. They tended to stay aloof from the natives, engaging them in neither a passionate nor destructive embrace. Indeed, one of the Indians' complaints about the English was that they refused to intermarry and establish alliances in the traditional native manner. Many Americans, such as Robert Beverley in seventeenth-century Virginia and Thomas Jefferson in eighteenth-century Virginia, urged the benefits of intermarriage with the Indians in bringing together the best qualities of both races as well as to establish

Sioux Indians of the Great Plains painted visions and other designs onto skins used to cover undecorated bison-hide shields. The two horsemen confronting each other with lances may symbolize the clash of the White and the Indian.

271

peace. But their aims were frustrated. The English colonists, who often included women, and who sought land to farm rather than people to exploit, were less directly hostile but ultimately more destructive of the Indian nations with which they interacted. Although America provided a vast extent of land (as English philosopher John Locke said, "In the beginning, all the world was America"), competition for it was robust and too often the cause of conflict and war between the races. With the technological edge provided by firearms, swords and the like, the English tended to be victorious, and unforgiving in their treatment of defeated enemies. Captured natives were often shipped off to the West Indies sugar cane plantations as slaves.

And yet it was the English, and not the Spanish or French, who dealt with the Indian tribes as autonomous powers, with whom treaties were made as with European nations. The English genius, as scholars have noted, was pragmatic; expedience was considered an appropriate guide (much to the contempt of the more logical French and autocratic Spanish). English recognition of the fact that the Indian nations existed as powers to be dealt with (however much such notions were inconsistent with the royal land grants and charters that tended to ignore the juridical rights of non-Christian powers) led to treaties that remain to this day as valid expressions of Anglo-American and Indian commitments and agreements. Although the treaty-making process was ended in 1871 by unilateral assertion of the U.S. Congress (exercising what it called its "plenary power" over American Indian affairs), the treaties made prior to that date were not invalidated but recognized as legally binding. The many disputes that have arisen from charges of violation of the provisions of these treaties are regularly considered and determined by the U.S. Supreme Court, sitting in confirmation of the fact that the Indian nations in the United States—unlike those in the rest of the Americas—exist in a government-to-government relationship with the federal government and with the states.

The "deed of gift" to the country, as Robert Frost put it in his poem "The Gift Outright," was "many deeds of war." The story of Indian-White warfare has both dark and bright chapters. Despite the mythologizing of intervening centuries and the numerous instances of treachery, the military conflicts between the intruders and the original occupants exhibited bravery, suffering and honor on both sides. While the historian, with 20/20 hindsight, can intone that the Indians lost and the invaders won, the contest was not so uneven as it now appears. Throughout the seventeenth century the numerical advantage remained with the natives. With the Indians' relatively rapid acquisition of firearms, the Europeans'

A grinding stone, symbol of life before the coming of the Europeans, lies on the grounds of the Mission San Antonio de Padua in Monterey County, California. The prehistoric Indians of California used such stones as mortars for grinding acorns into a nutritious flour.

technological advantage was minimized. Even in the eighteenth century, after the destruction or subordination of the coastal tribes by the English, the great inland confederacies of the Iroquois, Cherokees and Creeks proved reasonably successful in holding their own against the English colonies.

The American Revolution, which at first was described to the Indians as a family quarrel among English subjects in which they should take no part, soon involved the natives, most of whom chose to support King George against his aggressive colonists. The choice was tragic, for the successful rebels, with the silent acquiescence of the defeated mother country, asserted their claim to the vast reaches of "Indian Country" beyond the Appalachians to the Mississippi River. While that claim could not be finally secure until the successful conclusion of the War of 1812 and after American arms suffered humiliating defeats at the hands of the Indians in the 1790s, it was in fact asserted from the conclusion of the American Revolution.

How did the long history of Indian-White warfare affect the American people? For one thing, it gave the United States a tradition of citizens-in-

Indians of the western Subarctic crafted this eighteenth-century cedar-bark pouch with European glass beads as well as with traditional materials. Woven throughout are porcupine quills that have been soaked, flattened and dyed with pigments from berries and fungi.

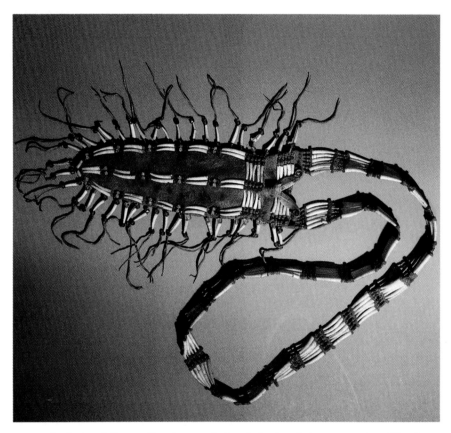

arms that stood the nation in good stead during later centuries. The long history of Indian-White conflict served as a symbolic model for the rigorous competition that lies at the heart of American economic and political life. The Indian wars taught Americans the importance of winning and the gravity of losing. The Indian, though defeated, provided symbolic references to the American spirit of achievement. The representation of Indians on American coins and stamps, and their symbolic identification with countless athletic teams, all celebrate virtues that the winner recognized in the defeated adversary. Just as many native peoples attempted to absorb the spirit and strength of brave enemies by ritual cannibalism, so did White Americans aim to absorb the virtues of the Indians by the symbolic recognition accorded their bravery.

No one can read the novels of James Fenimore Cooper or the treatment of Indians by other American writers, including Ernest Hemingway, without recognizing that the spirit of the Indian was — to use the phrase of D. H. Lawrence — absorbed in the blood of Americans. Critics have

274

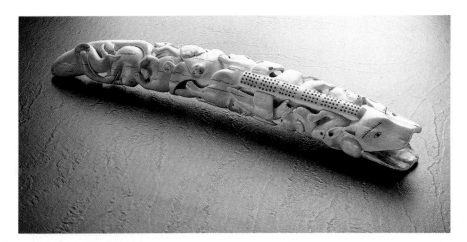

A menagerie of animals adorns a cribbage board from Nunivak Island, Alaska. Inuit artisans carved a number of these boards out of walrus tusks to sell to White visitors to Alaska during the late nineteenth and early twentieth centuries.

sometimes dismissed such celebrations of Indian traits by asserting that they accord less with Indian realities than with literary creators' attempts to criticize their own society. These two perspectives are not, however, inconsistent with each other. Perceptive observers, whether writers, military leaders, explorers or traders, were so often attracted to the lives of the natives and so critical of the restrictions of White society that they created images of "noble savages" and corrupt Europeans that can be seen as "mythical" on both sides. In fact, one can argue that while these characterizations may represent myths (in the sense of exemplars or ideals in the classical Greek tradition), they also represent reality. Why, otherwise, would history record the extraordinary fact that young Whites taken captive by the Indians so frequently resisted return to their natural parents, while Indians taken captive by Whites, or otherwise offered an opportunity to live in the White world, showed little corresponding desire to live like Whites?

There is another image in the White mind to match that of "Nature's nobleman": the drunken native wallowing in despair and poverty. Again, this stereotype has its roots in a grim reality: the effects of disease and alcohol upon the inhabitants of the Western Hemisphere. Because their ancestors had come to the New World before certain diseases ravaged the Old World, the native inhabitants of this hemisphere were left without the immunities acquired by Europeans in surviving the medieval plagues. When European settlers arrived in the New World, diseases traveled with them and spread mysteriously ahead of the carriers. Epidemics cut the populations of most tribes in half. The early Puritans interpreted the plagues that preceded their settlements as the work of God in clearing the land for His Elect. Because both parties were ignorant of the causes

275

of these illnesses, and because they disheartened as well as weakened the tribes that they struck, the Indians grew progressively less able to resist White encroachment.

Alcohol and refined sugar were substances unfamiliar to the inhabitants of the New World. They were unable to absorb them chemically and physically, as could Europeans. As a result, physical deterioration, sickness and death proceeded from these apparently neutral agents.

It is a curious fact that the "racial" feelings one assumes to have been prevalent from the start of the Indian-White relationship seem not to have been evident—at least in the form in which we are familiar with those feelings—throughout the first century or more of contact. Indians were not even seen as "red"—that is, physically different from Whites—until the eighteenth century. Rather, they were perceived as people who needed a little washing, a little education and a little Christianity to realize their potential as the equivalents of Europeans. Indeed, John White, in his compilation of drawings of Indians met in the course of the attempted settlement of Virginia, also included depictions of ancient Britons looking like the native Virginians he sketched in the New World. The literature of the period also emphasized that Indians seemed to be in a state similar to Europeans before the harsh rod of Roman civilization was laid upon them.

Native Americans, on the other hand, were often shocked by European social values (such as insensitivity to the plight of the poor) and offended by certain Christian principles (vicarious atonement was particularly bewildering to those who believed that a person could not escape responsibility for his or her actions). When the English (and Europeans generally) found that the process of conversion to Christianity and "civilization" was not necessarily desired or valued by the Indians, the stage was set for a more antagonistic relationship. Frustration over Indian "wickedness" in refusing to accept either Christ or "civilization" led English theorists ultimately to condemn the natives as hopeless, vicious and undeserving.

Given the confused and conflicting views of the Indian in the few centuries since the European "discovery" of America, is it possible to see in the Indians of today the Indians of the prehistoric past? One could as legitimately ask the same question of non-Indian Americans. Is there some norm or ideal of destiny or history that holds that a people ought to remain frozen in their life-style throughout time? On the contrary: change is the only constant in the history of all people. Many critics of American Indian policy complain that the system of democratic elections by which most (but not all) contemporary Indian tribes choose their

Red Cloud, opposite, leader of the Oglala Sioux in the mid-nineteenth century, fought against the United States government's efforts to develop a route through traditional hunting grounds into newly discovered goldfields in the Montana Territory. By the end of "Red Cloud's War" in 1868, the garrisons had been abandoned and the road closed, and Red Cloud had negotiated a treaty barring any further development of the Bozeman Trail. He wears the peace medal given him by President Ulysses S. Grant on one of several visits to Washington as a spokesman for Indian rights. Peace medals, such as the one issued by Franklin Pierce above, were given by all presidents from George Washington to Benjamin Harrison, with the exception of John Adams. Ceremonial gifts helped to cement Indian-White relations and acknowledged the status of the Indian recipient.

The Colorado River flows through a land now dominated by a patchwork of farms. White landownership and agriculture have done far more to change the land in the past 200 years than have native North Americans in over 100 centuries.

leaders was imposed by White society. Certainly the current system of tribal governments elected by the vote of tribal members is different from the system of choosing tribal leaders 300 years ago. But so is the system of choosing leaders in the White community. White Americans no longer have kings and queens to pledge their loyalty to (or to revolt against). Similarly, most native tribes no longer have traditional leaders distinguished by their military prowess, religious character or hereditary position. The burden of proof — short of being able to roll the film of time backward — lies with critics to propose what alternative system would be more appropriate in the context of today's tribal organization. Some tribes — such as the Pueblo of the Southwest — continue to organize themselves according to the will of their religious leaders. But among the Pueblo peoples, religion remains strong and central to the life of the community. In most tribes, the principal function of government is not to wage war, to determine the optimum conditions for the hunt or to organize the celebration of traditional religious ceremonies. It is, rather, to influence Congress to appropriate more funds, to urge the President to execute laws in the Indian interest and to persuade the Supreme Court to decide cases that will have the effect of protecting and enlarging Indian rights. It goes without saying that the skills of an English language education and a lawyer's training are better suited to these purposes than an ability to kill with a bow and arrow or to perform traditional sacred ceremonies.

We continue to think of the Indian as the human-in-Nature and of the White as urban, technological, a destroyer or manipulator of Nature. These images reflect a partial reality only. They reflect, to some extent, the sparse ratio of people to land in America and the more crowded conditions of Europe at the time of the White settlement of America. They also reflect the prevalence of relationships to Nature in native religious beliefs, in which the origin, life and future of humans is often tied to particular geographical areas. The religious beliefs of Europeans, on the other hand, relate more to Time than to Nature. Christian and Jewish traditions focus upon chronology, a sequence of events of significance that carries the believer from the Creation to the Last Judgment. European-derived religions have, moreover, been forced to share their hold on Western civilizations with Reason and the scientific method bequeathed by the Greeks.

But this does not mean that the Europeans transplanted to North America were unable to relate to Nature. While the "howling wilderness" filled with "wild men" that greeted the Pilgrims was, in Plymouth Governor William Bradford's words, frightening to behold, and while

the vast stretches of forests inspired both fear and hope, eventually the colonists adapted to the wilds, just as the Indians became familiar with European weapons and material culture. By 1776, James Adair, who had spent most of his life living with the Chickasaws of the Southeast, warned the general in command of British troops in the colonies to expect bad luck in dealing with the rebellious Americans because they had become "Indians" and knew how to fight in the forest.

We often assume that native Americans were the first ecologists, a notion reinforced by advertising campaigns. Scholars continue to debate the extent to which North American Indians were in fact ecologists. The best explanation is that they were not ecologists in the sense of twentieth-century interest groups that have made environmental protection their primary concern. Vine Deloria, Jr., of the University of Arizona, a leading Indian spokesman, has pointed out how Indians tend to despoil their reservations with casually tossed beer cans, auto carcasses left to deteriorate and so on. But even in the earlier, "unspoiled" phase of native existence on the continent, there is evidence, such as the bison herds driven off cliffs, to indicate that Indians were not the careful stewards of Mother Earth they are sometimes thought to be.

Most Indian religions, on the other hand, did emphasize the need to kill with what we might call "reverence," so as not to upset the powerful spirits that inhabited the universe of two-legged and four-legged creatures. Certainly the Indians, with their clan totems of animals, lived closer to and in a more intimate relationship with what we call the animal world.

Whatever the changes that have occurred over time to American Indians, one need only consider Indian achievements in the arts and literature to learn how vigorous and distinct the native heritage of America remains. This art and literature is not "traditional," one may argue. Certainly not. But it is nevertheless distinctively Indian. It is certainly not European Modern, European Gothic, European Baroque, European Post-Modern, or European "traditional" of any period (if one wishes to freeze the "true" art of a people into a particular time frame). Indians are changing as other peoples are changing. Yet they retain their identities while speaking English, wearing Western clothes, living in modern houses, borrowing techniques from the West and so on. Who but an out-of-touch intellectual would arrogantly assert that the American Indian, alone among peoples, should not change but should remain a textbook example of "the ethnographic present"? The Indians' survival in the contemporary world, different as that world is from the form uncovered by prehistoric archaeology and post-settlement ethnography, is itself a vindication of their Indianness. ✳

Peoples of Taos Pueblo, opposite, north of Santa Fe, New Mexico, maintain their traditional ways of life in the midst of late twentieth-century White society. Before her death in 1980, Maria Martinez, top, of San Ildefonso Pueblo near Taos, earned international acclaim for her traditional pottery — and her innovations of distinctive new styles. Members of the Martinez family have been potters for generations. Above, a boy draped in boughs participates in the winter Basket Dance near the Santa Clara Pueblo not far from San Ildefonso. The dance still serves to pass on important knowledge from one generation to the next.

281

INDEX

Numbers in italic signify picture references.

PICTURE CREDITS

Legend: B Bottom; C Center; L Left; R Right; T Top.

The following are abbreviations used to identify Smithsonian Institution museums and other collections.

SI Smithsonian Institution: NAA National Anthropological Archives; NMNH National Museum of Natural History; NPG National Portrait Gallery.

AIC Art Institute of Chicago; AMNH American Museum of Natural History; ASM-UA Arizona State Museum, University of Arizona; BM British Museum, London; DAM Denver Art Museum; EAF-JAM Enron Art Foundation, Joslyn Art Museum; FSM Florida State Museum; MAI-HF Museum of the American Indian, Heye Foundation; MNA Museum of Northern Arizona; NGS National Geographic Society; NMC-NMM National Museum of Canada, National Museum of Man; NP-MC National Palace, Mexico City; NYPL New York Public Library; OHS Ohio Historical Society, Columbus; PM-Harvard Peabody Museum, Harvard University; ROM Royal Ontario Museum; SLAM Saint Louis Art Museum; TGI Thomas Gilcrease Institute of American Art and History, Tulsa, Oklahoma; WSU Washington State University, Pullman.

Jacket: Jacket composite photo by Fil Hunter and Victor Krantz, NMNH/SI.

Front Matter: p. 2–3 "Landscape with Herd of Buffalo on the Upper Missouri," EAF-JAM; 4–5 David Muench; 6–7 Lowell Georgia/Photo Researchers; 10 Württembergisches Landesmuseum, Stuttgart, photo by Robert Harding Assoc., London; 11T reproduced from: Leland C. Wymar, *Southwest Indian Drypainting*, Santa Fe: School of American Research, 1983, drawing by Betsy James, photo by Ed Castle; 11C reproduced from: J. Eric & S. Thompson, *Maya Hieroglyphs Without Tears*, London: British Museum Publications, Ltd., 1950, photo by Ed Castle; 11B reproduced from: Philip Phillips & James A. Brown, *Pre-Columbian Shell Engravings*, Cambridge, MA: Peabody Museum Press, 1978, photo by Ed Castle; 12 OHS, photo by Dirk Bakker; 13 reproduced from: Philip Phillips & James A. Brown, *Pre-Columbian Shell Engravings*, Cambridge, MA: Peabody Museum Press, 1978, photo by Ed Castle.

The People: pp. 14–15 Ray A. Williamson; 16 NMNH/SI, photo by Aldo Tutino; 17L reproduced from: *Handbook of North American Indians*, Vol. 5, SI, 1984, photo by Ed Castle; 17TR FSM, photo for Lykes

Bros., Inc. by Rob Blount; 17B NMNH/SI, photo by Aldo Tutino; 18L reproduced from: Paul Hulton & David Beers Quinn, *The American Drawings of John White, 1577-1590*, Vol. I & II, London: BM, 1964, photo by Ed Castle; 18R PM-Harvard, photo by Hillel Burger, #T235; 19L,R reproduced from: Hulton & Quinn, *The American Drawings of John White. 1577-1590*, BM, 1964, photos by Ed Castle; 20T Kenneth Garrett/Woodfin Camp, Inc.: 20B art by Anne Morris "Sea Coast Village," 1927, PM-Harvard, photo by Hillel Burger, #T691; 21 art by William H. Holmes, "Cliff House in 1875," PM-Harvard, photo by Hillel Burger, #T8576; 22TL SLAM, gift of Morton D. May; 22TR University of Arkansas Museum, photo by Dirk Bakker; 22B private collection, photo by Justin Kerr; 23L The Gordon & Steven Hart Collection, Bluffton, IN, photo by Dirk Bakker; 23R PM-Harvard, photo by Hillel Burger, #T618; 24L ASM-UA, photo by Werner Forman Archive; 24R MAI-HF, photo by David Heald; 25T SLAM, gift; 25BL Georg Gerster/Photo Researchers; 25R Etowah Mounds Museum, GA Dept. of Natural Resources, photo by David J. Kaminsky; 26L OHS, photo by Dirk Bakker; 26TR MNA, photo by Werner Forman Archive; 26B Tom Bahti; 27 MAI-HF, photo by Werner Forman Archive; 28 courtesy of BM; 29 Tom Bahti; 30 Tom Falley/Alaska Photo; 31L reproduced from: Dean R. Snow, *The Archaeology of New England*, NY: Academic Press Inc., 1980, photo by Ed Castle; 31R Fred Bruemmer; 32 rendered by Walter Roberts; 33 J.& M. Ibbotson/ Alaska Photo; 34 mural by Jay H. Matternes, NMNH/SI, photo by NGS; 36T NMNH/SI, photo by Chip Clark; 36B courtesy of WSU, photo by Kerby Smith; 37 Bill Belknap/ Photo Researchers; 39 David C. Fritts; 40 Denver Museum of Natural History, Photo Archives; 41 Chip Clark; 42–43 Kenneth Garrett; 44L Chip Clark; 44–45 Joseph H. Bailey & Larry D. Kinney, ©NGS; 46 Denver Museum of Natural History, Photo Archives; 47 University of Colorado Museum, photo by Joe Ben Wheat; 48 "The Totonac Civilization" detail: "The Offering," NP-MC, photo by Andrew Rakoczy/Bruce Coleman; 49L reproduced from: *Handbook of North American Indians*, Vol. 5., SI, 1984, photo by Ed Castle; 49R Robert P. Carr/Bruce Coleman; 50 ASM-UA, photo by Helga Teiwes; 51 EAF-JAM; 52L John Running; 52R private collection, photo by Lee Boltin; 53 Walter H. Hodge/Peter Arnold Inc.; 54L TGI, photo by Dirk Bakker; 54R reproduced from: Stefan Lorant, *The New World, The First Pictures of America*, NY: Duell Sloan and Pearce, 1946, photo by Ed Castle; 55L ASM-UA, photo by Helga Teiwes; 55R MAI-HF, photo by David Heald; 56L Curt Schaafsma; 56R Field Museum of Natural History, Chicago, photo by Von Del Chamberlain; 57 Georg Gerster/Photo Researchers; 58 from *Revised American Ethnological Society Publication #20*, 1966,

rendered by Walter Roberts; 59 reproduced from: John L. Stephens, *Incidents of Travel in Central America Chiapas and Yucatán*, Vol. I, NY: Dover Publications, 1969; 60T MAI-HF, photo by David Heald; 60B Caribiner Corp., NY, photo by Peter White; 61T "Codice di Madrid,": Museo de America, Madrid, photo by Art Resource, NY; 61B NMNH/SI, photo by Ed Castle; 62 David Hiser/Photographers Aspen; 63L Ann Parks Hawthorne; 63R Kal Muller/ Woodfin Camp, Inc.; 64 Stuart Craig/Bruce Coleman; 65 courtesy of The Hand and Spirit Gallery, Scottsdale, AZ, photo by Jerry Jacka; 66 Richard H. Stewart ©1948 NGS; 67L reproduced from: E. G. Squier & E. H. Davis, *Ancient Monuments of the Mississippi Valley*, Washington, DC: SI, 1848, photo by Ed Castle; 67R Robert W. Parvin; 68 SI Libraries, photo by Ed Castle; 69 NAA/SI; 70 art by John J. Egan, "Panorama of the Monumental Grandeur of the Mississippi Valley," 1850, detail: SLAM, Eliza McMillan Fund Purchase; 72 Ed Castle; 73 NAA/SI, photo by Ed Castle; 74 NMNH/SI; 75L reproduced from: William H. Holmes, *Archaeological Studies Among the Ancient Cities of Mexico*, Vol. I. Chicago: Field Columbian Museum, 1895, photo by Ed Castle; 75R NMAA & NPG Library/SI; 76 Bowring Cartographic; 78 NAA/SI; 79 International Museum of Photography at George Eastman House; 80T NAA/SI; 80B Victor Krantz, NMNH/ SI; 81 NAA/SI, photo by Ed Castle; 82L Joan M. Walker/Thunderbird Museum, VA; 82R James A. Tuck/Memorial University of Newfoundland; 83–86L Robert W. Parvin; 86R Charles H. Phillips; 87 Robert W. Parvin; 88 Cotton Coulson/Woodfin Camp, Inc.; 89 Stephen La Blanc/Southwest Museum & Paul Minnis/Mimbres Foundation; 90 Glenn Van Nimwegen; 91 Kenneth Garrett/Woodfin Camp, Inc.

Land and Culture: pp. 92–93 Dallas Art Museum, photo by Justin Kerr; 94 Dan Guravich; 95L reproduced from: *Handbook of North American Indians*, Vol. 5, SI, 1984, photo by Ed Castle; 95R private collection/ photo by Justin Kerr; 96 Bowring Cartographic; 97L "Inhabitants of the Gulf of Kotzebue," 1816–17, Special Collections Division, University of Washington Libraries; 97R private collection, photo by Peter Furst; 98 MAI-HF; 99 art by F. H. von Kittlitz, "Inhabitants of Ounalachka with their Canoes," 1827, Special Collections Division, University of Washington Libraries; 99TR Holbrook Gallery, Santa Fe, photo by Peter Furst; 99BR NMNH/SI, photo by Ed Castle; 100–101 art by Greg Harlin/Stansbury, Ronsaville, Wood Inc.; 102 AMNH, photos by Werner Forman Archive; 103L MAI-HF, photo by David Heald; 103R NMNH/SI, photo by Ed Castle; 104 Fred Bruemmer; 105 NMC-NMM, #S86-400; 106 Sisse Brimberg/ Woodfin Camp, Inc.; 107 Chip Clark; 108 Sisse Brimberg/Woodfin Camp, Inc.;

109L NMC-NMM, #S86-398; 109R Kjell Sandved, NMNH/SI; 110–111 private collection, Toronto, photo by Peter Brown Photography, Ltd.; 112 Richard A. Cooke III; 113L Selwyn Dewdney, from *Ontario Prehistory Gallery*, Toronto: ROM, 1977, photo by Ed Castle; 113R NMNH/SI, photo by Ed Castle; 114 Bowring Cartographic; 115T Dan Guravich; 115B, 116L NMC-NMM, #74-18870, #S75-4279; 116R NMNH/SI; 117 NMC-NMM, #K73-141, #75-14085; 118 Library of Congress; 119L NMC-NMM, #S75-398; 119R Maine State Museum, photo by Greg Hart; 120 Lowell Georgia/Photo Researchers; 121L NMC-NMM, #K75-944; 121R Selwyn Dewdney, from *Ontario Prehistory Gallery*, ROM, 1977, photo by Ed Castle; 122 M. Serraillier/Photo Researchers; 123L reproduced from: Jesse D. Jennings, *Prehistory of North America*, 2nd ed. NY: McGraw-Hill, Inc., 1974, photo by Ed Castle; 123R MAI-HF, photo by David Heald; 124–125 Eleanor M. Kish; 126 Bowring Cartographic; 127L NMNH/SI, photo by Dirk Bakker; 127R D. R. Baston; 128 OHS, photo by Dirk Bakker; 129 TGI, photo by Dirk Bakker; 130TL OHS; 130TR MAI-HF, photo by David Heald; 130B PM-Harvard, photo by Hillel Burger, #T886; 131 reproduced from: E. G. Squier & E. H. Davis, *Ancient Monuments of the Mississippi Valley*, SI, 1848, photo by Ed Castle; 132 PM-Harvard, photo by Linton Watts; 133L OHS, photo by Dirk Bakker; 133R Victor Krantz, NMNH/SI; 134T NMNH/SI, photo by Ed Castle; 134B MAI-HF, photo by David Heald; 135L courtesy of BM, photo by Michael Holford; 135R Newfoundland Museum, photo by Lee Boltin; 136–137 art by Greg Harlin/Stansbury, Ronsaville, Wood Inc.; 138 NMNH/SI, photo by Ed Castle; 139 The British Library; 140 NMC-NMM, photo by Werner Forman Archive; 141T courtesy of DAM, photo by Lloyd Rule; 141B NYPL/Rare Books Division; 142 NMNH/SI, photo by Ed Castle; 143 courtesy of DAM, photo by Lloyd Rule; 144 NMNH/SI, photo by Aldo Tutino; 145L reproduced from: Phillip Phillips & James A. Brown, *Pre-Columbian Shell Engravings from the Craig Mound at Spiro, Oklahoma*, Peabody Museum Press, 1978, photo by Ed Castle; 145R MAI-HF; 146L Dr. Ripley P. Bullen/FSM, 1955; 146R art by Gordon Miller, from *Early Man*, 1982, Vol. 4, No. 4, photo by Ed Castle; 147 FSM, photo by Dirk Bakker; 148T Bowring Cartographic; 148B Georg Gerster/Photo Researchers; 149 reproduced from E. H. Davis, *Sketches of Monuments and Antiques: Found in the Mounds, Tombs and Ancient Cities of America*, NY, 1858. NAA/SI, photo by Ed Castle; 150 NASA; 151 reproduced from: Jon L. Gibson, *Poverty Point: A Culture of the Lower Mississippi Valley*, Baton Rouge, LA: Louisiana Office of Cultural Development, 1985, photo by Ed Castle; 152T art by William Iseminger, Cahokia Mounds State Historical Site; 152B Illinois State

Museum of Natural History & Art, Springfield, photo by Dirk Bakker; 153 St. Louis Museum of Science and Natural History, photo by Dirk Bakker; 155 Sisse Brimberg/Woodfin Camp, Inc.; 156T NMNH/SI, photo by Aldo Tutino; 156BL Victor Krantz, NMNH/SI; 156BC MAI-HF, photo by David Heald; 156BR NMNH/SI, photo by Aldo Tutino; 157T TGI, photo by Dirk Bakker; 157B MAI-HF, photo by David Heald; 158L reproduced from: *Transactions of the American Ethnological Society*, Vol. III, 1853, courtesy of University of Georgia Libraries, Special Collections; 158R George Catlin, "Tchung-Kee, A Mandan Game Played with a Ring and Pole," 1832–1833. NMAA/SI, gift of Mrs. Joseph Harrison, Jr.; 159T NMNH/SI, photo by Charles H. Phillips; 159B, 160, 161 Frank H. McClung Museum, University of Tennessee, Knoxville, photos by W. Miles Wright; 162–163 art by Greg Harlin/Stansbury, Ronsaville, Wood Inc.; 164 Museum of Natural History, University of Alabama, photos by Dirk Bakker; 165 Dan Guravich; 166 Kjell Sandved, NMNH/SI; 167 Victor Krantz, NMNH/SI; 168 Jim Brandenburg; 169L reproduced from: Peter T. & Jill L. Furst, *North American Indian Art*, NY: Rizzoli International Publications, Inc., 1982, photo by Ed Castle; 169R State Historical Society of Iowa, Charles Keyes Collection, photo by Thomas E. Moore/Iowa Public Television; 170L courtesy of Bob Edgar, Cody, WY, photo by Jack Richard Photo Studio; 170R Bowring Cartographic; 171 Robert W. Parvin; 172T "Prairie Bluffs Burning," 1832. NMAA/SI, gift of Mrs. Joseph Harrison, Jr.; 172B "Indian Hunters Pursuing the Buffalo in the Early Spring," 1825, courtesy of Public Archives of Canada; 173 courtesy of Montana Historical Society, Museum Collection; 174L art by Snowden Hodges, reproduced from: Ray A. Williamson, *Living the Sky: The Cosmos of the American Indian*, Boston: Houghton Mifflin Co., 1984, photo by Ed Castle; 174R NMNH/SI, photo by Chip Clark; 175 reproduced from: Robert H. Lowie, *Indians of the Plains*, Garden City, NY: Natural History Press, 1963, photo by Ed Castle; 176 Office of the State Archaeologist of Iowa; 177L Karl Bodmer, "Hidatsa Hoop-and-Pole Game," EAF-JAM; 177R reproduced from: Robert H. Lowie, *Indians of the Plains*, Natural History Press, 1963, photo by Ed Castle; 178 Jim Brandenburg; 179 "Interior of a Mandan Earth Lodge," EAF-JAM; 180 Karl Bodmer, "Mih-Tutta-Hang-Kush, Mandan Village," EAF-JAM; 181T NMNH/SI, photo by Ed Castle; 181R courtesy of the Southwest Museum, Los Angeles, photo by Justin Kerr; 182L Victor Krantz, NMNH/SI; 182T courtesy of Bob Edgar, Cody, WY, photo by Jack Richard Photo Studio; 182B courtesy of the Buffalo Bill Historical Center, Cody, WY; 183T NMNH/SI, photo by Ed Castle; 183C courtesy of the Southwest Museum, Los Angeles, photo by Justin Kerr; 183B

State Historical Society of Iowa, Charles Keyes Collection, photo by Thomas E. Moore/Iowa Public Television; 184 Larry Zimmerman; 185 Kjell Sandved, NMNH/SI; 186 NMNH/SI, photo by Ed Castle; 187L reproduced from: S. A. Barrett, *Pomo Indian Basketry*, Vol. 7. Glorietta, NM: Rio Grande Press, 1970, photo by Ed Castle; 187R Utah Museum of Natural History, photo by Laurel Casjens; 188L Utah Museum of Natural History, photo by Werner Forman Archive; 188R Bowring Cartographic; 189 David Muench; 190 MAI-HF; 191 MAI-HF, photo by David Heald; 192–193 NMNH/SI, photo by Ed Castle; 194L Tom Meyers; 194R reproduced from: Alexander Forbes, *California: A History of Upper & Lower California*, London: 1839, photo by Ed Castle; 195 David Muench; 196L NMNH/SI, photo by Ed Castle; 196–197 Ralph A. Clevenger/Wildshot; 197R MAI-HF, photo by David Heald; 198 NMNH/SI, photo by Ed Castle; 199 Edward S. Curtis, NAA/SI; 200 Ruth & Louis Kirk; 201L art by Hilary Stewart, reproduced from: Wilson Duff, *Images Stone B.C.* Seattle: Washington Press, 1975, photo by Ed Castle; 201R R. H. McClure; 202 Bowring Cartographic; 203L art by A. F. Postels, from *Voyage*, Atlas, by Litke, courtesy Lilly Library, Indiana University; 203R Fran Durner/Alaska Photo; 204T The Vancouver Museum, photo by Hilary Stewart; 204B NMNH/SI, photo by Ed Castle; 205 NMC-NMM, photo by Werner Forman Archive; 206L Dale Croes; 206–207, 207TR Ruth & Louis Kirk; 207BR art by John Webber, "A Man from Nootka Sound," James Cook, *A Voyage to the Pacific Ocean*, Atlas, London; 1784, PM-Harvard, photo by Hillel Burger, #T328; 208–209 art by Greg Harlin/Stansbury, Ronsaville, Wood Inc.; 210 Art Wolfe/Aperture; 211L Bill Bacon/Aperture; 211R Ruth & Louis Kirk; 212 art by Hilary Stewart; 212R NMC-NMM, #S85-3333; 213 Tom E. Roll, Montana State Museum; 214 reproduced from: Edward S. Curtis, *The North American Indian*, Seattle, WA: 1907–1930, SI Libraries, photo by Ed Castle; 215–216T PM-Harvard, photos by Hillel Burger, #T719A & T715A; 216B Ruth & Louis Kirk; 217 courtesy of BM, photo by Werner Forman Archive; 218 David Muench; 219L reproduced from: Kate Peck Kent, *Prehistoric Textiles of the Southwest*, Santa Fe: School of American Research, 1983, photo by Ed Castle; 219R MNA, photo by Jerry Jacka; 220 Bowring Cartographic; 221L ASM-UA, photo by Helga Teiwes; 221R ASM-UA, photo by David Arnold, ©1979, NGS; 222TL Victor Krantz, NMNH/SI; 222BL courtesy of Maxwell Museum of Anthropology, photo by Werner Forman Archive; 222–223 ASM-UA, photo by Helga Teiwes; 223TR, BR private collections, photos by Jerry Jacka; 224 Willard Clay; 225 John Running; 226 ASM-UA, photo by Helga Teiwes; 227 ASM-UA, photo by Jerry Jacka; 228 R. Van Nostrand/Photo

Researchers; 229 ASM-UA, photo by Jerry Jacka; 230 John Carter Brown Library, Brown University, photo from Museum of Art, Rhode Island School of Design; 231L ASM-UA, 231R ASM-UA, photo by Helga Teiwes; 232 ASM-UA, photo by Jerry Jacka; 233 ASM-UA, photo by Helga Teiwes; 234 ASM-UA, photo by John Running; 235L ASM-UA, photo by David Muench; 235R ASM-UA, photo by Jerry Jacka; 236L Mesa Verde National Park Museum, photo by Werner Forman Archive; 236R ASM-UA, photo by Helga Teiwes; 237 David Muench; 238BL John Running; 238–239, 239R David Muench; 240TL, Ray A. Williamson; 240BL Glenn Van Nimwegen; 240R, 241 John Running; 242–243 art by Greg Harlin/ Stansbury, Ronsaville, Wood Inc.; 244 MAI-HF; 245 AIC; 246 Metropolitan Museum of Art, bequest of Alice K. Bache; 247L reproduced courtesy of Dover Publications, NY: from Jamake Highwater, *Arts of the Indian Americas*, NY: Harper & Row, 1983, photo by Ed Castle; 247R Art Resource, NY; 248 Bowring Cartographic; 249 Justin Kerr; 250 art by Lloyd K. Townsend, photo by Ed Castle; 252 Norman Tomalin/Bruce Coleman; 253L Dana Hyde/ Photo Researchers; 253R Dick Davis/Photo Researchers; 254T Paolo Koch/Photo Researchers; 254B Lee Boltin; 255B detail from the mural, "Great Tenochtitlán the Market," NP-MC, photo by Alan Linn; 255T Alan Linn; 256 Metropolitan Museum of Art, Michael C. Rockefeller Collection; 257 Dunbarton Oaks, photo by Justin Kerr; 258 David Alan Harvey/Woodfin Camp, Inc.; 259TL W. H. Hodge/Peter Arnold, Inc.; 259TR Kenneth Garrett/Woodfin Camp, Inc.; 259B Gerard Murrell/Bruce Coleman; 260T David Alan Harvey/Woodfin Camp, Inc.; 260B Peter R. Dickerson/Art Resource, NY; 261 Carl Frank/Photo Researchers; 262–263R, courtesy of BM, photo by Lee Boltin; 263TR courtesy of BM, photo by Victor Boswell, ©1980, NGS; 263BR courtesy of BM, photo by Werner Forman Archive; 264 Kenneth Garrett/Woodfin Camp, Inc.; 265 David Hiser.

The Coming of the Europeans: pp. 266–267 Jerry Jacka; 268 EAF-JAM; 269L reproduced from: Zorro A. Bradley, *Canyon de Chelly, The Story of its Ruins and People*, Washington, DC: Dept. of the Interior, National Park Service, 1973, photo by Ed Castle; 269R Sisse Brimberg/Woodfin Camp, Inc.; 270 NYPL/Rare Books Division; 271 Victor Krantz, NMNH/SI; 273 Alexander Lowry/Photo Researchers; 274 University Museum, University of Alaska, photo by Werner Forman Archive; 275 NMNH/SI, photo by Aldo Tutino; 276 NAA/SI; 277 Paul Sequeira/Photo Researchers; 278–279 Glenn Van Nimwegen; 280 John Running; 281T George Haling/Photo Researchers; 281B John Running.

ACKNOWLEDGEMENTS

The Editors of Smithsonian Books thank the following people for their assistance in the preparation of this book:

Greg Hart, Maine State Museum; Joseph Tiffany, Office of the State Archaeologist of Iowa; Mary Kay Davies, Anthropology Library/Smithsonian Institution (SI); Paula Fleming and Kathleen Baxter, National Anthropological Archives/SI; Joseph S. Brown, Linda Eisenhart, Felicia Pickering, Anthropology Processing Lab, National Museum of Natural History/SI; Cynthia Nakamura, Denver Art Museum; Jefferson Chapman, Frank H. McClung Museum; Natasha Bonilla and Eugenie Laidler, Photography Department, Museum of the American Indian; Ian Brown, Curator, Peabody Museum/ Harvard University; Pat Lanza Field and Victor Boswell, National Geographic Society; Robert Stuckenrath, Smithsonian Environmental Research Center; Ray A. Williamson, Project Director, Office of Technology Assessment, United States Congress; Robert W. Parvin, Photographer, Bastrop, Texas.

While researching and writing this work, I had the good fortune to meet experts whose command of North American prehistory was crucial to my growing understanding of their specialties and whose willingness to share their knowledge was an inspiration in itself. Many of them are named in the text, but it is my pleasure to thank the following people in particular for their aid, instruction and encouragement:

At Chaco Canyon, Stephen Lekson and Dabney Ford; Phoenix City Archaeologist David E. Doyel; Richard S. MacNeish of the Andover Foundation for Archaeological Research; John Andresen, National Park Service Archaeologist at Casa Grande; Bennie Keel, the National Park Service's Chief Archaeologist; Eugene Sekaquaptewa and Milland Lomakema of the Hopi Nation; David S. Brose of the Cleveland Museum of Natural History; Jay Custer of the University of Delaware; Richard Krause and Joseph O. Vogel of the University of Alabama; Jon L. Gibson of the University of Southwestern Louisiana; James V. Wright and Richard E. Morlan of the National Museum of Canada; William Finlayson of the Museum of Archaeology in London, Ontario; Bruce G. Trigger of McGill University; Errett Callahan of Piltdown Productions; Historical Archaeologist Marley R. Brown III of Colonial Williamsburg; Dean R. Snow of the University of New York at Albany; New York State Archaeologist George R. Hamell; Hazel Dean-John of the Seneca Nation and the New York State Board of Education; Joe Ben Wheat of the University of Colorado; George C. Frison of the University of Wyoming; Moundville State Park Superintendent Phil Krebs; Poverty Point Manager Dennis LaBatt and Staff Archaeologist Mitchell Hillman.

At the Smithsonian's Anthropology Department, Curator Dennis Stanford and his associate Gary Haynes now at the University of Nevada at Reno; also at the National Museum of Natural History, Linguist Ives Goddard.

I wish to thank the publishers also for offering me this commission: Smithsonian Institution Press Director Felix C. Lowe; Smithsonian Books Editor-in-Chief Patricia Gallagher and Senior Editor Alexis Doster III, who conceived the book several years ago. A special word goes to Assistant Editor John Ross for his unflagging dedication and attention to tasks that might have felled a lesser man. Picture Editors Nancy Strader, Jenny Takacs and Frances Rowsell pursued and obtained the best possible illustrations; and thanks to the diligence and good-natured prodding of Patricia Upchurch and June G. Armstrong, the production schedule was met. I thank the members of the advisory committee for their close readings of the manuscript and their many suggestions: Don D. Fowler, Linda S. Cordell, Alice B. Kehoe and Vincas P. Steponaitis.

Finally I thank my wife, Mary Carll Kopper, for her unflagging support even when this work took longer than expected. But for her patience and loving grit, it might never have been finished.

Philip Kopper
Chevy Chase, Maryland